Routledge Revival.

I0130582

The Case for the Prosecution

Originally published in 1991, *The Case for the Prosecution* examines the entire process of arrest through to conviction. The book is a landmark in the study of criminal justice in Britain, and gives valuable information about the working of the police and the Crown Prosecution Service. The book provides strong empirical, theoretical and policy contributions to the field and should prompt lawyers to re-revaluate their role and the way they perform it. It is vital reading for anyone practising or studying criminal justice or law.

The Case for the Prosecution

Police Suspects and the Construction of Criminality

Mike McConville, Andrew Sanders and Roger Leng

Routledge
Taylor & Francis Group

First published in 1991
by Routledge

This edition first published in 2018 by Routledge
2 Park Square, Milton Park, Abingdon, Oxon, OX14 4RN
and by Routledge
711 Third Avenue, New York, NY 10017

Routledge is an imprint of the Taylor & Francis Group, an informa business

© 1991 Mike McConville, Andrew Sanders and Roger Leng

The right of Mike McConville, Andrew Sanders and Roger Leng to be identified
as the authors of this work has been asserted by them in accordance with
sections 77 and 78 of the Copyright, Designs and Patents Act 1988.

All rights reserved. No part of this book may be reprinted or reproduced or
utilised in any form or by any electronic, mechanical, or other means, now
known or hereafter invented, including photocopying and recording, or in any
information storage or retrieval system, without permission in writing from the
publishers.

Publisher's Note
The publisher has gone to great lengths to ensure the quality of this reprint but
points out that some imperfections in the original copies may be apparent.

Disclaimer
The publisher has made every effort to trace copyright holders and welcomes
correspondence from those they have been unable to contact.
A Library of Congress record is available under ISBN: 90023773

ISBN 13: 978-1-138-56546-3 (hbk)
ISBN 13: 978-0-8153-7246-2 (pbk)
ISBN 13: 978-1-351-24538-8 (ebk)

The Case for the Prosecution

Police suspects and the construction
of criminality

Mike McConville,
Andrew Sanders
and
Roger Leng

ROUTLEDGE

London and New York

First published in 1991
by Routledge
11 New Fetter Lane, London EC4P 4EE

Simultaneously published in the USA and Canada by Routledge
29 West 35th Street, New York, NY 10001

First published in paperback by Routledge in 1993

© 1991 Mike McConville, Andrew Sanders and Roger Leng

Typeset by NWL Editorial Services, Langport, Somerset

All rights reserved. No part of this book may be reprinted or
reproduced or utilized in any form or by any electronic,
mechanical, or other means, now known or hereafter invented,
including photocopying and recording, or in any information
storage or retrieval system, without permission in writing from
the publishers.

British Library Cataloguing in Publication Data
McConville, Michael
    The case for the prosecution.
    1. England. Police powers. Law   2. England. Offenders.
    Prosecution procedure
    I. Title   II. Sanders, Andrew *1952–*   III. Leng, Roger *1953–*
344.2055042

Library of Congress Cataloging in Publication Data
The case for the prosecution/by Mike McConville, Andrew
    Sanders, Roger Leng
    p. cm.
    Includes bibliographical references and index.
    1. Prosecution – Great Britain – Decision making
    2. Criminal procedure – Great Britain.   3. Police – Great
    Britain.   I. Sanders, Andrew   II. Leng, Roger, 1953–
    III. title.
    KD8348.M39   1991
    345.41′05042 – dc20   90–23773
    [344.1055042]   CIP

ISBN 0–415–10103–4

Contents

Tables

Preface

The field work for this book was carried out between 1986 and 1988. Our objective was to understand how police officers and prosecutors made decisions in respect of criminal cases. The Director of Public Prosecutions (DPP), as head of the Crown Prosecution Service, and the Chief Constables of the three police forces studied consented to the research and co-operated in all aspects of our study.

These were the first few years of the Crown Prosecution Service (CPS), and some practices may have changed since then. The CPS was established on the recommendation of the Royal Commission on Criminal Procedure (1981) as part of a package of reforms based on 'broad standards of fairness, openness, accountability and efficiency' (*Report*, para 6.8). A condition of the research imposed by the DPP, to which we reluctantly consented, was that we would not publish direct quotations from CPS employees without the prior approval of the DPP. Prior to publication we sent drafts of relevant sections of this book to the DPP. He chose not to approve publication of a number of quotations. We have noted in the text the occasions on which the DPP requested us not to use direct quotations.

Acknowledgements

All research projects rely on the help and support of countless numbers of people. This was no exception. Our greatest debt is to our two research associates, Vanessa Saxton and Robert Wight. Both dedicated themselves to the success of the research and undertook heavy fieldwork demands with patience and good humour. In addition, Gary Crozier, Sue Deebank, Jackie Hodgson, Dan Shepherd and Richard Young all provided valuable part-time research help at various stages of the project.

In Birmingham, Mary Blake, John Bosworth and Ian Scott (Dean of the Law Faculty) gave us all the support we could have wanted, and Hazel Bond acted throughout as project secretary, organizing our data retrieval systems and typing our field notes with skill and patience.

In Warwick, we were greatly helped by the support provided by Jolyon Hall and Sue Wallington of the university library and by the untiring efforts of Frances Halstead of the Computing Services Centre. Aileen Stockham typed (and re-typed) the manuscript with unfailing patience and accuracy.

We promised the police and Crown Prosecution Service (CPS) that complete confidentiality would be maintained regarding all persons, cases and areas. We have been happy to maintain this confidentiality, which has been secured in the text by conventional social science techniques. Unfortunately it prevents us from thanking all those people who gave us so much help. It really is true to say that both the police and CPS staff went out of their way both to expedite the research and to make our many months with them as comfortable as possible. We were welcomed in every police station and CPS office and had open access to all personnel and files. Special arrangements were often made to provide us with officers to interview, documentation and transport which made our job much easier than it would have otherwise been. If officers and prosecutors feel that we have been unduly critical of them in this book we can only hope that, having got to know us as well as we got know them, they take it in the spirit intended.

The Economic and Social Research Council (ESRC) funded the project and was very understanding when we went back for more time and money. The Home Office eased our way several times by negotiating access and providing unpublished case listings, and Mike Brogden read the manuscript, providing us with invaluable comments. Finally, we must thank our wives and families, who have lived with, and suffered for, this project for longer than any of us would have thought possible.

1 Criminal justice in England and Wales

The formal structure of English criminal justice is adversarial. That is, there are two sides – defence and prosecution – and cases which go to trial are judged by 'impartial' magistrates, judges and occasionally juries. This means that each side has a specific role to play. Rather than each seeking the 'truth', which would be a duplication of effort, each side argues its case as best it can within certain ethical limits. In this book we will be examining how one of these sides – the prosecution – constructs and presents its case, and the implications this has for our understanding of the adversarial process.

Our analysis arises from a long-term study of police and prosecution decision making which began in 1986 and which embraced three police forces in England and Wales. With the co-operation of those forces and of the CPS we collected 1080 cases on a random basis from arrest to their eventual disposition, whether by way of caution, prosecution or no action at all (see the Appendix for details of the research methods). As a result of undertaking this research, we have moved away from seeing criminal justice as a series of discrete stages, and have become committed instead to the view that they overlap in important ways so that the overall effect is larger than the sum of the parts. We now understand criminal justice not as a *system*, which implies a relatively static unity with fixed boundaries, but as a *process*. This process will be studied by looking at the way in which cases against individuals come into being. Before outlining our specific approach, however, it is first necessary to outline the place of the police in criminal justice and to describe the broad legal framework within which official actors operate.

POLICE AUTONOMY

The prosecution comprises two institutions: the police and the Crown Prosecution Service (CPS). The police have existed in their current form since the mid-nineteenth century. As well as being responsible for the investigation and prevention of crime and the arrest of suspected offenders, the police soon took on the additional role, in most cases, of prosecuting those suspects. The system of private prosecution which the police came to replace quickly fell into desuetude, and the next 150 years saw a remarkable growth in the dominance of police prosecutions (Hay and Snyder, 1989). Until the mid 1980s the police retained all of these functions within a framework of rules and guidelines gradually embellished by piecemeal Acts of Parliament, administrative guidelines and judicial rulings.

Whilst the police were, and are, nominally accountable to Police Authorities (or, in the case of the Metropolitan Police, to the Home Secretary) this is of the broadest nature and is irrelevant to arrest and prosecution decisions. The doctrine of 'constabulary independence' governs these decisions (Jefferson and Grimshaw, 1984). According to this doctrine each police officer has a legal right and duty to enforce the law as she sees fit, regardless even of the orders of her superior officers. Decisions to arrest, interrogate, prosecute and so forth are, in formal terms, those of the officer(s) concerned in the case. In reality many of these decisions are taken at the behest of senior officers, but constabulary independence continues to have two important consequences. First, even the rawest recruits exercise discretion in all these matters at least some of the time, having the responsibility of important decisions impinging on the rights and liberties of citizens. Second, the starting points of 99.9 per cent of the cases for the prosecution are in the middle and lower ranks of the police force, immune from the direct control of either political or bureaucratic officials.

Take the notorious case of *Confait*. In 1972 Maxwell Confait was found dead and his house set alight. Two days later a police constable patrolling the area saw two boys running away from the scene of a fire which had been started in a shed of a nearby park. This information was passed to other officers who ultimately arrested three boys on suspicion of the murder and arson. The boys were interrogated intensively without their parents or any other adults present, and then, the police alleged, they confessed to involvement in these offences. The police charged the youths and then sent the case papers to the Director of Public Prosecutions (DPP). When they were brought to trial, the prosecution eventually secured convictions. The youths alleged that their confessions were put into their mouths by the police who, they said, mistreated them. The police denied this, and their version of events, despite the formal control of the case by the DPP, constituted the core of the case for the prosecution.

Everything about the 'Confait affair', including the contested confessions, allegations of police mistreatment and convictions was, if not normal, far from exceptional. Unusually though, these defendants had their convictions quashed some years later. An independent inquiry conducted by a former High Court Judge, Sir Henry Fisher, was established to investigate what went wrong and it reported in 1977 (Fisher, 1977). Fisher accepted many of the boys' allegations, although he still concluded that the boys were, in some way, involved. Even this belief was dispelled some years later when another person, unconnected with the youths, confessed (Baxter and Koffman, 1983). More importantly, perhaps, Fisher criticized the practices which led to the wrongful result: the fudging of the time of Confait's death so as to nullify defence alibi evidence; breach of rules designed to protect suspects during interrogation, and ignorance of those rules by both police and senior barristers; and the failure of prosecution lawyers to subject the prosecution case, and the discrepancies therein, to careful scrutiny. The whole prosecution was geared simply to proving the case against the boys.

Was *Confait* simply one bad case, the exception which proves the rule? Was the eventual result a vindication of British justice? Or was the case a normal product of police autonomy within an adversarial process in which the balance of power and resources is strongly in favour of the prosecution and against the defence? More recently, the release of the 'Guildford Four' and the official vindication of the 'Maguire Seven' and the 'Birmingham Six' are further examples of conviction on the basis of fatally flawed prosecutions (McConville, 1989). Our present purpose is to consider whether such cases were simply aberrations or rather were the natural result of our adversarial process and the autonomy of the police.

THE LEGAL FRAMEWORK

Fisher's Inquiry was not able to uncover the systemic roots of miscarriages of justice like *Confait*, but as a result of his recommendations the Royal Commission on Criminal Procedure was established in 1978 to consider the investigation and prosecution of all crime. The Royal Commission reported in 1981, after which major changes to the criminal justice process were introduced by the Police and Criminal Evidence Act, 1984 (PACE), and the Prosecution of Offences Act, 1985 (POOA).

PACE replaces the mixture of statutory and common law rules which regulated police investigation. Powers of arrest, detention, stop and search of persons and vehicles, entry and search of premises and seizure of prohibited articles are extended. The provisions of the Act are complemented by Codes of Practice made by the Home Secretary under section 66. The Royal Commission's aspirations to fairness and openness are expressed in new safeguards for suspects, which complement the additional powers conferred on the police. The safeguards take three forms. First, there are provisions for recording the reasons for exercising a particular coercive power such as stop and search. Second, there are provisions for reviewing the exercise of such powers. For instance, detention following arrest is subject to review at set intervals by a senior officer who must be satisfied that there continue to be grounds to detain at the time of the review. Third, there are provisions which confer rights on suspects, such as access to legal advice in the police station (section 58).

The safeguards are bolstered by provisions requiring that certain powers may be exercised only by a senior officer or a designated custody officer who must be independent of the relevant investigation. The custody officer has overall responsibility for the welfare of all suspects in custody and for ensuring that the provisions of PACE and of the Codes of Practice are observed. These responsibilities include authorising and releasing from detention, informing suspects of their rights, keeping detailed custody records and deciding whether suspects should be charged or not.

A central principle of English law is that the accused has a right to be silent in the face of police questioning. Although the right is not directly expressed in PACE it is implicit in the requirement that a suspect should be cautioned when arrested or charged, and at the beginning of any interview, that she or he is not obliged to say anything. The right to silence is protected by the rule of evidence that no adverse inferences should be drawn from an accused's silence in interview or failure to mention any fact which is later relied upon at trial (Cross, 1985 pp. 541–2; Mirfield, 1985).

A process which unequivocally embodied these principles would tend towards an ideal type system of the sort labelled by Herbert Packer as 'Due Process'. For Packer (1968), the foundations of a Due Process system are: (i) a value statement that the interests in protecting the citizen from unjustified punishment and general diminution in civil liberty outweigh the community interest in effectively apprehending and punishing criminals; and (ii) a recognition of the fallibility of human institutions (i.e. the police and the courts) and a corresponding need for checks, safeguards and reviewing procedures.

Packer compared this Due Process model with a second ideal type which he called the 'Crime Control Model'. The principal value statement underlying this model is that the interests of citizens are best protected by repressing crime and rooting out offenders by any efficient means. The emphasis is upon confidence in the abilities of the police to detect offenders and to release any innocent people who wrongly fall under suspicion. Once the police make their initial judgment about guilt and innocence therefore, there is little need for further checks; the rest of the process, including the court stage of the procedures, can operate on administrative rather than judicial principles. Whereas Due Process was likened to an obstacle course, Packer compared the Crime Control Model to a conveyor belt.

THE PROSECUTION SYSTEM

The POOA created the Crown Prosecution Service (CPS), headed by the Director of Public Prosecutions, and organised in 31 areas; each area office is headed by a Chief Crown Prosecutor, and most cover one or two police force areas. The two major functions of the CPS are to take over all criminal proceedings instituted by the police and to advise on any cases referred to them by the police prior to charge. Although the power of ordinary citizens to institute private prosecutions is retained, the CPS may take over any such prosecution at any stage where it is considered that it is in the public interest to do so. As well as the power to prosecute cases, the CPS is given a power under section 23 to discontinue cases without leave of the court. In performing this function the prosecutor is formally independent of the police, although the prosecutor is required to inform the police of the fact of and reasons for discontinuance, and the police may in effect appeal the decision by requiring that the case be reconsidered by a more senior prosecutor, with ultimate recourse to the local Chief Crown Prosecutor. These changes extend the DPP's former jurisdiction over serious cases to *all* police-initiated cases: none the less, the DPP and CPS have no greater role in any one case now than the DPP had in the *Confait, Birmingham Six* and *Guildford Four* cases (Sanders, 1986).

The Prosecution of Offences Act does not prescribe the criteria for prosecution decision making. These are set out in general terms in the *Code for Crown Prosecutors*, a public document issued by the CPS. Together with the Home Office Guidelines on cautioning (Home Office, 1985) the Code supersedes the Attorney-General's Guidelines issued in 1983 (Sanders, 1985a). Home Office circulars addressed to the police are not formally binding (otherwise 'constabulary independence' would be eroded), but the cautioning guidelines were developed after consul- tation with Chief Constables. All police forces have made efforts to implement the guidelines and many forces have simply incorporated them within force standing orders (Wilkinson and Evans, 1990). The starting point for the Code and cautioning guidelines is that there is no rule that suspected offenders must be prosecuted, and cautioning should be considered a possible course of action for both adults and juveniles. Since prosecution is not automatic, and the police retain autonomy in arrest and prosecution decisions, their discretion and control of the prosecution process (in its early stages, at least) are virtually absolute. This suggests that there are 'Crime Control' elements in our criminal justice process. However, the *formal* independence of the CPS from the police and the *formal* function of the CPS to review police decisions evidences a formal commitment to 'Due Process' values. This tension between form and substance will be a major theme of this book.

THE ROLE OF THE DEFENCE

The defence lawyer has always had some influence on pre-trial decision making by virtue of presence at the suspect's interview (where this occurred) and by the general freedom to communicate with the police or prosecutor about the case pre-trial. However, traditionally the focus of defence activity has been the court. Modern reforms have had the effect of increasing opportunities for defence activism before the case is dealt with in full court. The right to legal advice in the police station, coupled with increased provision for legal aid and the setting up of schemes to provide such advice, has meant that more solicitors have active involvement in the case at an early stage and the opportunity to make representations about the appropriate disposition of the case. Also the requirement that the prosecution should disclose at least an outline of its case pre-trial has provided the opportunity for more meaningful exchange about the strength of evidence or appropriateness of the charges. This has been further bolstered in some areas by the institution of pre-trial reviews, under the auspices of the courts, which have the express purpose of bringing lawyers from the two sides together to discuss the case in the presence of a court officer. Although ostensibly designed to clarify the area of dispute and to deal with administrative matters like agreeing lists of witnesses, a major objective of all participants is to achieve a settlement without recourse to contested trial.

FILES, CASES AND ACCOUNTS

When a person is arrested on suspicion of a crime, an official file is created. This file is an account of what happened, of who the arrested person is and of the role of the arrested person in what is alleged to have happened. The file is not created at one moment but is subject to continual additions and revisions so long as the suspect remains within the system. This working and reworking of information ultimately leads to the production of an official account of what happened, against which other accounts (such as those from the defence) have to struggle for acceptance. As the *Confait, Guildford Four* and *Maguire Seven* cases show, such other accounts may take years to become accepted, while in many other cases they never are.

We are concerned in this book to understand such official accounts of investigated criminality, to show that official accounts are problematic, selective renderings of complex realities and to examine the consequences of this for the criminal justice process. The problematic nature of official accounts can be demonstrated by examining three apparently straightforward cases drawn from our research, the first two relating to juveniles, the third an adult cautioned for being drunk and disorderly.

AH-J14[1] – As a result of a call from a member of the public, the police went to the rear of a shop in the early evening and found J14 in the back garden with some milk drinks which had been taken from the shop. J14, a 12-year-old schoolboy made a full admission at the scene that he had stolen the drinks from the shop. The incident appeared to have been opportunist in character (the boy having come across an open door) rather than pre-planned, and the goods taken, all of which were recovered, were valued at less than £2. The police officer from the Juvenile Liaison Bureau who carried out a home visit noted that J14 had played truant from school and found J14's mother to be not very supportive. The officer described J14, who had no prior criminal record, as very polite and well dressed, if somewhat 'disinterested'. On the basis of the character of the incident and what had been learned on the home visit, the officer recommended that a caution was appropriate, a course supported by the Detective Sergeant of the Bureau.

CC-J52 – J52 was allegedly seen by a store detective to examine some goods valued at £6, hide them up the sleeve of his jacket and leave the store without paying. He was stopped outside the store and made a full admission to the theft. According to the arresting officer, this was a planned offence in which J52 'secreted' the goods up his sleeve. J52 was a 14-year-old boy with several prior convictions and was in breach of a conditional discharge imposed by the court within the last year. The arresting officer told us that a prosecution was 'automatic' in these circumstances and the Inspector in charge of reviewing the case noted on his file that court proceedings 'must follow'.

The Home Office Guidelines appear to make the resolution of these cases unproblematic. They lay down, among other things, that as 'a general principle in the case of first time juvenile offenders where the offence is not serious, it is unlikely that prosecution will be a justifiable course. Specifically it will not be right to prosecute a juvenile solely to secure access to the welfare powers of the courts.' This would seem to require a caution for *AH-J14* and prosecution for *CC-J52*. This impression is reinforced by the detailed rules which encourage quick decisions on cautions where the offence is 'not serious' and the 'offender's record is not serious'.

In fact, however, *AH-J14* was prosecuted for burglary of the shop and *CC-J52* was cautioned by the police and not prosecuted. *AH-J14* was prosecuted because the Juvenile Liaison Bureau Inspector, on reviewing the recommendations of the other officers, decided that the boy needed a quick and sharp shock to stop him falling into worse ways. So far as *CC-J52* was concerned the 'automatic' prosecution was avoided after social services proposed a caution based upon the offence being 'minor', different in character from the last offence (namely, unlawful wounding), and on the fact that *CC-J52* had not previously received a caution. The details of the third case are as follows:

> *AH-A058* – The circumstances of this case are set out in the incident report book of the police signed by the arresting officer:
>
> 'From the information received, I attended a house where outside the premises I saw a man I now know to be [A058]. Noticed he was unsteady on his feet and he smelled strongly of intoxicating liquor. I said 'what are you doing here?' His reply was incoherent. I said 'where have you been?' Answer – 'I've had a few drinks down the pub.' I noticed that his speech was slurred. He was drunk. Arrested and cautioned.'

Under interview with us, the arresting officer in this case disclosed a rather different story. According to the officer the police were called to A058's house by neighbours concerned about an incident involving screaming and shouting and damage to the door of the house. When the police arrived, A058 was standing outside the house next to the damaged door. The officer was asked whether he had considered any alternative to arresting A058 and said: 'No. There was the damage and he was still at the door and [I felt] the behaviour would continue if [A058] was not arrested.' The officer told us that A058 had been drinking when he was arrested but that 'he would not have arrested him for drunkenness'. When asked to explain why A058 had been cautioned for drunk and disorderly, the officer could not account for this, saying 'It does seem strange'.

UNDERSTANDING SOCIO-LEGAL PHENOMENA

It is tempting to draw from these three case examples conclusions which are in line with traditional critiques of police (or prosecutorial) behaviour. Thus, the counter-intuitive outcomes of the juvenile cases appear to demonstrate inconsistent or aberrational police decision making, explicable in terms of uncontrolled discretion, questionable judgment or even disregard of clear legal precepts. Similarly, the adult case, *AH-A058*, might be taken to show the incompleteness of official records arising perhaps from the lack of external accountability. However, no form of analysis is 'obvious', and choices have to be made about how to subject any process to systematic scrutiny. In this section, we describe some of the forms of analysis that we considered adopting and outline the broad method which informs our own account. The forms of analysis we deal with are positivism, interactionism and structuralism.

Positivism evaluates behaviour against standards, not usually made explicit, which enables a judgment to be reached that the behaviour is, or is not, in conformity to the standards. Significant departure from the standards thus founds an argument for a different outcome than that which occurred. The assumption is that there is a set of standards which are clear, objective and determinative of action; the discretion exercised is accordingly 'weak', i.e. bounded by clear standards. Since prosecution decision making is subject to standards of evidence and criteria for cautions, positivist critiques would appear at first sight to be useful.

Positivism has its problems, both in general and in this context. Assumptions of ability and willingness to change behaviour, as well as of clear standards by which to judge behaviour, may all be faulty. We shall see that in reality the police have their own reasons for deviating from supposedly set standards, and that these standards are actually not at all clear. Moreover, to apply rules to facts requires that the facts themselves be clear. In principle this is no problem for positivism which draws a sharp fact/value distinction. But even positivists would recognise that in reality the facts are often unclear.

In view of all this, we argue that positivist analysis is ultimately unprofitable. If we return to the three cases outlined above we can see that attempts to understand the behaviour of the police, or other official actors, purely in terms of legal rules, precepts or guidelines is inadequate, for the official guidelines alone pointed to outcomes other than those which occurred. It is necessary instead to take into account the rules, legal *and* social, which the actors choose to follow. As William Sanders (1977) put it in relation to studying the work of detectives:

> Examining police conduct in terms of the statutory requirements can explain very little, for exceptions to the rules are so pervasive that police actions almost appear to be arbitrary. On the other hand, if we follow a sociological approach, concentrating on formal bureaucratic rules and policies *and* informal norms within the police organization, we can begin to discern and understand patterns in police actions. (Sanders, 1977, p. 78, original emphasis)

Second, the cases show that there is no single reality but rather competing versions of reality and this may be so even *within* the official records or the police organization itself. So, was A058 'disorderly' or not, or even 'drunk'? Third, for official purposes, the police have a pivotal role in deciding which reality will be accorded dominance and, in this way, are central 'definers of reality'. Was J14 in danger of sliding into criminality? The belief of the ultimate decision-making officer defined J14's reality in the form of a criminal record. Fourth, in the process of creating this official reality the 'facts' as well as the 'rules' are malleable: rules are there to be used and the 'facts' which ultimately triumph are those needed to justify the desired outcome. Fifth, the way in which the official reality is arrived at may not be apparent or discoverable from the official records and, indeed, official actors may have an interest in suppressing the process which led to the official reality gaining dominance. So, there was no way of discovering from official records either that A058 had allegedly damaged a door, or that the caution was for an offence which no-one had alleged he had committed.

Uncritical legalistic approaches to the analysis of how official actors behave, which assume a complete congruence between 'the law' and 'reality', and do so on the basis that the law itself is an unproblematic, fixed, certain and ascertainable entity, are thus unhelpful. There are various alternatives. First, there is *interactionism*. This stresses the ambiguity and uncertainty of information, and indeed of all social life. One problem with micro-sociological approaches (of which interactionism is one) is, as Jefferson and Grimshaw (1987, ch. 1) point out, that they focus so closely on subculture that they take little or no account of broader socio-economic structures or legal rules. Interactionism 'sometimes amounts to an extreme rule scepticism' (Reiner, 1985, p. 175).

One consequence of this is that interactionism pins the explanation for 'deviant' behaviour on middle and lower rank actors, the agents of social control. But if the police act out socio-economic policies, as expressed in legal and other bureaucratic rules, to focus on police subculture alone is to miss the point. Interactionism, in the last analysis, is as reformist as positivism: change the subculture (rather than, as in positivism, the rules) and police behaviour will change. This assumption, that the particular forms of particular subcultures are autonomous and arbitrary, is surely too simplistic.

Another perspective is *structuralism*, which does focus on socio-economic structures, legal-bureaucratic rules, and on the 'senior officers, judges and the state elite' (Reiner, 1985, p. 176) who mediate between those structures and rules. McBarnet (1981) and Jefferson and Grimshaw (1987) are major structuralists who argue for the political role and permissive character of legal rules.

Whilst our approach is broadly structuralist we have reservations about McBarnet's analysis (see Chapter 9). In part this is because of the need for an interactionist methodology. With Henry (1983) our approach is an *integrated* one, exploring 'the interpenetration of the micro-structures with the macro and vice versa' (p. 62). We need to recognise the complexity of the micro-social world, the dynamic way in which cases reflect external 'realities' and the way that cases are *social constructions* which further broad socio-political objectives.

CASE CONSTRUCTION

The essence of *social construction* is that its purpose is not necessarily to fulfil some assumed objective of the law, but to attempt to achieve a particular objective through the use of *the legal form*. The concept of case construction has no perjorative overtones. Construction does not require or imply that cases are necessarily unworthy, unmeritorious or against the interest of the object of the construction, the suspect or defendant. Whilst case construction is a feature of *any* criminal justice system, the adversary system, as we shall see, makes case construction a particularly partial and partisan process.

Construction may be achieved at one moment and by one act, but often it will be an ongoing task in the course of which the objectives may change and in so doing render earlier constructions redundant or unsuccessful, at least for the moment. The nuances of this process were set down in the early study of Aaron Cicourel, *The Social Organization of Juvenile Justice* (1968). Cicourel stressed the necessity of seeking:

> an organizational context for understanding how law-enforcement justifies practices that may have little to do with the implied rationality of ideals of legality and justice. . . . Specifically, therefore, the actor in law-enforcement organizations makes decisions in terms of his situation and way of thinking that govern his encounter with suspects. These decisions may vary with subsequent encounters, and the accounts of 'what happened' will vary accordingly, especially as they assume a formal written status.
>
> Each successive stage of legal decision-making transforms the object or event (as, for example, with rumour transmission) so that the contingencies, the situation in which the actor interprets what is going on, the kind of 'theorizing' or thinking employed are progressively altered, eliminated, and reified, as the case proceeds 'up' the legal machinery and reaches the stage of a hearing, trial or appellate jurisdiction. At each stage the various participants select from available 'facts' or created interpretations about motives, intent, and the like, those propositions which are to be accorded a factual status in their particular explanation, whether this be from the standpoint of the police, witnesses, lawyers, members of the jury, or judge. (Cicourel, 1968, p. 53)

In what follows, our principal task will be to lay bare the process by which a case is constructed, from the moment the suspect becomes an object of police suspicion. It must be emphasized that at each point of the criminal justice process 'what happened' is the subject of interpretation, addition, subtraction, selection and reformulation. This process is a *continuous* process, so that the meaning and status of 'a case' are to be understood in terms of the particular time and context in which it is viewed, a meaning and status that it may not have possessed earlier or continue to possess thereafter. The construction of a case is not confined to one aspect of the process, such as the creation of an internal record or the compilation of evidence, but infuses every action and activity of official actors from the initial selection of the suspect to final case disposition. Case construction implicates the actors in a discourse with legal rules and guidelines and involves them in using rules, manipulating rules and interpreting rules. It involves not simply the selection and interpretation of evidence but its *creation*. Understanding the selections made and the decisions taken requires, therefore, analyis of the motivations of the actors, their value systems and ideologies.

The complexities of this process are usually not apparent to the observer because police and prosecutors structure their accounts of cases to fit into accepted legal categories. These categories are simple, often dichotomous (guilty/not guilty; sane/insane; intentional/not intentional; reckless/not reckless; voluntary/involuntary) and deny the ambiguities and uncertainties of the world of our experience. As Ericson pointed out, in dealing with the work of detectives, the process of transforming the complex into the simple has distinct instrumental effects for other actors in the system:

> [T]he detective is involved in a process of transforming an individual event into categories which have a character of permanence and exactness. These categories are drawn from the available stock of categories stored within the police and wider legal organizations. Use of these categories allows the detective to assume that everyone else will know what this case consists of. It allows the detective, his superordinates, the prosecutor, and other court officials, to accept his account as 'the facts', and therefore to act '*as if*' they are in a state of perfect knowledge, and *as if* this "perfect knowledge" has fairly stable constitutive elements. . .'. (Ericson, 1981a, p. 18, citing Carlen, 1976, p. 88. Emphasis added by Ericson)

This process of rendering down the complex to the simple is not only enabling for other actors, but also gives the official version a dominant place in the hierarchy of possible accounts, conferring on competing realities a presumptively illegitimate status. Thus, A058 would have found it difficult, if not impossible, to argue successfully that he was not 'really' drunk and disorderly, particularly since 'drunks' (along with other negative social stereotypes) find that the label itself de-legitimizes their arguments about those very labels (Box and Russell, 1975). Further, in the world of case construction, facts, values and rules become inextricably fused (Ericson, 1981b, p. 45). Whilst it is true that, within the legal world, facts, values and rules often appear to take on separate lives, this speaks only to the success of the method and grammar of law in creating an image of scientism and rationality through a claimed discourse of objective and discrete categorizations.

The account which follows is *our* account not in the trivial sense that someone else did not write it but in the important sense that no-one else could have written it. The account, and the data upon which it relies are not separate from ourselves, the methods and strategies adopted, the choices and selections made and the meanings and interpretations adopted or imposed. Research, like the world of its subjects, is a process of construction. In describing the 'realities' presented by police and prosecution, we set up another 'reality'. The fact that researchers do not and cannot have unmediated access to the 'truth' is not a strength or a weakness of the research and is not a deficiency in our method: it is an epistemological reality.

NOTES

1 Throughout this book, cases are assigned an identification code based on the Police Force and sub-division from which they were collected, and divided according to each adult and juvenile within the samples. The first two letters identify the Force area and sub-division (basic details of which are given in the Appendix), with adults classified in each sub-division from A001 to A120, and juveniles from J01 to J60. Thus, for example, case *AH-J14* was drawn from Force A, sub- division H, and involves the fourteenth juvenile collected in the juvenile sample in that sub-division.

   In all case accounts in this book, insignificant details have been varied using well- established social science techniques in order to ensure that none of the individuals involved can be identified.

2 Constructing the suspect population

What makes someone a 'suspect'? Most people assume that the simple answer to this is anyone who breaks the law and/or who excites police suspicion that they have done so. The constitution of the suspect population seems, at first glance, to be unproblematic – a naturally occurring group which any successful and efficient police force would encounter. Criminals are those who break the law, and suspects are those whose conduct suggests that they fall into this criminal category. No-one would expect a complete correspondence between these two categories, if only because low detection rates suggest that there are many criminals who never become suspects. But people do expect substantial overlap. They also expect that police investigation would aim to differentiate 'normal' people from suspects (through logic, evidence, classic 'detective' skills and so forth), and then ascertain whether the evidence against suspects warrants a public accusation that they fall into the criminal category.

This chapter will show that this picture is too simplistic. Although the police begin investigation with many actual offenders and many who have behaved 'suspiciously', the raw material with which the police work is a police construct. The suspect population is *not* a sub-set of the criminal population. Indeed, as this book unfolds we shall see that the reverse is true: the 'criminal' population (that is, people who are convicted of criminal offences) is a sub-set of the suspect population. Some years ago the 'labelling theorists' posited a 'societal reaction' perspective on crime (Erikson, 1964; Lemert, 1967). This argues that

> deviance is not a quality of the act the person commits, but rather a consequence of the application by others of rules and sanctions to an 'offender'. The deviant is one to whom that label has successfully been applied. (Becker, 1963)

We do not argue that criminality consists solely in the reaction of the police or the wider society. This would deny both the intentionality of 'primary deviance' and 'the structure of power and interest' within which action and reaction occur (Taylor *et al.*, 1973, ch. 5). However, the major insight of the labelling theorists remains valid: that suspicion, accusation, conviction and criminal self-identity are not objective characteristics of 'criminals', but are the products of law enforcers as well. Thus, once initially selected, suspects are further classified and sorted on the basis of police-driven criteria. In this grading process some are released unconditionally (whether or not there is strong evidence of offending) some are subjected to a police sanction (whether or not there is strong evidence of offending) and some are sent for prosecution (whether or not there is strong evidence of offending).

These processes are not random or arbitrary. The suspect population is constructed on the basis of a complex interaction of rules and principles. But they are *police* – rather than *legal* – rules and principles. They are not *illegal*, but simply arise from the discretion which the police enjoy. The police do not *have* to stop and search an individual in the street, but they *may* do so; they do not *have* to arrest individuals, but they *may* do so; and they do not *have* to detain and process individuals, but they *may* do so. The way in which the police choose to exercise these discretions explains why they take the action they do – to stop or not, to search or not, to arrest or not, and so forth.

It may be thought that we give too much emphasis to the coercive law enforcement role of the police, to the exclusion of their 'service' and 'peace-keeping' roles in which they are said to work with, rather than against, the 'community', and to persuade rather than prosecute (Banton, 1964; Chatterton, 1983; McCabe and Sutcliffe, 1978). However, this emphasis is deliberate, for our current interest lies in the use of the coercive powers provided by law to the police. Other aspects of police work may be important, but they are not our current concern. On the other hand, since different aspects of police work all emerge from one policing mandate, one policing institution and one set of social relations, we would argue that our case construction approach would yield similar results if applied to other aspects of policing, as other works with comparable perspectives suggest (Bittner, 1967; Piliavin and Briar, 1964; Smith and Gray, 1983, vol. IV).

ENTERING THE FRAME: CITIZEN OR POLICE INITIATION?

Low visibility discretion

The research on which this book is based was primarily a study of arrested individuals (see Appendix). This limited (but did not eliminate) the extent to which we could explore what influenced officers to *not* stop and search, or to *not* arrest. However, a mass of research which has concentrated on this 'low visibility' discretion already exists and provides the context for our own work. A number of uncontentious conclusions can be drawn from this body of work:

– When confronted with situations requiring immediate decision, officers decide what they want to do and then fit their legal powers around that decision, rather than assessing their legal powers first and then seeing what action might be lawful (Bittner, 1967; Willis, 1983; Dixon *et al.*, 1989).

– The law in general, and the requirement that stop-search and arrest be based on 'reasonable suspicion' in particular, does not constrain the police from taking most of the actions which they consider desirable. The law is sufficiently vague and flexible to allow the police very extensive discretion (Goldstein, 1960; Davis, 1969; McBarnet, 1981; Dixon *et al.*, 1989).

– Discretion is exercised according to police criteria, rather than officially announced legal criteria. That is, not all suspected offenders are stopped or arrested, many stops and arrests are not based on 'reasonable suspicion' and arrest decisions are not based solely on grounds of evidence and seriousness of suspected offence. The perceived character of the suspect, for instance – often based on stereotypical cues – is at least as influential (Piliavin and Briar, 1964; Smith and Gray, 1983).

– The police use the law as a control device. The aims of stops and arrests are often not to enforce the law *per se*, but to secure broader objectives: the imposition of order, the assertion of authority, the acquisition of information (Holdaway, 1983; Chatterton, 1976; Bittner, 1967).

The broad thrust of the above is encompassed by Egon Bittner (1967, p. 701) in his study of public order on skid-row:

Patrolmen do not really enforce the law, even when they do invoke it, but merely use it as a resource to solve certain pressing problems in keeping the peace. . . . The problem patrolmen confront is not which drunks, beggars, or disturbers of the peace should be arrested and which can be let go as exceptions to the rule. Rather, the problem is whether, when someone 'needs' to be arrested, he should be charged with drunkenness, begging or disturbing the peace.

Thus the law makes it possible to proceed by way of arrest but it does not dictate that an arrest should be made nor determine it: the reason for the arrest has to be sought elsewhere.

We will see that Bittner's observation is generalizable. It is not confined to public order situations or to arrest but pervades all police (and prosecutorial) decision making relating to initial apprehension, warnings, cautions, charging and so on. It does not follow, of course, that there are no variations in practice. Police culture and police norms are not monolithic or static, but major patterns are discernible within and between localities.

Another pattern which can be discerned from the policing research relates to wider social structures. Police powers are not exercised randomly or representatively across society. They bear most heavily on young working-class males, especially young black males. Demeanour – the basis for judging character in street encounters – is also socially and racially patterned. Thus, after considering these and related factors, Box concludes that 'it is not to be wondered at that the official profile of criminals suggests that they derive from the lower strata' (1981, p. 163).

This patterning is not primarily a product of deliberate bias, but of the criteria and objectives discussed earlier, along with certain institutional pressures (Cain, 1973; Reiner, 1985). For example, it is easier to police public than private spaces, and so those people who most inhabit the former – young working-class males – are most 'at risk'.

Thus, for example, it is not surprising that only one in seven adults (13.6 per cent) and one in eight juveniles (11.7 per cent) in our official suspect population were females. Whilst this ratio approximates to the male–female offending ratio in the official statistics, the offending ratio measured in self-report studies is much lower at 2:1 (Riley, 1986). The construction of official suspect populations is very much a product of broad societal gender divisions, with women generally denied access to the 'public' domain, thus having reduced opportunities to participate in those crimes upon which police attention has been historically directed. Given equal opportunities, 'sex differences in crime participation by young people – as offenders or victims – are minimal' (Riley, 1986, p. 38).

The most obvious sphere where structured gender discrimination relating to 'acceptable' presence in the public sphere is less operative is in such places as shops and work settings, and it is precisely these public areas which produced the significant proportions of female suspects within our suspect population. Thus, of female juveniles 66.7 per cent were arrested in respect of shoplifting, compared with only 18.9 per cent of male juveniles; the equivalent figures in respect of adults being 27.6 per cent females, 9.3 per cent males.

It is not just the law which fails to structure discretion. 'Official' police policy (in the form of Home Office circulars and the 'Standing Orders' of individual forces) is similarly ineffective. This is because in the police service, almost unique among complex organizations, 'discretion increases as one moves *down* the hierarchy' (Wilson, 1968, p. 7). Police discretion on the street is 'low visibility' (Goldstein, 1960). Shapland and Vagg (1988), for instance, report that most beat officers see a supervising officer just once a day on average, and that this is often because they seek the assistance of the supervisor. The discretion exercised in everyday policing can therefore be controlled only within very broad limits, and officers can, after the event, easily characterize their action in terms of official norms (Ericson, 1981b). It is 'cop culture' (as Reiner, 1985, describes it) which actually structures discretion, albeit within a broad political framework in which 'official' police norms and legal rules play a part. The collective set of decisions taken by the police, on the basis of these complex networks of rules and influences, defines the suspect population.

The role of the citizen

It would be misleading, however, to suggest that arrests are solely a product of police street discretion. Other institutions and social processes play a major part. This realization some years ago (e.g. Banton, 1964; Bottomley and Coleman, 1976; Mawby, 1979; Steer, 1980; McConville and Baldwin, 1981) has even led some to argue that police discretion is of little importance in shaping the suspect population. In order to evaluate this view, we need to consider the main methods by which people come to be arrested.

First, the police may see the suspect acting suspiciously or 'in the act'. Table 1 presents the sources of initial information linking suspects to their alleged offences in our sample.

As in our sample, other research has found police initiation to account for a minority of arrests (e.g. Zander, 1979; McConville and Baldwin, 1981). Second, the police may adopt the 'bureaucratic' mode of detection, whereby the police cull 'known' offenders for crimes fitting their 'modus operandi' which are known to have been committed (Matza, 1969). This is even less significant proportionately, but it relies upon the same types of police 'knowledge' of suspicion and so forth as the first method. Third, the police may adopt other 'detective' methods – either systematically investigating forensic evidence (the 'classic' method) or securing information from co-defendants or informants. Very few arrests are the product of the classic method but 'information',

Table 1 The source of initial information linking the suspect to the alleged offence in both adult and juvenile cases

	n	*%*
Suspect apprehended by civilian	189	18.1
Police called to scene by civilian	163	15.6
Civilian gave name of suspect or other identification to the police	253	24.2
'Information received'	65	6.2
Police witness offence	138	13.2
Police see suspect at crime scene	55	5.3
Suspect apprehended after police stop of person/vehicle	74	7.1
Co-suspect giving information	56	5.4
Other	51	4.9
No information	36	–
Total	1080	100.0

as Table 1 shows, is significant. Reiner (1985, p. 122) suggests that 'real detective work' accounts for less (probably considerably less) than one quarter of CID arrests – and CID arrests are themselves a minority of all arrests. As Table 1 shows, police initiative overall, whilst important, accounted for a minority of cases. The police either witnessed the offence, saw the suspect at the scene of the crime or apprehended the suspect following a stop in just 25.6 per cent of all our arrests.

Most information comes from civilians. As Reiner points out, empirical studies agree that 'the prime determinant of success is information immediately provided by members of the public (usually the victim)' (1985, p. 121). Thus Table 1 shows that in our sample civilians initiated police action or identified the suspect in 57.9 per cent of all arrests. Hence it is common to find arguments on these lines in the literature:

> The demands made upon the police by the public form the largest single 'input' to which the police react. Police work is largely generated by the decision making of individuals. (Shapland and Vagg, 1988, p. 7)

> Most of the knowledge that contributes to solution through investigation is based upon citizen information on the identity of the suspects. (Reiss, 1971, p. 109)

> [I]t has been shown that the police are largely dependent on the public not only for the initial discovery of the offence but also for the information that will lead to its detection. (Steer, 1980, p. 121)

Steer goes on to argue that the role of police suspicion is further diminished because most arrests are made immediately or almost immediately. He concludes that the 'sociological tradition' – by which he means the research on street discretion and stereotyping – 'does not stand the test of empirical examination' (p. 126).

The following case, drawn from our sample, is the type of case on which Steer bases his view:

> *BK-A056/A057* – Responding to a call, the police found a man bleeding profusely on the ground. They set off to look for the assailants and in the words of the arresting officer 'saw [A056/7] walking down the pavement covered in blood'.

However, as McConville and Baldwin (1981) point out, police initiative is more pronounced in non-indictable offences, 'victimless' crimes in particular (e.g. public order, prostitution, drunkenness), than in indictable offences. Thus studies based only on the latter – such as McConville and Baldwin's own, Steer's and Zander's – will significantly understate the 'proactive' role of the police. Yet these offences account for around half of all prosecutions.

Further, when civilians believe that a particular person committed an offence, they are as influenced by stereotypical cues as are police officers. Whilst it may be that the police are a microcosm of society (albeit skewed towards the lower-middle-class white male conservative section: Box, 1981), this does mean that civilians and police officers are subject to similar influences. Indeed, the police play a large part in shaping stereotypical views of crime and criminals (Hall *et al.*, 1978). Thus, in the USA, Cameron (1964) found that store detectives observed, followed and prosecuted juveniles and black people disproportionately. In England, too, store detectives stereotype 'typical' shoplifters (Murphy, 1986). So although civilians help to construct the suspect population, they do so through stereotyping as much as do the police.

Constructing information from the citizen

Apart from in shoplifting cases (18.1 per cent of all the arrests in our sample), civilians rarely make arrests themselves. The civilian role is more usually to transmit information to the police. This transmission process is not necessarily, or even usually, unproblematic. Thus Steer makes a logical jump from the proposition that citizens initiate most police action to the conclusion that police discretion is minimal, without considering how the police exercise their discretion in deciding how to respond to citizens and to the information they provide.

First, the police have to decide whether to respond at all. The police are increasingly acknowledging officially that they are adopting 'graded responses', and police and public definitions of crime seriousness do not correspond (e.g. Jones *et al.*, 1986). Even if they do respond by sending an officer, the complainant's information will range from highly specific identification to very vague impressions. The vaguer the information the more reliant upon police skills, preconceptions and so forth the eventual arrest (where there is one) will be. Even if the suspect has been apprehended by the civilian, the police still need to sift and evaluate what they are told. They need to decide:

Whether to do anything: is it a crime? Is it sufficiently serious? Is there any evidence against the suspect?
What to do: is the suspect really likely to be guilty? Are there other equally plausible suspects? Is arrest the best strategy?

If the suspect has not been apprehended, but identification evidence has been provided, the same questions arise. In either case prior police attitudes are important.

The police receive enormous amounts of information, some of which does not really relate to crime, or does so only indirectly, as in the following case:

CE-A089 – A089 was circulated on a 'wanted' list for shoplifting from an off-licence. He was arrested. According to the police he 'had been identified as entering a shop ... with two of his friends. ... He was the only one on the video. One of the shop staff recognized the other two and saw the third one, his colleague, take this bottle of wine and they all walked out together you see. As yet we've spoken to [A089] but he can't identify this man. You see, they are all dossers ...'.

Since the shop staff saw someone else take the wine, A089 was arrested solely in an effort to catch the 'real' criminal. Citizen information is often wrong, or at least unproductive. Thus Black (1970) in the USA found that, of 500 citizen complaints, only two-thirds were taken seriously or accepted as genuine by the police. And, in England, Shapland and Vagg point out that:

1 message pads are likely not to contain calls which do not, in the view of the controller taking the call, require police attendance;
2 the way in which the matter is referred to in the written record is an amalgam of the way it is presented by the public ... and the controller's view of the possibilities for police action. (1988, p. 35)

Even when complaints are taken seriously, the police must still set priorities and the nature of their response, as is clear also from McCabe and Sutcliffe (1978), is a matter of complete discretion for them. The result is that the suspect population is constructed by the police even when they are responding to citizen complaints:

CC-A074/A075/A076 – A restaurant called the police to deal with three lads who disputed their bill. After some argument they were arrested. As the arresting officer explained: 'Had their attitude towards the police been different we could have dealt with it in a different way . . . but there were another five, perhaps six, customers in the restaurant . . . these people are watching to see what was going on. And if we are seen to take a soft line at that stage then where the hell does it stop? So as far as I was concerned it had got to be taken away from there.'

The police sometimes create official suspects only reluctantly:

BW-A118 – The AO (arresting officer) was sent to a domestic disturbance. A118 had moved out of the house in which he had been lodging with V but returned to collect personal property which V denied having. A118 refused to leave at first and the AO heard him threaten 'to smash every window in the house'.

Res:	'You didn't consider arresting him at that point?'
Officer:	'Came close to it but managed to talk him out of it and talk him into going. I must have spent 20–30 minutes there in order to avoid a further breach of the peace.'

As we shall see when we discuss this case again, A118 was eventually arrested. But this was only after further incidents and a remarkable exercise of patience on the AO's part.

Despite Steer's argument to the contrary, there is, then, no contradiction between, on the one hand, the view that police investigation is filtered through their own values, prejudices and preconceptions and, on the other hand, the view that most arrests are made on the (partial) basis of information from the public. Even when they are 'reactive' the police use their discretion as fully as when they are 'proactive'. Citizen information, then, is another *resource* for the police. Whether it leads to any police action and, if it does, what kind of action are matters largely in the hands of the police and not citizens. Information provided to the police by citizens is mediated through police values and priorities, and it is at this point that case construction begins.

POLICE WORKING RULES

It is clear that few constraints on police discretion are imposed by legal rules. Take the legal requirement that, in order to stop/search or to arrest, the police must have 'reasonable suspicion'. There is no definition in either statute or case law, and so 'even the people in here don't know exactly what it means' (Detective in *CE-A074*). The legal vacuum is filled, not by random or patternless policing, but by the structuring of discretion according to working rules developed by policing on the ground (see also the 'recipe rules' of Ericson, 1981a). In this section, we deal with six working rules of the police.

Previous

Being 'known to the police' is all that is sometimes needed to make someone an official suspect. The arresting officer in *AT-J52* thought it vital to see prisoners, spend time with them, get to know them in order to recognize them in future: 'I think that's our stock in trade . . . recognizing people who were arrested in the past has got to be what we do for a living'. This knowledge can be used by the police in at least three ways: to provide the first lead in a reported crime, to follow the individual to see if anything suspicious is done and simply as a basis for arrest in itself.

Smith and Gray provide a good example of the first, when reporting a Crime Squad discussion; the police decided to crack down on burglaries as follows: 'Let's go round and nick Danny' (1983, p. 345). This was purely because Danny had previous convictions for burglary, a shop had been burgled three nights running and only Danny was thought stupid enough to do this. Similarly, Sanders and Bridges (1990) discuss a juvenile (BA094) who was arrested for deception, to which he confessed, solely because of the particular 'modus operandi'. *BW-A098* (in Chapter 8), *BW-A031* (see p. 27) and the following example are all similar, although less successful for the police:

BK-A110 – A private garage had been damaged by fire. A110, who had several previous convictions, had in the past had a liaison with the complainant. On several occasions in the past he was said to have pestered her. A110 denied any involvement but was arrested for criminal damage. A search of his house was unproductive. The investigating officer said that 'it was obvious that [the defendant] was responsible. . . . I would say that he has done it out of spite because his approaches have been spurned. He is an objectionable little creature. He's dirty, he's a drunkard, he's of low intelligence. It's a racing certainty he's done it.' At the very outset of the case (on which there was eventually 'no further action'), the CID note on the case file was open about the grounds of arrest and the lack of evidence:

'Recently there have been numerous occasions when [he] has visited this address whereby a breach of peace has been occasioned or public order offences have occurred, it was on this basis that [he] was arrested, there was no concrete evidence that could place him in the vicinity. . . . There are no witnesses who are able to assist in any way. . . . When interviewed [he] adamantly denied any involvement . . . examination of his clothing failed to disclose any possible connection and indeed an inquiry was made with the forensic science laboratory to establish whether they may be able to assist, unfortunately they could not.'

Whilst this is a good example of a case where the reasons for arrest were of no legal-evidential value at all (which does not in itself invalidate the arrest), it is also a good example of how citizen complaints do not remove the need for the police to exercise their own rules of suspicion. Although the complainant may well have pointed to A110 as the likely offender, the police chose to act on the complainant's information because of A110's antecedents and perceived character.

The second way in which someone with 'previous' is more likely to come under suspicion is that the person can be followed when noticed. The offender's status is, for the police, enough to make the person a suspect – for something. This, in its simplest form, happened in *AT-A047*. Here the arresting officer had been looking for 'dippers' (or pickpockets) in a street market when

> 'up walks this chap who we knew was one of the suspects. . . . He'd been seen there before, he fitted the description, he was an associate of someone who'd already been arrested. . . . You tend to follow the ones you know. If I hadn't known him to tail him he'd have probably got away with it.'

The third way is stated by the arresting officer in *AH-A115*: 'when you get to know an area, and see a villain about at 2.00 a.m. in the morning, you will always stop him to see what he is about.' The products of stops (materials found, things said and so forth) sometimes lead to suspects becoming 'official' suspects (i.e. arrested). In very serious cases, no more need be known about someone than the fact that the person has been previously convicted: in such cases, a 'record' *is* the basis for the arrest. In Area AT, five suspects in our sample were arrested as part of a major rape enquiry. The Detective Inspector (DI) leading the enquiry explained:

> DI: 'All five, together with hundreds of others, were put up to us as suspects, and we are dealing with them on the basis of elimination on a positive basis, taking blood samples and verifying alibis.'
> Res: 'How did they come to be arrested?'
> DI: 'On information supplied to us.'
> These particular five, though, were arrested, he said, solely on the basis of information from criminal records and police collators.

'Reasonable suspicion', it seems, means even less than usual in cases like this. The alibis of these suspects could have been checked first, which would have led to considerably fewer arrests. On the other hand this could have alerted the actual criminal, and so police action – whereby 'previous' alone justified arrest – was based on real Crime Control concerns. Whilst recognizing this we must also recognize the subordination of Due Process concerns.

Disorder and police authority

As part of their public order mandate (Brogden, 1982) the police put up
with disorderliness only if it ceases on their arrival. In fact it usually does
cease. Shapland and Hobbs (1989) found that only 19–25 per cent of
'disturbances' attended by the police led to arrests. But if it does not
cease, arrest powers are used to crush the disorder. This was found on a
large scale in the miners' strike (McCabe *et al.*, 1988, pp. 42–4), with the
'hippie convoy' (Vincent-Jones, 1986) and, more generally, in our
sample:

> *BW-A032/A033/A034* – The police were called to a disturbance outside a club.
> The suspects were, according to the arresting officer, threatening the bouncers
> 'which is quite a laugh if you saw the gorillas on the door and these little lads'.
> When the police arrived the suspects turned their insults on the police. One
> 'made a very rude gesture and called us a load of wankers and he had to come
> in for that really . . . you come to a point like a parent with a child where if you
> don't do something the others will all join in . . . so you have to be perhaps a
> little bit extra strong, for want of a better word, in that situation than you might
> be with these people at 10.00 a.m.'.

The police have the same working rules everywhere. So, in *CE-A083*,
where a driver was stopped for not wearing a seat belt, 'my suspicions
were raised immediately because his friend tried to walk away . . . so I
decided to do a full street interview. . . I asked him for his details under
PACE, he refused his details and challenged me to arrest him, so I did.'

This kind of response is also displayed in less confrontational
situations:

> *CE-A039* – The police were called to deal with a drunk. 'Even when we
> approached him', the arresting officer said 'he was offensive towards us and
> generally acting in a disorderly fashion.' So he was arrested.

If disorderliness is interpreted by the police as an attack on their
authority – that is, their *personal* authority as well as the abstract
authority of Law and Order (Westley, 1953) – they rarely accept it. This
was the situation in *CC-A074/A075/A076* (see p. 22) and in the following
case:

> *AT-A053* – The arresting officer was called to a party. A053 refused to turn off
> his 'ghetto blaster'. The arresting officer said to the researcher: 'It would have
> been all right if he'd just gone away but he had to be Jack the Lad and wanted
> to be put down. So I put him down . . . I grabbed him and arrested him.'
> Res: 'On what basis?'
> AO: 'Well it's hard to explain. Anyone in the police would under-
>   stand but you wouldn't. . . . It's a way of dealing with the
>   situation. You get him off the street and make the residents
>   happy. It's "Ways and Means", just to get him away, control

the situation and show the neighbours you're doing
something. . . . It's touchy and I don't want to say any more.'
[The case was the subject of a complaint by A053's friend, and
A053 was cautioned for insulting behaviour.]

Many police officers do not try to avoid confrontations and the
consequences which follow. All police officers seek excitement in their
work. Some therefore look for a 'ruck'. (Smith and Gray, 1983, p. 341;
Jefferson and Grimshaw, 1987, p. 54; Shapland and Hobbs, 1987,
p. 141).

It follows from this that most officers accept that a few bruises go
along with the job. It is all part of the 'machismo syndrome' (Reiner,
1985, p. 89). Thus, an officer explained to us:

CE-J04 – 'I tend personally to accept a few scuffles and bruises. . . . There are
times when to be honest you would charge sometimes to cover yourself
because you have to put an injury-on-duty form in. . . . I know one or two
bobbies who'd cry "assault police" if somebody pushed them in the chest but
as far as I'm concerned that just goes down in the statement as a violent
struggle or something like that – a struggle, that's it. If you get a bruise, so be
it, that's the way it is.'

So arrest may be the consequence of a fight but it need not be. Officers
who do not wish to arrest and charge for assaults made in the course of
a 'ruck' need not do so, but the option is always there, no matter how
trivial the injury, if arrest serves a policing purpose such as the
imposition of authority.

General suspiciousness

As we saw earlier, stereotypical cues that make individuals or groups
'suspicious' are the partial or total basis for law enforcement decisions
by police officers, non-police agencies and ordinary citizens alike. As
one officer put it to us: 'The police service itself tends to put people in
boxes. If your lifestyle or appearance is out of the ordinary then they
stick another label on you' (*AT-A017*). Apart from the factors already
examined, which relate to the person or the specific conduct, there are
also situational attributes – being in certain areas, having certain
associates (seen with certain people), incongruity at a particular time or
place and so forth (Manning, 1977, p. 117).

Piliavin and Briar (1964), for instance, report that when they asked
why one person was stopped on the street the answer was 'he was a negro
wearing dark glasses at midnight', and Box reports being stopped
because with his demeanour and appearance (late-1960s, hippy)
carrying golf clubs in a middle-class suburb looked distinctly suspicious

(1981, p. 212). In these examples the police found nothing else to justify action, so no arrests were made and the suspects did not enter the 'official' category. Jefferson and Grimshaw (1987), however, show that the situation is not simply one of 'finding' a justification, for justifications can be constructed. They discuss a call to a football ground where intruders were reported. D was seen leaning against the wall of the ground around midnight. 'I bet he's something to do with it', said an officer. When it was found that his friends had been arrested, he was arrested too. He refused to confess (to that incident) and so two officers claimed they had seen him climb out of the ground.

The nature of our research was such that pure fabrication of this sort would not usually be apparent. However, it is probably rare, if only because it is rarely needed. Cases can usually be successfully constructed through ambiguities, assumptions and confessions. But to reach that stage the initial stop or arrest is needed, and many are on pretexts which are as thin as those given above.

> *CC-J30/J31* – The arresting officer explained: 'I saw [J30/1] walking through [X] store with several other youths. [J30] was carrying a jumper which was obviously new.... I followed them out.... I went and questioned him about it and he became very agitated. His first words to me were 'I haven't stolen it' so I immediately thought it's obviously stolen. As a result of what he told me I arrested him.' He also arrested J31 (despite securing no admissions from J31 or other evidence of him assisting J30). Later he became convinced that J31 was *not* in fact guilty, despite being – he added darkly and obscurely – 'involved in the group's activities earlier'. Ultimately, no action was taken against either.

As we shall see in Chapter 6, the police accept that many individuals will be NFA (no further action) if the *cases* about which they are concerned can be prosecuted. Thus many arrests are on general suspicion; the police hope that evidence will be forthcoming, but are philosophical if it is not.

> *BW-A031* – A031 was hanging around near a school where there was a reported break-in. The custody officer told us: 'A031 is known to us ... and we are quite sure that on the night he was with them [his co-accused]'. As another officer put it: 'he's got previous convictions for burglary so I had the suspicion there. He was in the right place at the right time and as I say he gave a lame excuse for being there.' A031 was NFA, and his friends were prosecuted.

At other times strong grounds which can be used to justify the arrest are discovered only after a legally baseless stop-search:

> *AH-A079* – The officers saw A079 sitting with his girlfriend in a parked car. When they returned A079 was still in the car. It was 'just a matter of instinct ... something undefinable' which made them check A079. When searched they found drugs on him.

Associates often provide the basis of fruitless arrests:

> *AT-A043/A044/A045* – A complaint was made about A043 approaching people and asking them if they wanted to buy cannabis. He was with the two other arrestees, although no-one claimed that they had approached anyone. The police, however, arrested all three: 'Obviously all three denied any involvement but because all three seemed to be together . . . albeit that [A043] was the only one seen to be doing the approaching, they were all arrested. . . . Let's face it, they obviously knew what was going on . . . but at the end of the day it's all about evidence.'

Dixon *et al.* (1989) and *AT-A041/A042* (in Chapter 6) are good discussions of general incongruity – and are all drawn from research done after the introduction of PACE. So the new, or more specific, rules ushered in by PACE have made little difference to the working rules adopted by the police. Thus in *AH-A101*, in which A101 was stop-searched simply because he walked away when he saw the police officer, the prosecutor told us that he suspected that this would not have stood up in court as reasonable grounds. This did not inhibit the prosecutor from prosecuting, and so the absence of 'reasonable suspicion' does not inhibit police officers from undertaking a stop-search.

Police working rules relating to 'suspicion' can be rather like proverbs or canons of statutory interpretation: for every maxim there is an opposite, thus justifying virtually any course of action. The result, quite often, is an arrest on virtually no evidence and nothing which the police are able or willing to prove, leading to no further action:

> *AH-A082* – When A082 saw the officers approach he ran off. When he was caught he said he ran because he thought they were looking for him after he had assaulted his girlfriend. He was searched, found in possession of a Krugerrand, arrested on suspicion of theft or handling, and released when his lawful possession was proved (the assault was NFA as the woman refused to pursue it).

Officers in such cases regard more or less any activity they choose as 'reasonably suspicious'. There is some pattern though because people in middle-class areas (if they look as though they 'belong') are not regarded with outright suspicion. In working-class areas nearly everyone is fair game. In *AH-A100* the arresting officer was asked how he decided which cars to stop. He laughed: 'We check cars when we see people sitting inside them for a period. We stop when we see three men in a car. Basically it's impossible to say, we just use our instincts.'

In another part of the country, according to the police, 'nobody ever admits the truth, not in this area anyway. If you find anyone without a criminal record in this area it's like trying to find a needle in a haystack, but worse . . . you are dealing with the dregs of society' (arresting officer in *CE-A032*). And so in this case the arresting officer, searching for two youths suspected of causing criminal damage, saw 'two lads who were likely suspects' simply because they were out late in the right area. They were stopped, questioned, arrested and positively identified. These were the right 'type' of lads to stop in this 'type' of area, but for every 'successful' stop there are of course ten or more unsuccessful stops (Willis, 1983; McConville, 1983).

Being uncooperative is a very important indicator of 'suspicion' as in many of these cases. This evokes the police objection to the suspect's 'right of silence': the only suspects who wish to be uncooperative, the argument runs, are those with something to hide. Thus in one case (*AT-J46*) we asked: 'Was he co-operative?' to which the arresting officer replied 'He denied it' as though this was all that there was to the matter. The following case, however, shows that even the police recognize that co-operativeness is not the sole determinant of guilt, although this does not displace their working rules to this effect:

> *BW-A099* – The police visited A099's home at 7.00 a.m. in connection with an attempted robbery as a result of information received. 'He wasn't exactly being co-operative at that stage . . . so he was arrested.' The officer went on: 'I formed the opinion later on that it wasn't him. . . . His reaction initially was one of, perhaps, shock, and aggravation I think. The fact that his name had been associated with an offence like that, considering he had settled down with his girl and all the rest of it.'

Information received

Information comes from a variety of sources, including informants to whom money or other forms of favour are provided (see Cain, 1973, p. 51 and *BK-A095* and *CE-A113* in Chapter 6). Information is often the starting point of an investigation. In a serious case, like suspected drug dealing (e.g. *CE-A074*), it can lead to police surveillance teams, video cameras and so forth. In other cases the police may simply arrest, wholly or largely on this basis. This is not necessarily in breach of 'reasonable suspicion' requirements, even when it secures no 'result' – as in *CE-A113*, where A113 was chased because of 'information received' that he was selling cannabis, but no drugs were found on him. In circumstances like this, the police often give more credence to complainants than to alleged criminals. It is for the suspect(s) to demonstrate innocence, through alibis for instance, rather than for the police to discover any more incriminating evidence, as in the major rape enquiry discussed on p. 24 and in the following case:

BW-A099 – This was the attempted robbery discussed above. Several days after it, on 'information received', A099 was arrested. As the officer put it: 'From first hearing the information it sounded quite good but I will admit that later on knowing all the circumstances it didn't sound so good. But obviously you have to react on what you hear initially.' In fact A099 did not fit the description of the attacker, and nothing at all linked him to the offence. So why was he arrested? 'You are not in a position to know exactly what the bloke is going to say and what he's going to do until you actually go and see him.'

In fact, there was something more in this case, as indeed there may usually be when 'information received' is taken seriously by the police:

'He certainly wasn't in the frame to start with, in fact he was virtually non-existent – we would never have thought of him. But as I said the information that came forward was quite good and when we checked his form we thought there might be a chance; the name even rang a bell to the lads in the office from something which occurred some time ago.'

Very often it will be a cluster of factors that come together around a suspect which leads to his or her arrest. This may seem to provide a more sound basis of 'reasonable suspicion' than just one factor, but it will only do so when these factors are independent of each other. Often they are not. The sort of people about whom the police receive tip-offs simply do tend to have records and live in high crime areas and – for all these reasons – dislike the police (especially when woken in the early hours of the morning). Stereotypes tend to be self-perpetuating.

Workload

Volume of work influences arrests in different ways, depending on the circumstances. Arrest and prosecution figures are still the principal measures of 'success' for police officers, particularly probationers (Smith and Gray, 1983, p. 343). When an officer, or a shift, has a particularly low total they will seek arrests in quantity, with an obvious effect on the nature of the offence mix in the official suspect population and on the amount of evidence. Changes in the way particular types of offence are processed also affect the arrest pattern:

AT-A009 – The police were called to a woman slumped in a doorway: 'lying in her own vomit, the usual thing. It's one of those cases where if you can't do anything else, bring her in for her own safety . . . since they've started cautioning drunks, you don't get many drunks arrested any more as a police constable thinks it's a waste of time. The ones who are just lying in the street have to be brought in really for their own safety; and the disorderly ones. . . . Of course lots of them now get cautioned. It defeats the object as far as lots of PCs are concerned. They can't be bothered with them unless they're disorderly, so leave them to their own means.'

On the other hand, officers who do not need to raise their arrest total at any particular time, and who want to have an easy shift or want to avoid overtime and so forth, will avoid arrest in the absence of strong imperatives.

When not subject to any of these pressures, the police are most interested in 'quality' work. Although most police officers seek 'quality' arrests, this is not just CID work. It will include vice, as far as members of a vice squad are concerned. Any special squad will treat the subject of its concern as 'quality' work. Hence shoplifting is not 'quality crime' for the CID, but it is for the shoplifting squad.

However, alleged crimes can be constructed in ways that boost their 'quality' content, or reduce it, according to the officers' wishes. In *AT-J52* (discussed earlier), for instance, J52 was originally arrested for shoplifting. The amount involved was assessed to be too small to be worth pursuing (the other kids involved were not even arrested). But J52 was arrested because he was in possession of a lock knife and a spark-plug:

> Arresting officer: 'Yes he was quite an interesting little touch really. We arrested him initially for the theft . . . he was questioned further regarding the offensive weapon. CID were advised as to the other matters and they decided they were not really interested.'

Victim

It is usual in the policing literature to acknowledge the influence of the victim in deciding whether to arrest and whether to prosecute and so forth (Ericson, 1981a; Shapland and Hobbs, 1987). All the applicable rules and guidelines – apart from actual legal rules – confirm this. Two important qualifications to this 'rule' are, however, less frequently acknowledged. The first is that the concept of the victim is itself a construction: in many situations the labels 'victim', 'offender' and 'witness' could all be interchangeable:

> *BW-A059/A060* – There was a pub brawl and fight between an employee A059 and a customer A060. A060, who had a scratched face and a black eye, reported A059 to the police. A059 was arrested, interviewed and reported for summons. However, during interview, A059 claimed that A060 started the fight. Whatever the police originally thought, they ended up believing A059, and NFAed the case: 'it's quite clear that A059 was in the right and if I'd have been there I'd have bloody lamped him [A060] too.'

BK-A056/A057 (mentioned on p. 20) is another example. The police arrested only those participants in a fight who were still standing, even though according to the arresting officer the 'victim' was 'quite frankly as bad as [A056/A057] are, if not worse' (AO). How do the police decide who is to be 'victim' and who the 'criminal', especially if their ascriptions of moral character are not decisive?

> *BW-J33* – Four girls were fighting. The 'victim' complained to the police about J33, who, however, claimed that she hit the 'victim' only once and in self-defence. We asked the arresting officer why J33 alone, who was cautioned, was reported for the fight.
>
> *Officer:*   'When you present the facts they are pointed towards a particular defendant. They have to be because you put the defendant's name on the front of it [the file] in case they want to take it to court. It is in fact a court brief as well, so it is not an all-encompassing thing. This is the case pointing towards [J33] and this is the evidence against her.'
>
> *Res:*   'Is this because [J33] was the one originally complained about?'
>
> *Officer:*   'That's right.'
>
> *Res:*   'If she had come to the station first, would the complainant's name have been on the front?'
>
> *Officer:*   'Yes, more than likely. That's the way the system works.'

So the person who makes the initial complaint is often of determining importance unless the police discover or construct facts to clearly rebut the complainant's story. Where there is no complainant the police often just arrest everyone, particularly if neither side appeared to 'win' or 'lose'.

The second qualification to the 'victim rule' is that some 'victims' are more influential than others.

Influential victims

As the officer in *AT-A009* (see p. 30) indicated, police officers would often be content to leave drunkenness, in particular, alone were it not for the effect on members of the public – i.e. the *complaining* and *powerful* public. This may often mean local traders:

> *AT-A032* – The arresting officer was called to a restaurant. A032 was 'lying prostrate across a dining table very drunk, vomit all down his front, his clothes were a mess and he obviously upset all the people. I mean, there was no-one in the fish and chip shop any more. So he had to be arrested . . . you wouldn't have much option. You've been called by a member of the public, a restauranteur, this man has gone in there absolutely out of his brains, vomited up in the place. He'd been arrested for his own safety and for the convenience of everybody else.'

Public drunkenness can offend tourists too:

> *AT-A031* – 'We get a lot of tourists in this area and obviously it doesn't look good for the tourists themselves that these people are out causing a nuisance. If they're just sitting there and drinking and not actually causing any

disturbance, which nine times out of ten they actually are, you'll say 'Come on lads, move away, we don't want to *see* you on the streets'. Give them that sort of warning and if they're there later, drank more, then in that case they're a little bit more rowdy, getting into people, you know, not physically but just causing a nuisance – in that case you've got to take them off the streets, so you arrest them, bring them to the station.' (emphasis supplied)

Both A31 and A32 were cautioned. The point of arrest is not necessarily, as later chapters will show, to prosecute. It is to deal with the immediate problem. In most drunkenness cases the problem is not drunkenness *per se*, but the *visibility* of the drunk – that is, offensiveness to influential others. What kind of police action would be best for the drunks themselves is difficult to say, but this is never the subject of police or prosecutor discussion.

It is not just drunkenness cases in which certain types of victim are influential. As we shall see, domestic and many other types of interpersonal violence are treated dismissively by the police. Lack of witnesses, the ending of the disturbance before or when the police arrive and the 'triviality' of the actual injury (sometimes 'only' a common assault) are all reasons not to arrest (Sanders, 1988a; Shapland and Hobbs, 1989). For traders, however, much more than mere bodily integrity is at stake. Money speaks.

AT-A005/A006 – A restauranteur who was allegedly threatened by two customers (one was said to have picked up a sauce bottle) called the police. According to the arresting officer: 'On our arrival there was no fight in progress … both men by their behaviour had committed minor assaults – common assaults … in that they had not merely made threatening remarks to the manager; they had actually made gestures towards committing an assault.' So both were arrested.

Non-influential victims

The policing literature has now documented in great detail how domestic cases are treated as 'rubbish' work by police, who therefore avoid arresting assaultative partners (Smith and Gray, 1983; Edwards, 1989; Hamer *et al.*, 1989). As with all policing, though, categories are not natural entities, but are police constructions. Thus Shapland and Hobbs (1987) discuss a 'reported burglary' which was 'cuffed' by the officer, i.e. not dealt with as a crime, but in which the officer simply gave advice to the victim. This was because the victim had a history of 'domestics' for which she had sought police assistance, and this alleged burglary also arose out of a personal relationship. Instead of the initial burglary construction being reinforced by the officer it was re-defined as a 'domestic', allowing no action to be taken.

Although the parties to any domestic dispute are, by definition, non-influential, female victims of violence *in general* are especially non-influential (Chambers and Millar, 1983, 1986). The problem is not simply one of domestic disputes but of interpersonal disputes with no public order implications (Sanders, 1988a). Shapland and Hobbs comment that 'the officer is likely to respond not so much to the facts of the alleged incident, as to the social context in which it is alleged to have taken place' (1987, p. 148). However, it is not quite this simple. The 'facts' have to be sought, elicited and constructed by, for instance, questions and observations (Sanders, 1987). The police definition of the situation structures that initial construction process. Investigating officers usually have the situation defined in advance for them:

> Controllers receiving information that suggested that an incident might be of a domestic nature would normally relay this perception to patrol officers as part of the despatching process. Indeed this was regarded by most officers as an essential part of the message. (Shapland and Hobbs, 1987, p. 150)

So in 'domestics' certain types of fact would not be sought, leading to different types of construction for different types of context. The result is that suspects who prey on non-influential victims are, all other things being equal, less likely to be arrested than are other suspects.

Since the problem of the non-influential victim is largely one of non-arrest, and our research was based on an arrest sample, our data are of limited use in exploring this problem. However, a few of our cases shed light on this. In *BW-A118* (discussed on p. 22) A118 had created a domestic disturbance then returned to the house and allegedly smashed a window. Only then was he arrested, but NFA because the victim did not wish to pursue the matter. This was not the inevitable result, however, according to the custody officer: 'His actions did constitute a breach of the peace, he could have feasibly been reported for a breach of the peace without her complaint.' Without the damage to the window A118 would not have been arrested even though the disturbance he was causing must have been comparable with, for instance, that of *AT-A005/6* (p. 33) or *AT-A053* (p. 25), all of whom were arrested.

CONCLUSION

It is impossible to estimate the proportion of cases in which arrest of the suspect was inevitable by any standard because of what the police saw or were told by a citizen, and the proportion in which a significant amount of judgment and discretion was used in deciding whether or not to arrest. What we have sought to show is that police discretion is far more important in shaping the suspect population than might be imagined by simply analysing the sources of police information about their suspects. The mere existence of, for instance, direct 'eye witness' evidence does not determine arrest. Many arrests take place on the basis of no 'evidence' at all and, without other reasons for arrest, 'evidence' alone often will not suffice.

But it is not sufficient simply to state that police officers exercise discretion on the basis of the factors outlined in order to deal with situations in the 'best' way. Many of these disparate factors come together in class, race and gender terms. Again, most convicted criminals are working class (Sanders, 1985b). Since most people associate with people of a similar background, the associates of 'known' criminals – who are always liable to be arrested – will generally be working class as well. Working-class people are therefore more likely to be drawn into the 'official' suspect population than are other people. Male members of the ethnic minorities encounter similar problems.

To anticipate the argument in later chapters, class and race bias intensifies as the suspect population is sifted into NFA, caution and prosecution categories (the 'previous' thus created then feeding back into criteria of 'suspicion' which influence future arrest decisions).

It is for these reasons that we stated at the start of this chapter that the criminal – i.e. convicted – population is a sub-set of the official suspect population. Whilst convicted criminals may be broadly representative of suspects, there is good reason to believe that they are very dissimilar to the 'real criminal population', insofar as the constitution of that group could ever be determined. The make-up of the convicted population is, therefore, like the make-up of the suspect population: a police construction.

3   In the police station

In legal rhetoric, police and prosecutors are depicted as impartial investigators, neither striving officiously to seek convictions nor trying to set free those believed to be guilty, whose task is to put before the court those defendants against whom there is sufficient evidence of guilt on legally acceptable criteria. Under this view, police investigators respond to evidence which exists or which has been assiduously gathered: their mission is to give effect to the actualities of evidence, to present that which already is in being.

However, in pursuance of their chosen goals, the police participate in the *construction* of evidence. Evidence is not something 'discovered' or 'unearthed', but is produced by all the parties (victims, witnesses, suspect, lawyers and police) involved in the investigation of the case, and in this process the police are the key actors. Before the police are able to construct evidence, however, it is necessary for them to create the social and environmental conditions which enable them to do this in the circumstances most favourable to *them*. They do this by processing suspects in particular ways. In this chapter, we explain how the police seek to create and control the environment which makes it possible for them to produce 'cases' in the manner of their own choosing.

As we saw in Chapter 1 the police have been accorded a high degree of autonomy over significant aspects of the criminal justice process through laws which confer authority on them and provide them with discretion in the use of that authority. Their control over the selection of suspects and witnesses is of fundamental importance in determining who is charged and the evidence to be presented; their choice of summons or arrest provides them with the power to decide where interviewing will occur, in the police station or outside; their ability to subject a person to various styles of interrogation or to exempt them from questioning altogether enables them to alter the nature of the product by varying the process; their power to exclude third parties gives them the ability to determine whether the process will be open to inspection by others or take place in secret; and their right to charge or release without charge enables them to decide the immediate course of the case.

The degree of control enjoyed by the police over case production is not constant but varies according to a host of factors, including case seriousness, the nature of internal supervision, the structure of legal provisions and so on. In some situations the police have absolute powers. There can be, for example, very little, if any, external regulation of police encounters with citizens on the street or in an individual's home. What officers choose to record in their notebooks, in incident report books, and in refused charge books generally cannot be effectively challenged. The most remarkable and public demonstration of this in recent years is the revelation that Kent CID were manufacturing crime en masse (albeit on paper only), and attributing it to previously convicted persons with their consent. This practice of creating 'write-offs' became known only when one of their own number 'blew the whistle' (*Observer*, 8 October, 1989; see also Gill, 1987). In all of these situations, the police decide how 'reality' is officially determined: their case-building decisions are *autonomous*.

In other circumstances their freedom of action is more limited. Where the decision-making freedom of police is potentially more restricted, this may be a function of a rule or it may arise from the presence of some third party or the fact that the report prepared of the relevant encounter has to be reviewed by another before it can be validated. Thus, although the police may subject a citizen to interrogation, legal rules limit the duration of detention, require the creation of a contemporaneous record of what is said and permit a legal representative, parent or other responsible person to be present except where excluding conditions are fulfilled. Although police decision making may thus be potentially only *semi-autonomous* in such situations, it is vital to understand that, when this is the case, maximisation of control often becomes a police project. The task for the police is to mitigate the effect of the restriction (as where the suspect is re-interviewed after the departure of the solicitor from the police station) or to seek exemption from it altogether (by not recording every interaction or persuading the suspect to waive access to legal advice).

The degree of control which police have over the construction of reality and over the legal and procedural rules which empower them, then, is absolutely basic to the functioning of police and their ability to create case files. Control over the case-building environment is secured by creating a set of conditions which define the relationship of a citizen as suspect to the police. Those conditions are marked by: *territorial control*, the suspect being removed from socially supportive environments and compelled to attend the police station; *enforced detention*, the suspect losing the basic freedom of movement and being placed under restraint at the police station; *isolation*, the suspect being denied access to any ally, whether family, friends or others, and being forced to confront the police alone; and *enhanced vulnerability*, the suspect being exposed to actions designed to lower self-esteem and undermine resistance to undesirable or unpleasant choices. The ability of the police to take control over the body of the citizen, to control conditions in which questioning will take place and to manipulate a system of reward and punishment enables them to secure the production of evidence. In the following pages, we illustrate how the police are given or seek to acquire control over the case-manufacturing process through consideration of three aspects of the investigatory process: (i) the choice of report for summons or arrest; (ii) the decision to release or place in detention; and (iii) the decision to allow the suspect access to legal advice.

THE CHOICE OF REPORT FOR SUMMONS OR ARREST

The police have two methods by which they may make a person into an official suspect: report for summons and arrest. The former is literally a report from the officer concerned to a senior officer about the alleged offence and alleged offender. It can be made after an interview (conducted anywhere) and may be made following arrest, although this is not necessarily so. Because arrest involves depriving individuals of their liberty, the Royal Commission on Criminal Procedure (1981) called this a 'coercive power' and recommended that the circumstances in which the police can exercise the power of arrest without warrant be restricted to those in which it is genuinely *necessary* to enable them to prevent the commission of offences, to investigate crime and to bring suspected offenders before the courts. Historically the police tended to favour the arrest power, and the Royal Commission found that of those proceeded against for indictable offences, 76 per cent had been arrested and charged. Research conducted on behalf of the Commission by Gemmill and Morgan-Giles (1980) showed further that of the residue brought to court by summons (24 per cent), a majority had at some point been first subject to a police arrest. That research also showed that juveniles were on the whole less likely to be arrested than adults (and, if arrested, less likely to be detained and charged): RCCP, *Report*, para. 3.72. The Royal Commission set out to alter the practice:

whereby the inevitable sequence on the creation of reasonable suspicion is arrest, followed by being taken to the police station, often to be searched, fingerprinted and photographed. The evidence submitted to us supports the view of the Police Complaints Board . . . that police officers are so involved with the powers of arrest and detention that they fail at times to understand the sense of alarm and dismay felt by some of those who suffer such treatment. (*Report*, para 3.75, citation omitted)

The Commission's restraining proposal, that arrest should not be used unless it was *necessary* to do so was not, however, adopted by the Police and Criminal Evidence Act, 1984, in relation to the power to arrest for 'arrestable offences'. This means, therefore, that while the police powers of summary arrest are conditional upon the existence of 'reasonable grounds', no other constraints operate to limit the use of arrest or to encourage reliance upon a report for summons.

Our research discloses that the position which concerned the Royal Commission has deteriorated since its *Report* in 1981. The Commission emphasized that it 'is not always necessary to detain a person in custody in order to question him or to carry out other enquiries' and stated that 'the current police practice of dealing with juveniles without resorting to the use of custody, for example by questioning them at home, should be encouraged' (RCCP, *Report*, para. 3.77). Despite this, police reliance upon arrest is now almost total, as Table 2 demonstrates.

Indeed, in three of the sub-divisions studied, *all* defendants in the samples (n = 540), adult and juvenile alike, were arrested. Nor were our sub-divisions untypical of urban and semi-urban areas. In earlier research, Sanders (1985a) was assured by a senior officer that in his sub-division *all* adult suspects were arrested: 'The lads round here lift everyone!'

The police found it difficult to explain to us why they had arrested individuals. This was not, of course, because the police are not fully aware of the benefits to them of placing citizens under restraint: they, more than anyone, appreciate the coercive potential of arrest and detention. As one police officer stated, in advising others as to the significance of interrogation tactics: 'A prisoner interviewed at a police

Table 2 Mode of apprehension of adults and juveniles

	Adults		*Juveniles*	
	n	*%*	*n*	*%*
Arrested	705	98.2	327	90.8
Report for summons	13	1.8	33	9.2
Not known	2	–	0	–
Total	720	100.0	360	100.0

station is at a distinct psychological disadvantage' (Firth, 1975, p. 1507). Rather, for the police, arrest is such a routine response that they cannot be said to be taking 'decisions' in any real sense. Arrest is not for them an option to be considered but the standard strategy used to get persons to the place where they wish to question them – the police station.

> CC-A053 – The police wished to interview A053 in connection with an offence of deception arising out of the cashing by A053's husband of a cheque for £27 wrongly sent to her address. A053's husband made a statement of admission in which he implied that A053 knew about the transaction in question. The police visited her home, arrested her there, and took her to the police station.
>
> Res: 'Would you have thought at any point of interviewing her at her home, rather than taking her to the police station?'
> Police: 'It's very difficult to interview her at home when she had three or four children running about, and it's an offence, it's a criminal offence, it's deception so there was no way I was going to interview her at her home address, where a criminal offence had taken place, i.e. a deception.'
> Res: 'Why's that, tell me....'
> Police (interrupting): 'It's an arrestable offence! So I arrested her to get her to the police station, so I could interview her, do the necessary paperwork, and then take her home to the children.'

We see here a clear contradiction between the principles and goals espoused by the Royal Commission and those held by the police. For the Commission, the expressed goals of law reform were to *restrict* the circumstances in which the police could exercise the power of arrest because the Commission sought to hold a balance between, on the one hand, the duties of the police to investigate crime and to bring suspected offenders before the courts and, on the other hand, the legitimate interests of individuals in going about their business without fear of arbitrary or unnecessary arrest. The police, however, in the interests of increasing the vulnerability of suspects wish to *maximize* the use of arrest powers. The Royal Commission was chary of the power because arrest was seen as 'coercive'; the police resort to the power precisely because it is coercive.

THE DECISION TO RELEASE OR DETAIN

Before PACE, an arrested person would be taken to a police station and brought before a charge sergeant whose decision it was whether or not to accept the charge. This system attracted criticism partly because of the perceived identity of interests between the arresting officer and the station sergeant and partly because the sergeant seemed structurally unable to provide that neutral and rigorous view that would constitute a genuine 'second opinion'. The Prosecuting Solicitors' Society summarised the basic criticisms in the following terms in its evidence to the Royal Commission:

> Under the arrest and charge procedure the obligation of the charging officer to lay his case before the charge sergeant is little or no safeguard to the arrested individual.... It would be exceptional for the charging officer to have had time, by that stage of his investigation, to take formal written statements from the witnesses. The view of the charge sergeant or other officer accepting the charge must therefore be gained from what he is told by the investigating officer. As an independent check this must be almost without value.
> (Prosecuting Solicitors' Society, 1979, para. 3.3)

Despite such criticisms, the Royal Commission continued the tradition of internal regulation of the police by proposing that, once an arrest had occurred, the arrestee must (unless de-arrested) be brought to a designated police station where a station or charge officer would have responsibility for deciding whether continued detention was necessary. The Commission took the view that such continued detention should depend upon 'the necessity principle'. The PACE Act gives partial effect to this by providing that *custody officers* should be responsible for decisions relating to arrest and detention and that where there is insufficient evidence to charge when the arrestee is brought into the station:

> the person arrested shall be released either on bail or without bail, unless the custody officer has reasonable grounds for believing that his detention without being charged is necessary to secure or preserve evidence relating to an offence for which he is under arrest or to obtain such evidence by questioning him.
> (PACE Act, s.37(2))

If, in the view of the custody officer, there is sufficient evidence to charge, the person may be detained for such period as is necessary to enable a charge to be prepared: *ibid.*, s.37(1). The PACE Act, therefore, places clear duties upon custody officers to make important decisions in respect of each suspect brought before them. The decision to detain an individual at the police station should be an *individual* decision, specific to the circumstances of the case before the custody officer.

The police, however, know full well that locking a person in a cell may constitute sufficient psychological pressure to secure an admission. It is understandable, therefore, that arresting officers (or officers in charge of the case) should want the suspect detained in order to exert pressure for a confession. However, as we have seen, the PACE Act provides that the detention decision should be made by a 'custody officer', who is supposed to be a quasi-judicial figure 'not involved in the investigation of an offence for which [the suspect] is in police detention' (PACE Act, s.36(5)). In theory, therefore, custody officers should not be caught up in the investigation and should make the detention decision only on the basis of the necessity principle. The custody officer is to be a bulwark between the officer seeking an admission and the suspect. It is the custody officer's job to balance the interests of the police in investigating crime against the individual interests in liberty. Detention following arrest is supposed to be, in the words of the then Home Secretary to Parliament, 'necessary – not desirable, convenient or a good idea but necessary' (*Hansard*, H.C. col. 1229, 1984).

In practice, however, custody officers are unable to divorce themselves from the 'needs' of policing and are unable to stand back from their institutional and collegial ties with other officers. At the end of the day, a custody officer is a *police* officer. Contrary to early indications following the introduction of PACE that custody officers could display independence from investigating officers (Maguire, 1988; Irving and McKenzie, 1989), our research clearly showed that custody officers, with some exceptions, readily go along with the wishes of the case officers because they are emotionally committed to believing their version of events, and because they share the instrumental goals of case clearance which underpins all police work. This is so in respect of the detention decision and, we shall see in Chapter 6, in terms of the decision whether or not to charge as well:

> *AT-J28* – In this interview, the custody officer demonstrates the routine nature of his detention decisions and his working assumption that the 'facts' are to be found in the narrative of the arresting officer:
>
> *Res:* 'When the officer brings the suspect in, do you question the officer?'
>
> *Police:* 'Only if I'm unclear as to why he's been arrested. I find I don't ask questions because the officers are good.'
>
> *Res:* 'What do you do next?'
>
> *Police:* 'I have my own procedure. I like to book them in first, get all the personal details, hear what has happened from the officer and then I decide on what grounds I will authorise detention.'
>
> *Res:* 'So you first complete the front page of the custody record [to obtain personal details, etc.]?'
>
> *Police:* 'Yes.'
>
> *Res:* 'And then you ask the officer. . . .'
>
> *Police (interrupting):* 'to relate the facts, and then I read them their rights after the detention has been authorized.'

Here we see the collaborative role of the custody officer, assisting the arresting officer in detaining the suspect by resort to *ex facie* compliance with the Act. It has become unnecessary for officers to examine the substance of the case: the Act has not restricted the circumstances under which they can authorize detention but instead has provided a means by which detention may be *justified* in all cases.

In practice, therefore, we found, as had McKenzie *et al.* (1990), that the police use detention as a *routine* response, to be displaced only by exceptional circumstances. Where the law contemplates an individual decision, the police apply a working rule tied to case-building needs. The legal requirement – that the custody officer should decide whether or not detention is necessary to secure or preserve evidence relating to an offence for which the person is under arrest, or to obtain such evidence by questioning – is displaced by the working rule that arrestees should be detained.

CC-J04
Res: 'What was the basis upon which you authorised her detention?'
Officer: 'On most offences like this, by the PACE Act you are detaining
            to secure evidence by questioning; that's basically on all
            persons arrested no matter what they've been brought in for.'

Although some custody officers understood their role as *theoretically* involving the possibility of the non-acceptance of a suspect, this was a postulate unrelated to their everyday experiences and was almost unimaginable where the arresting officer sought detention. The working philosophies of custody officers involve a set of assumptions about the integrity and good judgment of fellow officers and a particular conceptualization of their own role. In their working world, police officers relate the 'facts' of a case and their account is a faithful reproduction of a reality that happened. If there is a competing account of reality offered by the arrestee, then either the view of the officer must prevail (because arrestees are expected to lie and contest 'the truth') or the 'truth' has to be ascertained. But that task is not one for the custody officer, and is not to be carried out immediately. It is to be done by interview – for which, of course, detention can be authorized anyway.

Independence, in the role-definition of custody officers, does not mean a capacity to form an objective judgment about what is being presented: it means, instead, that custody officers have no responsibility to attempt any such judgment. In their world, 'independence' requires them to stand aloof from the case, not to get involved, not to become any part of the inquiry and not, therefore, to obstruct the process of investigation by refusing detention against the wishes of the arresting officer. The question: 'Should I authorize the detention of this suspect?' is therefore displaced by the question: 'Which reason shall I use to justify detaining this person?' The provisions of the PACE Act are *not evaded* by the police: they are *used* by them, to justify detention in virtually every case. The following examples illustrate this working world of custody officers:

> BW-A044 – Interview of custody officer:
> Res: 'Is there any time you would not detain somebody?'
> Police: 'Probably not in practice, no.'
>
> BW-A048 – Custody officer interview:
> Res: 'Would you ever say "No" to a CID officer, you cannot detain this man?'
> Police: 'Bearing in mind I have the CID man and the potential prisoner with me, I would always initially accept what the policeman tells me. When I say "always", 99.9 per cent of the time. I mean if things are clearly wrong then I would say "No, I won't accept him of this minute". Often the bloke's remonstrating saying "Not me, it wasn't me. I haven't done it, you've got the wrong man" but *of course* I have to take the policeman's word, so I accept him on what the policeman tells me.'
> (emphasis supplied)

Time and time again custody officers explained their role in terms of ensuring that the individual had been arrested for an offence known to the law and *then authorizing detention*, and were baffled by our questioning them about this 'decision'. For them it was not a separate decision: a person lawfully arrested would be detained. To *not* detain would undermine the authority of arresting officers and question their judgment and ability. Custody officers are not prepared to do this: group solidarity, police culture and professional friendships dictate mutual reinforcement of authority. 'Independence' does not bring an objective judgment to the case: instead it prevents a merits test being applied at all and converts the custody officer into a functionary who assists in case movement.

Case-building demands dictate that the suspect be detained. Custody officers know that detention and interrogation are often accompanied by a confession and the prospect of an admission is much more important to them than the 'rights' of any suspect. And after all, as the quotations make clear, the custody officer accepts whatever the arresting officer says and disbelieves whatever the suspect says. The result is that custody officers do not make individualized decisions: *they detain as a matter of routine* even where, as in juvenile cases, detention is supposed to be discouraged:

> CC-J57 – In this case a juvenile was arrested at his home in the presence of his parents. When we asked why arrest and detention were necessary in this case the custody officer said:
>
> '[W]hen he was initially brought in, I queried the reason why it was

necessary to arrest a juvenile at home address when the parents were there, and basically the reason was he wouldn't cough it, i.e., he wouldn't admit to it.'

The arresting officer confirmed this in a separate interview:

'He denied it to start with when I was asking him about it, so I arrested him on suspicion of theft, brought him down to the police station, interviewed him with his dad and he admitted it in the end.'

In the light of such sentiments, it is hardly surprising that we found that the overwhelming majority of adults and juveniles had been detained by custody officers. In the few cases where detention was *not* authorized, it had become obvious to the arresting officers that detention was unsuitable or unnecessary, as where the suspect had shown clear signs of senility on the way to the station and the arresting officers had concluded that he was simply confused.

There was, thus, a *consensus* between custody officers and arresting officers about the disposal of *all* arrestees, and, in almost all cases, this consensus dictated that the suspect be detained as Table 3 shows.

This compares with detention being authorized in 99.9 per cent of the cases in McKenzie *et al.*'s (1990) research. In only 13 cases in our entire sample was a suspect initially detained in order to allow time for the preparation of a charge. In most other cases, the basic grounds for detention were given as to obtain evidence by questioning (n = 534), to secure and preserve evidence (n = 27), or a combination of both (n = 146). The suspects in 84 cases were detained by virtue of s.37(9) PACE because they were drunk (n = 84). However, the reasons given in the custody record for detention in 127 cases were non-PACE Act (i.e. illegal) reasons. These reasons included 'investigations', 'on suspicion' and the like – in other words, any reasons which the custody officer felt at the time to be reasonable, regardless of the controlling legislation.

The recording of illegal reasons by custody officers is a further indication of the *unimportance* they attached to this particular interaction. Although conscious of the need to justify their decisions,

Table 3 Detention practices of custody officers following arrival of suspects at the police station

	Adults		Juveniles	
	n	*%*	*n*	*%*
Detention authorised	700	99.4	318	99.7
Detention not authorised	4	0.6	1	0.3
Not known/not applicable	16	–	41	–
Total	720	100.0	360	100.0

they had quickly learned that not only would *any* of the reasons provided by PACE (whether they actually applied in the instant case or not) be sufficient to 'protect' them but that a wide variety of other reasons could also be used. In cases where custody officers were pulled up about recording 'errors', the sole purpose was to prevent adverse comment on the force from Her Majesty's Inspectors of Constabulary. Slipshod recording thus indicated routine decision making and collusive supervision.

Prior to the PACE Act, the police could exert pressure on the suspect by prolonged detention, exploiting the fact that the law regarding the length of time for which a person could be detained by the police prior to charge was unclear. All cases of detention following arrest were subject to a requirement to bring the detainee before a magistrates' court 'as soon as practicable'. For 'non-serious' cases the police were under a duty to release if it appeared that the detainee could not be brought before the court within 24 hours (Magistrates' Court Act, 1980, s.43). Seriousness was not defined and the courts interpreted practicability in terms of the needs of the investigation (*Hudson*, 1980, 72 Cr. App. R.163). There is now less opportunity to use extended periods of detention as a means of pressure in so far as limits on detention under the PACE Act are clear: a person cannot be kept in police detention without charge for more than 24 hours (s.41) unless in respect of a 'serious arrestable offence' and authorised by a superintendent (or rank above this) when there may be a further 12 hours detention. We found, as had Maguire (1988) and Irving and McKenzie (1989), that prolonged detention, extending over three days or more, is infrequent, as Table 4 shows.

Table 4 The duration of detention per suspect for adults and juveniles

	Adults		Juveniles	
	n	%	*n*	%
Less than 1 hour	48	7.0	16	5.2
1 hour less than 4 hours	318	46.5	206	66.6
4 hours less than 6 hours	119	17.4	45	14.6
6 hours less than 9 hours	78	11.4	24	7.8
9 hours less than 12 hours	44	6.4	6	1.9
12 hours less than 24 hours	69	10.1	12	3.9
24 hours less than 36 hours	7	1.0	0	0.0
36 hours or more	1	0.2	0	0.0
Not applicable (not arrested/not detained)	17	–	34	–
Not known	19	–	17	–
Total	720	100.0	360	100.0

However, two points need to be made here. First the *fact* of detention is as important as its duration; indeed most suspects historically have been released in less than four hours (Softley, 1980; Barnes and Webster, 1981; RCCP, *Report* para. 3.96). As many police officers made clear to us, confinement of any duration exerts powerful pressures upon most suspects, for, as the suspect is aware, detention is totally in the control of the police and is thus *indeterminate*.

This became apparent in other research recently conducted, where one suspect said that, without a solicitor to protect him, the police 'can do anything they want. They can keep you in overnight if they want' (Sanders *et al.*, 1989, p. 77). That research also revealed a second point. Four hours may not seem long to an outside observer, but to a suspect in a cell it can be torture. And 24 hours is an eternity. So the (apparently) tight limits on periods of detention in PACE are, as subjectively experienced, no such thing.

CONTROL OVER ACCESS TO LEGAL ADVICE ETC.

Access to legal advice whilst in police custody has always been regarded as of fundamental importance to the police–suspect relationship. Legal reformers have seen a solicitor as the suspect's ally in an alienating and hostile environment, providing comfort and support, and giving advice as to what should be done. Solicitors have been seen as individuals who are able to protect the innocent from making inadvertent admissions when under severe psychological stress, and as people who provide a link with the outside world, easing worries by reassuring the suspect that family and friends will be told of the suspect's whereabouts and safety. In the police view, solicitors are seen as obstacles to gaining an admission precisely because legal representatives bring strength and support to the suspect. The solicitor is also seen as a disruptive influence by coming between suspect and police and thus inhibiting the creation and development of that bond between detainee and officer which is basic to many 'effective' interrogations. For the police, solicitors are outsiders who suppress the truth and whose mission is inconsistent with the pursuit of justice.

Police who felt antipathy toward solicitors were always able to exploit the uncertain state of the law prior to PACE as well as the ignorance of suspects as to their 'rights'. The pioneering study of Zander (1972) showed that few suspects were allowed to consult a lawyer before or during interrogation, a finding that was reinforced by later studies (Baldwin and McConville, 1979b; Softley, 1980). In Softley's study, for example, no mention was made of the right of access to a solicitor in 84 per cent of interrogations observed and solicitors attended in only two of 168 interrogations. The police were able, therefore, to shut out legal advisers from the police station, as they had done in the *Confait*, *Guildford Four* and *Birmingham Six* cases.

The Royal Commission (1981) considered the merits of allowing suspects access to legal advice and concluded that the balance between 'the interests of the community and those of the suspect' (*Report*, para. 4.90) dictated that the power of the police to refuse access should be exercised only in *exceptional* circumstances. The Commission emphasized that, in conferring on the police a discretion to withhold access, there must be no risk that it will be used improperly, and continued: 'In particular, we do not consider it sufficient justification for withholding access that a solicitor may advise his client not to speak: that is the suspect's right' (*ibid.* para. 4.90).

Where a person has been arrested and is being held in custody at a police station, the PACE Act confers certain rights upon the detainee. These rights include the right to have one friend or relative or other person told of the suspect's arrest and where she is being held (section 56); and the right to consult a solicitor privately at any time (section 58). Custody officers are required by the Code of Practice to inform suspects of the right of access, actual access being dependent upon a request by the arrested person. As recommended by the Royal Commission, the right of access is absolute for non-serious arrestable offences and can be delayed only in limited circumstances in respect of serious arrestable offences. It is the duty of the custody officer to ensure that suspects are treated in accordance with the PACE Act and its accompanying codes of practice (s.39). Softley (1980) found that suspects were far more likely to request a solicitor if they were advised of their rights than if they were not. Nearly ten years later, Sanders *et al.* (1989) found the same. The police, therefore, control access to solicitors in part through their notification to suspects of their rights (and, indeed, the way those rights are stated).

According to the custody records created by custody officers, almost all suspects in the sample were advised of their rights and comparatively few were, for policy reasons, not told of their rights: see Table 5.

On the face of it this appears to confirm the findings of Irving and McKenzie (1989) and Maguire (1988) that custody officers did everything 'by the book'. Such a conclusion would, however, be wholly misleading.

Suspects have to sign to indicate that they have been read their rights, and should not sign if they have not been notified. But in police stations, as elsewhere, people often sign when and where they are told without

Table 5 Whether suspects advised of rights, based upon analysis of police custody records

	Adults		Juveniles	
	n	*%*	*n*	*%*
Advised of rights	609	98.2	278	95.2
Not told of rights (policy, etc.)	11	1.8	14	4.8
Incapable of understanding by reason of drink, etc.	63	–	3	–
Not known/not applicable	37	–	65	–
Total	720	100.0	360	100.0

knowing precisely what they are signing for. And if they are not told all of their rights, or are told them incorrectly, how are suspects to know that they have been misled – and thus refuse to sign – unless they have first been notified clearly, fully and correctly?

In one case from Sanders *et al.*'s (1989) study, a suspect was handed the official leaflet containing suspects' rights, but they were not explained to him. The custody officer then said: 'Sign there to say that I've given you these forms' and he indicated that he was also to sign that he did not want a solicitor. This officer said that he never read suspects their rights and had never heard any other custody officer do so. Moreover, suspects were rarely given time to read these leaflets either! One suspect in another station (noted on the custody record as 'refused to sign') was also given a leaflet but did not have his rights read aloud. The custody officer began filling in the custody record and the suspect said: 'What's that for? Is it for that bit of paper which you won't give me time to read?' He was hustled away to a cell! Custody records, then, *validate* what the police do, rather than act as a constraint upon them. They enable the police both to treat suspects as they wish (within certain self-imposed boundaries) *and* to justify their actions afterwards, thus creating perfect conditions for constructing cases on the most unshakeable foundations. Sanders *et al.*'s (1989) research provides some quantitative evidence on this. Sanders observed the notification of rights to suspects and compared his observations with what was recorded in the custody records. Rights were recorded as not being provided in 7.6 per cent of cases (only half in accordance with PACE) but were *observed* to be not provided in some 15 per cent of cases. In other words, only around one half of all failures to provide rights were admitted as such in the custody records.

The same is true in respect of requests for access to legal advice. Custody records contain a box which the suspect is asked to sign stating 'I do/do not' wish to see a solicitor. According to the custody records

Table 6 Whether suspects requested a solicitor, based upon analysis of police custody records and police response to any request

	Adults		Juveniles	
	n	%	n	%
Requested solicitor granted	97	14.9	28	9.6
Requested solicitor delayed	7	1.1	0	0.0
Requested solicitor refused	2	0.3	0	0.0
Requested solicitor but agreed to be interviewed without solicitor	23	3.5	7	2.4
Requested solicitor but only after interview commenced	19	2.9	3	1.0
Waived right to solicitor	432	66.3	242	82.9
Suspect too drunk, etc.	68	10.4	2	0.7
Suspect not given rights and no request for solicitor	4	0.6	10	3.4
Not known/not applicable	68	–	68	–
Total	720	100.0	360	100.0

only a small proportion of suspects ask to see a solicitor, with the overwhelming majority waiving their right to do so, as can be seen from Table 6.

Again, Sanders *et al.* (1989) found that custody records simply under-record requests for advice. This does not happen often (only some 6 per cent of all requests were not so recorded), but these cases are presumably those in which the police most want to prevent the attendance of solicitors.

Actually, the police rarely have to rely on falsification of custody records. They can adopt numerous ploys to ensure that suspects do not understand their rights, to discourage them from requesting a solicitor or to encourage them to cancel their request. If all else fails, the police sometimes simply fail to pass on the request (one in ten of recorded requests which were not cancelled). The structure of PACE assists the police in this situation: advice is triggered only by a *positive* request. Yet many suspects are either silent or inarticulate when they are asked if they want advice. In one typical case in the Sanders *et al.* (1989) study, the suspect said that he didn't know if he wanted a solicitor. The custody officer replied: 'Well, I've put you down as "no" for the moment.'

None of these practices would be evident from analysis of the custody records in question, thus rendering nugatory later review by senior officers, HM Inspectorate of Constabulary and others. Custody records, by their insistence upon fairness and rectitude, *mislead* rather than inform.

The way in which 'waivers' are obtained means that little reliance can be placed upon the answers given. The police exercise considerable influence over, and even sometimes determine, whether access will be accorded. Thus, the arrestee may be persuaded to waive the right to a lawyer by the custody officer saying that this will cause delay and mean longer incarceration, stating that the named solicitor does not come out at night or urging that legal advice is not needed in this case. In other cases, the right might not be mentioned at all and a 'waiver' elicited without the suspect being aware of what is being agreed. Thus:

> *CE-A055* – An officer was asked whether the provisions in PACE had made a difference to requests for a solicitor, and replied:
> 'I think it all depends on the way it's put over to them, when they're asked the question you're entitled to a solicitor, which way it's put over to them: you can have a solicitor or you're entitled to a solicitor if you want one. If you say to them "you can have one" it obviously makes them think they've got to have one. A lot of it relies on how it's put over to them when they're initially asked.'

> *CE-A093*
> *Res:* 'Do you find that many [arrestees] ask for a solicitor these days?'
> *Custody Officer:* 'A lot do. I'd just say on that, it's nevertheless true that it's usually the known toe-rags ask for a solicitor, in fact, demand a solicitor as they are coming through the door.'
> *Res:* 'As soon as they arrive at the police station?'
> *Custody Officer:* 'They tell you their rights and list them in what order they want them doing. Then it's a battle of wills!' (*laughing heartily*).

Similar examples are given by Maguire (1988), Sanders *et al.* (1989) and by a judge in a letter to the *Criminal Law Review* (1989, p. 763). In some forces, the police have sought to use (out of context) Law Society guidelines to solicitors to undermine a suspect's express wish to remain silent, even in cases where the solicitor has advised the suspect not to answer questions (MacKenzie, 1990). Discouraging access to a solicitor enhances police control and lowers the potential resistance of the suspect. As an instruction manual for British police interrogators put it: 'Pressures to conform exercised by a dominant persuader are more likely to be effective if the subject is isolated from his peers' (Walkley, 1987, p. 20). The manual, dealing specifically with access to solicitors, continues: 'It has to be said that the presence of a solicitor, even if he is not positively obstructive ... is likely to be counter productive' (*ibid*, p. 21). Interrogation is very dependent upon creating an atmosphere in which the suspect is more likely to co-operate with the interrogators, and the presence of any third party is generally seen as inhibiting this. As the police manual observes:

> [E]ven if the solicitor does not interrupt the flow of the interview, the suspect will look at him at critical points in the interview, and mere eye contact will be sufficient to give the suspect sufficient moral support to negate the influence of the interviewer. (Walkley, 1987, p. 89)

This was a point brought home to us by the police in our research:

> 'But even where a man's talking to us, before he answers certain questions he'll look at his "brief" and a man takes strength from having a "brief" there. Whether that's right or whether that's wrong I wouldn't like to say, but it's a pain in the arse for us.' (Detective Sergeant, *CC-A003*)

The police do not isolate the suspect simply to ensure maximum psychological vulnerability but also to limit the constructive potential of the defence. There is concern that the suspect may be advised to exercise silence, to refuse to answer police questions. Whilst the Royal Commission might have felt that it was the right of a suspect to remain silent and that the likelihood of a solicitor advising silence must not be a reason for denying access to legal advice, a view consistently endorsed by the courts (*Samuel* [1988] 1 All E.R. 135; *Davidson* [1988] Crim. L.R. 442), the police continue to see this as *the principal reason* for excluding solicitors from the police station. Solicitors who advise silence are seen as obstructive or 'bent':

> *CC-A009* – In this case a solicitor was present for the interrogation of the suspect. The police attitude to what occurred came across clearly in our interview with the officer:
>
> *Police*:   'The solicitor we had, I daren't really say, I'd get done for libel, but he's a, you know, I won't say it. . . .'
> *Res*:   'It's confidential.'
> *Police*:   'Well, I think he's bent. It's a rough word really, I know. . . . He had a word with them and they'd changed completely when I came in; they didn't want to know. He'd obviously had a word with them and said 'don't say nothing' and told them how far to go etc. and all that. . . . He wasn't straight down the line, unbiased, he was on their side.'

Solicitors just get in the way:

> *CC-A016* – The arresting officer expressed concern over the presence of solicitors during interrogation:
>
> *Police*:   'It's obviously a lot easier interviewing someone without a solicitor because, well I know this is basically wrong but, when interviewing somebody you're supposed to write down everything that's said, but nine times out of ten you say many things that you don't write down, which you don't if the solicitor's there. . . . There's no way you can do this job by the book.'

Where a request for a solicitor is made and agreed to, it does not follow that a solicitor will attend the police station or, if attending, be present for any or all interrogations. The police are assisted in their control of the case-building process by a reluctance on the part of some legal practitioners to attend the police station, particularly at unsociable hours. This is not entirely fortuitous or the fault of the profession because the police can exploit the known propensities of lawyers and effect arrests in the early or late hours of the day. They can, moreover, exploit the *fear* suspects will experience that solicitors will not come out for some time or, indeed, at all. This helps the police discourage requests and secure cancellations of requests.

Where solicitors do attend interrogations the police may seek to co-opt the solicitor into encouraging the suspect to make an admission. This is achieved by disclosing to the solicitor that the suspect is 'bang to rights' or facing overwhelming evidence of guilt. The police do not attempt this with solicitors who are known to be resistant to such approaches, and, even where it is attempted, it may not be successful. Nevertheless, the police strategy is designed at all points to maximize their influence over the suspect and to turn to their own advantage any potential obstacles.

CC-A068
Police: 'If you've got a little bit of something about you, you'll have
             five minutes with the defence solicitor and let him know
             exactly what you've got if you've got a strong hand and you've
             got a strong case then you inform him so he can tell his client
             and maybe come down on the amount of time you're all
             going to waste .... It depends on the circumstances. ...
             Let's put it this way, whenever I've approached a solicitor and
             I've said "look this is what I've got" it's because I'm confident
             of what I'm dealing with and I'm confident at the end of the
             day, and if I can win the solicitor over to that point of view it's
             going to be a lot easier to win the defendant over.'

If solicitors are present during interrogations, it does not follow that they will 'obstruct' the police. Some will advise the client to speak, even where the answers given constitute a full admission to the offence under investigation. And some, whilst expressing the intention to protect the client through use of the right to silence, are ineffective.

Overall, in terms of access to legal advice, it is hardly surprising that we found proportionately few cases in which a solicitor attended the police station. The police were highly successful in isolating suspects from the outside world and enhancing their influence at interrogations. To determine the extent to which requests actually led to advice, we

Table 7 Solicitor attendance at police interrogations

	Adults		Juveniles	
	n	%	n	%
Solicitor attended all interviews	48	8.9	20	6.9
Solicitor present for only some interviews	10	1.9	2	0.7
No solicitor attended any interviews	479	89.2	266	92.4
Total custodial interview cases for which information available	537	100.0	288	100.0

examined both the custody records and the records made of interrogations. In a small number of cases (n = 15 for adults; n = 2 for juveniles) solicitors provided telephone advice only and the overall presence of solicitors at police interviews was low: see Table 7.

Just as the police are hostile to solicitors being present at interrogations, so also there is some resistance to a parent or guardian attending in juvenile cases. Police resistance is, however, much reduced because it is felt that parents are less inhibiting than legal advisers, are less knowledgeable of police procedures and of the 'rights' of suspects and are more easily co-opted into assisting the police. This has long been acknowledged by police themselves:

> The interrogator is at a disadvantage when he is required to have a parent or guardian present. . . . It is advisable to explain to a parent (out of hearing of a child) that the interrogator will be firm in order that the truth may be ascertained. (Firth, 1975, p. 1507)

Elements of this resistance emerged from time to time in our conversations with police officers, and we can note that in a small number of our sample cases (n = 27) no responsible adult (parent, social worker, solicitor or the like) attended police interviews of juveniles.

Police practice is not, therefore, designed to ensure that the maximum possible reliance for evidential purposes can be placed upon suspects' statements in all cases where they are made, but instead to ensure that statements of confession are made in the maximum number of cases. Through experience, the police have learned that statements are more likely to be made when the suspect is psychologically most vulnerable, a state best achieved by compulsory confinement, isolation and manipulation of self-esteem. It is to these features that they direct their attention rather than to questions of the reliability of statements.

CONCLUSION

Contrary to the rhetoric of law, which depicts the police as neutral investigators earnestly seeking 'the truth' in an impartial setting, the first concern of the police is to place the suspect into an environment which is hostile for the suspect and favourable to the police themselves. In this way, the police lay the foundations for the construction of a case *against* the suspect rather than for an impartial inquiry. The police are able to achieve control over the suspect in large measure because the custody officer, designated in legal rhetoric to be the guardian of the suspect's interests, is a *facilitator* and not simply a doorkeeper. It is the custody officer who expresses embedded police values through the automatic detention of suspects and their isolation from those who might provide comfort and assistance. Custody officers so much share police cultural values that they will connive with investigating officers in bending or breaking the rules if this will weaken the suspect's position or give a further push to the emergent police case.

4   Building the case: interrogation

In previous chapters we saw how the police seek to manipulate the social environment of the suspect to increase their control and influence over the suspect's decision making and to prepare the ground for building a case against the suspect. Here, we are concerned to demonstrate how the police build cases and create evidence, and to consider the strategies they use and the techniques they employ.

Of course it is commonly thought that evidence is 'discovered' by the police and that such discoveries are the mark of a good investigator. It is also imagined that the nature and quality of evidence is unaffected by what the police do: an interrogator may elicit a confession, but it was 'there' waiting to be missed by a poor interrogator or to be unearthed by an expert; the product is not influenced by what the interrogator does. In this chapter, we show that this is far from the case, and that, in a very real sense, the police construct evidence (and sometimes more than evidence). The police have, at a most fundamental level, the ability to select facts, to reject facts, to not seek facts, to evaluate facts and to generate facts. Facts, in this sense, are not objective entities which exist independently of the social actors but are *created* by them.

The principal investigative strategy employed by the police is the interrogation. Shielded from external scrutiny, police interrogation has historically been viewed with deep suspicion, and accusations of torture, third-degree, trickery and blandishments of various kinds have been levelled against the police with more or less credibility at frequent intervals. Whatever the force of these accusations, it is quite clear that the secrecy of interrogation and the structural features of power associated with it must always remain a matter of concern. Since we did not witness interrogations and since the police themselves constitute the source of much of our information, we do not have adequate foundations for systematically testing the merits of this historical argument. Instead, we focus our attention on a little noticed, though fundamentally important, aspect of interrogation – its function as an instrument for creating evidence.

Many commentators have, of course, drawn attention to the importance of interrogation in generating confessions. Other forms of evidence, such as that resulting from forensic examination, do occur but are exceptional rather than standard (Greenwood *et al.*, 1977; Silberman, 1978; McConville and Baldwin, 1981; Mason, 1986; Samuels, 1989) and only rarely prove successful (Steer, 1980; Ramsay, 1987). There is general consensus that admissions during police questioning (together with information provided by civilian witnesses) are the most useful sources of obtaining police detections (Mawby, 1979; Softley, 1980; Bottomley and Coleman, 1981; McConville and Baldwin, 1981; Mitchell, 1983). Although confessions are not always necessary to the prosecution case (McConville and Baldwin, 1981) and may be disputed at trial (Mitchell, 1983; Vennard, 1985), none the less the interrogation is *the* central investigative strategy of the police.

In contrast, comparatively little attention has been paid to understanding the structure and nature of confessions. To what extent is interrogation a process of 'extracting' a confession from a suspect? Can it be said that confessions 'pre-exist' to be elicited by the skilled interviewer? How far if at all are confessions a product of the suspect, a product of the police or a joint product of the interaction of interviewer and suspect? These are important questions because the answers to them speak to our understanding of what a confession is and to our willingness to accord confession evidence a central place in the system of investigation and in trials.

INEQUALITY OF POWER IN INTERROGATIONS

Before we look at how confessions are created it is necessary to re-emphasize that the interrogation environment is police controlled and to examine two particular aspects of the interview context: the completeness of the official record; and the 'trading' context within which much police business is transacted.

Integrity of the official record

In the rhetoric of the law, police interrogations take place in circumstances which enable prosecutors, defence lawyers, magistrates, judges and juries to be fully informed as to what took place. Custody officers are given the responsibility of authorizing the release of a suspect for interview, keeping a record of the time taken for interview and ensuring that there is full compliance with rules relating to the duration of interrogation. Officers undertaking the interview must keep a contemporaneous record of the questions and answers and invite the accused to verify the accuracy of the record. The rules do not permit interrogating officers to have access to the suspect outside these circumstances and do not authorize or condone non-recorded interviews.

Despite this rhetoric, and contrary to early findings on the impact of PACE suggesting that custody officers were willing to stand up to other officers who wish to stretch the rules in order to obtain a confession (Maguire, 1988; Irving and McKenzie, 1989), it is quite clear that official records of interrogations, even if 'verified' by contemporaneous notes and attested to by third parties such as solicitors, constitute only a partial representation of what transpired. This is clear not only from our present research, but also from that of Sanders *et al.* (1989) and Dixon *et al.* (1989). The integrity of the record is compromised by the fact that it ignores the police/suspect questioning that often precedes it. Police control over the authentication process is such that 'informal interviews' may take place 'off the record'. This is sanctioned where officers feel that the 'official' interview will be unduly constraining or where it has been unproductive, and where case construction will be assisted by an unofficial encounter.

CE-A015 – The officer in the case explained that he could 'get round' the requirement of contemporaneous interview notes:
'by trying to have a few words that aren't on the record, i.e. on the way in [to the police station], in the car, on the way to the cell – give them something to think about – or before the start of an interview.'

One detective, reflecting the views of many we spoke to, told us that defendants were spoken to 'off the record' and that if the suspect did want to talk in these circumstances 'no policemen who did his job is going to say no' (CE-A046).

In other cases, the custody officer is complicitous in the creation of an off-the-record interview by permitting the case officer to visit the suspect in the cells or by authorising the suspect's release to the interview room without any record being made for the purposes of the custody sheet.

CC-A048
Res: 'How do you find the custody officers, do you find that you can work with them?'
Police: 'Some of them are more strict than others. But I can get on with them all anyway. But some are really all PACE, PACE, PACE, PACE. Some will just bend a little bit, if you want a

	quick word with them to see, you know, if somebody wants a solicitor and you haven't had chance to chat and don't want him to have a solicitor yet.'
Res:	'So they'll help you, some of them will?'
Police:	'Some of them, for just a quick word with them, yes.'
Res:	'Has that changed a bit from the old Station Sergeant or did you have the same there?'
Police:	'No, you could always have a quick word with a juvenile before his parents come.'
Res:	'Just to get to know them, to get the picture?'
Police:	'The facts, to get the facts.'
Res:	'The facts?'
Police:	'Yes. But now you can't talk to a juvenile until his parents are there, or you aren't supposed to!' *(laughs)*

These practices are dependent upon the individual custody officer, the relationship between the case officer and the custody officer and the police determination of how 'necessary' it is that the suspect should be seen informally. Even so, there are other ways of interrogating suspects informally, such as in the car on the way to the station.

There need be nothing sinister in these off-the-record exchanges, whatever the official, legal, position is. A powerful element of police culture is 'knowing your suspect', learning the suspect's habits and lifestyle, problems and worries, hopes and fears. This is believed to be useful not as criminal intelligence in any real or direct sense but as an essential strategy for 'getting under the skin' of the suspect, reading the suspect's mind, finding out what makes the suspect tick. The clinical system of contemporaneous notes or tape-recording is seen as inimical to this process.

Field Note Extract: Area AT
An experienced Detective Sergeant was asked how the police had come to terms with contemporaneous note-taking during interrogations:

Police:	'Well, it's not that easy in some ways, it's not natural. You need a rapport with the person first; it's no good otherwise.'
Res:	'Can you get information that way?'
Police:	'Look, I never do it that way. I'd never go cold into an interview. I always have a run over first with the person, do an informal chat without taking notes. Then I do the formal interview with the note taking being done. I'd write up some notes of the informal later.'
Res:	'Why do it like that?'
Police:	'Because it's not natural otherwise. You can't ask the question, write it down and wait for the answer, write it and then ask another. Its no good. You have to get a rapport.'

When asked about the introduction of tape-recording the Detective Sergeant showed immediate hostility:

Police: 'It would wreck the way we do interviews. We could go on there
             swearing and yet you have to. You'd always say things like
             "Don't fuck me about" but you couldn't on tape which would
             be in front of a judge and jury really. You'd have to do an
             informal interview first.'

The importance of these low-visibility exchanges between police and
suspect cannot be overestimated. The more successful in manipulating
the decision making of the suspect, the less apparent will be the influence of the police when the official interrogation takes place. It is at this
covert level that the police are able to utilise those strategies which, if
discovered, would or might incur the disapproval of courts and endanger
the admissibility of any confession arising therefrom. Of their nature,
many of these tactics remain hidden from anyone's view and only very rarely
are exposed to public gaze. One of the less extreme tactics favoured by
the police is to attempt to induce the suspect to confess by resort to
'information bluff' or some other trick which suggests that the police
'know' the suspect is guilty or already possess incontrovertible evidence
of guilt. An example of this tactic is supplied by the following case:

> CC-A070/A071/A072 – There was a report to the police that three or four lads
> were hanging around the door of a building, perhaps attempting to get in.
> Three lads were found in the area, arrested and brought to the police station.
> According to the police, the door in question was 'almost a wrecked door
> anyway' from previous treatment and there was 'absolutely nothing in the
> building'. The person who made the initial report was not prepared to say more
> than that some lads were near the door and could not identify these three as
> the lads in question. The police attempted to get an admission. They explained
> to us that the door was covered by security cameras, although these were not
> linked to a video system:
>
> Police: 'The cameras, although they are running all the time, they don't
>   have a linked video system. So there's no video, that would
>   have been ideal. If you want to trick them and tell them they
>   were all on video, cameras and that. . . .'
> Res: 'Did you try that?'
> Police: 'Oh yes. I tried all sorts to get them to admit but they just said
>   "no, we weren't even near the place, we saw some other lads
>   up there". . . .'

The use of bargaining tools

Although the police control the social and psychological environment
of the suspect, it is their ability to *manipulate* it in their discussions with
the suspect that is perhaps the most significant of their discretions. The
police–suspect relationship is not fixed or constant: it is always
negotiable. What determines the precise nature of the relationship at any

one time is the trading chips that each possess and the extent to which what is possessed by one side is wanted by the other. The suspect may possess information about the instant offence, about other offences or about other offenders, all of which may be sought after by the police. For the police, every suspect is a possible source of confession evidence and every suspect is a possible informant (Banton, 1964). Suspects, for their part, may wish to get the benefit of various police discretions, such as those relating to caution, prosecution, charge selection and bail. The suspect–police relationship is, therefore, in many cases characterized by 'dealing', 'trading' and 'bargaining'.

Some officers maintained that bargaining could not take place with suspects, but this was unusual, with officers in general not only admitting to deals but also claiming that such transactions were *essential* to good police work. Before we detail the general picture, we give an example of an officer who stated that there were no deals with suspects:

CC-A096

Police: 'I certainly haven't ever made a deal with anybody. You do have a number of offenders who still think that the officer can; they'll ask kind of "will you get me bail?" and you have to be perfectly honest and tell them there's nothing you can do. That I suppose is the most standard sort of question. It wasn't possible before [PACE] and it isn't possible now. You can certainly approach the custody officer and let him know that the course of action you wish to follow is to bail your prisoner, but it depends entirely on the custody officer and I don't think it's changed a great deal really.'

Before the PACE Act, research pointed to the fact that the principal negotiating currency was bail (see Dell, 1971; Bottoms and McClean, 1976; Softley, 1980; Irving, 1980). Today, it remains the case that the police have absolute command over the release/custody decision and use this to influence the decision-making process of the suspect. Detention at the police station is not welcomed by suspects. As we have seen, most are intimidated and frightened by the idea of being locked up, and the police are constantly aware of the power of their discretion over bail. But, in addition to bail, deals may be struck on the basis of charge reduction, offences taken into consideration (TICs) and general criminal intelligence.

CE-A006 – A detective sergeant complained to us that the use of solicitors in police stations was a major hindrance to the police but that 'often with more seasoned criminals who knew the ropes deals were struck when the solicitor was not present'. He explained that the solicitor would come in, be present for the interview and then 'as they go out of the door a deal might be struck'. When the solicitor leaves, he said, 'you go back and see if you can have a word with them about it all and sort it all out.' He described the 'bargaining tools' as bail and offences taken into consideration.

CC-J36 – An experienced detective pointed to some of the difficulties:
'You can't make deals with the solicitor present but you can when he's not there. It needs watching that, but you can still do it.'

In this case, the suspect was interrogated and made a complete denial. Later, at the start of a second interview, the suspect *immediately* confessed. We were told that, some time after the end of the first 'unproductive' interview, it had been made clear to the suspect that bail would be available if the matter were cleared up. This was a pattern that we were to see repeated in a number of cases.

CE-A074 – An experienced drug squad officer told us that bargaining was fundamental to this line of police work:
'There's always wheeling and dealing. If we didn't wheel and deal and use informants, then I would tell you we'd have a crap drug squad or we'd have no drug squad. But bail isn't always the answer: money is very often the answer, or they've got trouble with a traffic policeman who's given them a ticket. If they want something and they want it badly enough, be what it is, they will help you, but you've got to be very careful about the people you choose to help you, especially if they are users of drugs.'

Bargaining of this kind is marked by its low visibility. Outsiders, especially solicitors, are usually seen by the police *and by some suspects* as threats to this system of 'dealing'.

CC-A062 – A police officer told us how deals were done with suspects:

Police:	'PACE is there and I'm not saying it's abused, it's not; but there'll still be times when you're talking to the chap that won't be recorded, and that's when deals and bail are discussed. They understand that as well as you understand it. We say "Well, if you want to talk about that, that's fine, but we can't officially." But then he might be the one who wants to talk about it. It's not evidence, it'll never be presented in any way so it's not terribly awful not to write it down. It's not like you're taking him away and beating him up sort of thing.'
Res:	'Do you still get criminal intelligence like this?'
Police:	'Yes, as far as it ever did, but that's more on the street.'
Res:	'Won't tape-recording inhibit you?'
Police:	'No.'
Res:	'Not from leaning on suspects?'
Police:	'Not really because you do that sort of thing in a situation where the tape-recorder isn't there. It sounds bent, I know.'

Bargaining involves *relationships*. If the conditions are right, relationships may be cultivated in a single encounter, but this would be unusual (Banton, 1964). Instead, they arise out of an extended set of encounters between suspect and police in which understandings develop, favours are exchanged and trust is negotiated within a particular context (Hobbs, 1988). Relationships are cultivated by the police on a *long-term* basis. This requires a degree of forward thinking which might involve making a concession even without a reciprocal gesture on the part of the suspect, as the following example shows:

Field Note Extract: Area CC
A detective explained the complexities that dealings with suspects could involve:
'I'll give you an example yesterday. He's on bail for an offence, OK, which is taking away [a car]. He's on curfew 7.00 p.m. – 7.00 a.m. Now, at 2.38 in the morning a police car disturbs him near a car and he runs away. They chase him and catch him and go back to the car to find the speakers and things have been taken out. Now he says: "I was going to hospital to have my arm fixed and it's nowt to do with me, the car", and he's on curfew. . . . Now we said to him, without the solicitor present: "Look, you're on curfew. We are going to put you before the court tomorrow, which you've got to go before the court, and we'll ask for a remand in custody because you've broke the conditions of your curfew or we could ask that the conditions be re-imposed but a bit tougher", I said, "and that's the choice. You admit it and stay out or you can deny it and be remanded in custody." Now we can't say that to him with his solicitor present, you see. . . . He thinks about it at that stage and more or less is ready to admit it but he didn't trust us because he had a bad experience the last time he was dealt with [by other officers], with promises made that they didn't deliver. If you promise, you've got to deliver. . . . I did work till half past nine at night: if he had admitted it in the morning, he could have gone to court in the afternoon and got bail. Whereas he didn't go to court until today and I had to do all them enquiries to prove the case and at the end of the day when I got all the evidence he said: "Okay, I'll have it." I still said to him "I'm going to recommend you get back on bail anyway." So I wasn't doing that because he'd admitted it but I said: "I'm doing it because I know that you've been dealt with badly in the past and I'm trying to show you we're not all like that and if we promise you something we'd have delivered. So you can have it [bail] anyway, even though you put me to trouble."'
Res: 'But the suspect would normally have been in custody?'
Detective: 'Well, that's all part of the relationship.'

Bargaining with suspects is not to be understood as a crude, coercive process in which the police confront the suspect with a way out of an unpleasant dilemma. Bargaining is a subtle process and it may be the suspect who initiates the discussion and who seeks to strike up a deal.

CC-A092 – A detective talked about his relationship with 'criminals':
Police: 'Your job isn't worth "fixing anyone up" as the saying used to be, because it should never be a personal vendetta like that. But invariably these people seem to come and come again, and you do build up a sort of rapport. . . . I mean, they know you by your first name. They know that they got a fair deal last

time so they say "Look, let's sort it out". They know that if they sort it out they are going to get treated properly. . . . Without making threats and intimidations: they just want to be treated as a person would expect to be treated. That's the way to be: it's no good being high and mighty with anybody. They've done something wrong and you are there to sort them out. You know, you are the one who's talking to them and you've got to sort their problem out. They can go away from the station thinking "well, I've sorted that out. He's a prat! I've done something else I haven't told him about", but if he's happy and we've got the offence we want, and 90 per cent of the time they tell you a lot more than we originally have.'

Often the police trade on ignorance or seek to gain an advantage by enhancing the suspect's self-esteem (Powis, 1977). In these negotiations, 'face' may be a vital consideration for a successful bargain. The following case illustrates some of the subtleties:

CC-A034 – The officer in charge explained how advantage could be taken of the suspect's ignorance in striking a 'deal':

Police: 'I mean, you know if somebody's going to get bail or not and if they think they're not going to get bail then you can always say to them, "Look, I'll get you bail if you admit it", but if they're going to get bail anyway then that's all right. But I wouldn't tell them that unless they were going to get bail, because they would never tell you anything again after that.'

Res: 'So you've got to have that sort of basis of trust then if you're going to give them anything like that. . . .'

Police: 'You've got to give them truth.'

Although the use of 'bargaining' was openly acknowledged by many officers its precise role in the construction of cases is of its nature hard to detect: the more successful the bargain the less likely that any other social actors apart from the officer and suspect will uncover the existence of the deal or trace its impact. Sometimes it results in the selection of some defendants for prosecution with other suspects being released. Thus:

AT-A075/A077/A104 – Four suspects were arrested in connection with a burglary, all four being apprehended in a van containing the stolen goods. The two women suspects, A075 and A077, were described by the police as the 'girlfriends' of the two male suspects, and both women were released no further action. The officer in charge said that the police 'weren't particularly interested in the two girls' and continued:

'So we wrote them out. Sometimes you can play the part of the woman to give you an edge over the prisoner.'

Res: 'What do you mean?'

Officer: 'If you get a man and wife arrested and it's obvious that it's the man who committed the offence and the wife has only played a small part in it to such a degree that you'll be able to release her anyway, I mean you play on the man saying "She'll get into trouble". It's not used to make people plead to things they haven't done but it's an edge and you use any edge you can when you interview people. . . . So you know sometimes that the part of the woman is so small that really and truly there is no point in going ahead with it. So what you do is say: "Well, there she is languishing in a cell, how about telling us about it?"'

Usually, the only manifestation of a bargain is where a confession follows on from an earlier non-inculpatory interview, where a charge is reduced in return for a plea of guilty or where some other deal is struck. But, whatever form it takes, bargaining is endemic to police work, is absent from official records and shapes and moulds cases in largely unseen ways.

CREATING 'FACTS' THROUGH INTERROGATION

The establishment of 'a case' against an individual requires acceptance of or proof of certain basic facts and circumstances, the essential building blocks of a legally sustainable case. These basic building blocks, the prohibited act (the *actus reus*) and the forbidden state of mind (the *mens rea*), are the 'primary facts' of the case. Although it is assumed in black-letter law books (and in many sociological studies) that these primary facts 'exist', they are the outcome of a process of construction.

The principal forum for case construction is the *interrogation* and, though there is an increasing presence of third parties such as solicitors, parents and social workers, these interactions are still very much under police control. In legal theory, while the police are free to question any citizen, there is only a moral and not a legal duty to answer. Indeed, unless subject to an arrest, the citizen is not obliged to submit to questioning at all. Suspects, however, are placed in a very different position. They too have a legal right to remain silent but they are obliged to submit to police detention and to police questioning.

In the rhetoric of the law, police questioning is a process by which the police extract 'the facts', pure and undiluted. In the rhetoric of the law, the *purpose* of interrogation is to elicit *from the suspect* those facts which are relevant to resolution of the case, at least so far as the suspect is concerned. The accused is seen as the repository of information which can confirm or dispel police suspicion, and it is the task of the police to uncover this hidden data-bank.

Now, of course, legal rhetoric acknowledges that this process is not unproblematic and that, in particular, a suspect may on rare occasions be induced to disclose false information, such as a wrongful admission. Where this occurs, however, the false information is seen as an *inadvertent* product of an otherwise valid process. In such cases, 'errors' occur *despite* the wishes of the investigators to arrive at the 'truth' and are not in any way a deliberate or predictable product of the investigatory process.

The claims of the law cannot, however, withstand scrutiny. The literature on interrogation is replete with examples of the dangers of interview practices which can produce such anxiety and stress in suspects that, in the words of Williams, 'in order to end an atmosphere of suspicion and hostility they will say and sign anything that seems to produce for a moment a more favourable feeling' (1979, p. 8).

Coercion and 'voluntariness'

In a review of the problems arising out of police interrogation, Gudjonsson and MacKeith (1982) concluded that 'widespread and accepted police interrogation practices may sometimes result in definite psychiatric disorders' and that, although false confessions may not frequently occur and not many people may be psychologically disordered as a direct result of police interrogation, 'both do occasionally happen' (p. 253). Whilst we cannot say how frequently if at all suspects in our case samples falsely confessed or were adversely affected by the stress of interrogation, it is clear from what officers told us that many police officers thought it perfectly acceptable to put at least a measure of pressure on suspects. Thus, for example:

> CC-A003 – A detective explained why it was sometimes necessary to put pressure on a suspect during interrogation:
> 'There's nothing wrong with [pressure]. . . . So long as it's all related to the job, you won't be accused of being over the top and causing stress, unnecessary stress, no. I mean that's part of the interview, shouting; everybody's different and everybody has to be interviewed in a different way. There's the old idea about detective ability – one of the main things is interview technique and [you need to remember that] everybody's interview [involves dealing with] a different personality before you go about how you're going to interview him. Some people need a bit of shouting at, like kids really at school, at home, and then there's some people you've got to soft talk, sort of like a father's talk, and that's the whole art of it. Sometimes it's necessary to shout at people, especially the ones who are abusive and you know are restless, and the heat's on and you have to keep up the pressure.'

There is nothing surprising in this. It is a commonplace that police officers are deeply committed to apprehending offenders and securing the conviction of those believed to be guilty. Convictions confirm the correctness of their investigation, just as acquittals throw doubt upon their judgment, their efficiency and their 'knowledge' of crime, as Lambert (1970, p. 38) has pointed out.

Interrogation is, however, a highly problematic process quite apart from the issue of psychological pressure or physical coercion. It is an error to assume that the suspect is the repository for 'the facts' and that these flow in a unidirectional manner from suspect to officer. 'Facts' are not elicited, they are *created*. The 'facts' generated during interrogation are the product of a complex process of interaction between suspect and officer, much of which is directly traceable to the style and manner of police questions. The creation of such 'facts' is not an unusual or aberrant feature but absolutely endemic to police interrogation. Nor are such 'facts' accidentally created: they are precisely what the process sets out to achieve. We now detail these processes.

Proof of states of mind, such as 'intention' and 'recklessness', is conventionally understood to present investigators and courts with a very difficult challenge achievable only by establishing circumstances so compelling that they lead to an irresistible inference that the accused must have intended or foreseen the forbidden consequence. In legal mythology this might mean in an assault case, accumulating evidence relating to the suspect's motives (such as bad blood between suspect and victim), the suspect's statements at the time of the incident ('I'm going to kill you'), the statements of eyewitnesses and the victim (who testify that the suspect was the assailant doing various acts and saying various things) and forensic evidence of the fact and nature of the victim's injuries. It is a bonus if the suspect does anything to assist the prosecution, such as by stating that there was an intention to frighten, to injure or to kill.

In practice, however, the weight of evidence often comes not from 'independent' sources but from the suspect, apparently voluntarily; and the police put most of their efforts into producing by way of interrogation admission statements that will lead to conviction, usually by way of plea. Often, however, these 'admissions' are not volunteered by the suspect nor are they the work of the suspect; they are very directly created by the form and style of police questioning.

Psychologists have identified two general categories of erroneous confession evidence: the *'coerced-compliant confession'* and the *'coerced-internalized confession'* (Gudjonsson and MacKeith, 1988). The former is elicited by the nature of the interrogation process but the suspects remain fully aware that they did not commit the crime in question. Thus, the suspect may confess in order to achieve some immediate instrumental gain, for example, to gain release from custody after an inducement of bail. In the coerced-internalized confession, however, suspects become persuaded (at least temporarily) during the interrogation that they might have or did in fact commit the crime and begin to accept suggestions offered by the police.

Our research indicates an important third category: the '*coerced-passive confession*'. Confessions of this kind occur when the process of questioning induces suspects to adopt the *confession form* without necessarily adopting or even *understanding* the substance of what has been accepted or adopted. In this situation, suspects may internalize the confession by taking on trust the police assertion that they have committed a crime, but equally they may simply adopt words which amount to a confession without even appreciating that they have made an admission.

One of the central features which assist in the production of these kinds of confession is the approach adopted by the police. Although very little interview training is given to the police, officers soon adopt various strategies which are believed to 'work'. These are well documented in the literature (Inbau and Reid, 1967; O'Hara, 1970; Royal and Schutt, 1976; Irving and Hilgendorf, 1980) and include, for example, confronting suspects with damaging evidence; using information bluffs; manipulating self-esteem; befriending the suspect; persuading the suspect that it is in the suspect's best interests to confess; and employing the Mutt and Jeff or Mr Nasty and Mr Nice routine. These strategies are forged in the day to day empirical world of the police officer.

What has been less noticed, however, is the influence exerted by the form and style of police questions. The core of police interrogation only rarely relies upon simple information-seeking questions ('What did you say?', 'What did you do?', 'Did you take any goods?'). Instead, police questioning is best understood as involving a heightened form of *interrogative suggestibility*. Interrogative suggestibility has been defined as 'the extent to which, within a closed social interaction, people come to accept messages communicated during formal questioning, as a result of which their subsequent behavioural response is affected' (Gudjonsson and Clark, 1986). Custodial police questioning is highly *directive* in nature, with the suspect being influenced by cues expressed in questions about what the interrogator expects the 'correct' answer to be, the whole situation being enhanced by the closed nature of the social interaction (Tully and Cahill, 1984). That closed social interaction, in which police authority and control is at the forefront of every encounter and in which the roles of questioner and respondent are so pre-ordered that there is an *expectation* that the suspect can only *answer* not question and *must* answer not remain silent, has been described by Irving (1985) in the language of games:

> [E]ach question and answer are turns, the object of the game is for the interrogator to so manipulate the decision-making of the suspect that he progressively decides in favour first of speaking, then giving true detail, then providing, if appropriate, a signed confession statement. The suspect ... is trying to read the situation from the incoming data, and either exculpate himself or deceive the interrogator. The whole game is played out in a biased environment which puts in the hand of the interrogator some potential ways of lowering the suspect's ability or will to resist manipulation. (p. 59)

Whilst the background account described by Irving is broadly acceptable, we seek to show that the effect of manipulating the suspect's decision making and influencing the kinds of answers allowable gives no confidence that the resultant answers predictably lead to the suspect 'giving true detail'. In fact, we should expect the opposite to be the case in many situations given the manipulative power of the police and the situational vulnerability of the suspect.

In addition to this balance of advantage lying with the interrogator, the very form and structure of police questions increases the likelihood of a confession consistent with the police-desired account and irrespective of 'true detail'. Commentators have drawn attention to one kind of question – the leading question – as creating interrogative suggestibility (Stern, 1938; Richardson *et al.*, 1965; Marquis *et al.*, 1972; Lipton, 1977; Powers *et al.* 1979; Cahill and Mingay, 1986; for a defence of leading questions, see Walkley, 1987, p. 76), but the situation is much more complex than this. We set out below four kinds of question form that are encountered in police interrogations and which overtly manipulate the suspect's decision making:

1 *Leading questions*   These seek to persuade the suspect to give a *particular* answer and to foreclose other possible answers. 'You intended to injure him, didn't you?'; 'You set fire to the house deliberately, isn't that so?' are typical such questions.

2 *Statement questions*   These are statements which masquerade as questions: the suspect is confronted with a 'statement of fact' which the suspect is defied to contradict or invited to confirm. 'You took the money after displaying a knife and threatening the victim, didn't you?'; 'You went out today looking for easy money, saw this person as an easy victim, pushed him to the ground, grabbed his wallet, took the money, ran off and went home as if you had been out for a walk. That's right, isn't it?'

3 *Legal-closure questions*   These purport to invite the suspect to provide information but in reality force information into a legally significant category in the hope that the suspect will 'adopt' it. This may involve introducing some matter not previously mentioned or it may reshape what has been said so that it now 'fits' into an appropriate legal category. Thus, for example, where a suspect states that she took goods from a shelf in a shop and was apprehended outside the shop and had not paid but has not admitted that this was an intentionally dishonest act, the interrogation might continue 'So you *stole* the goods?', apparently re-stating what is already disclosed but in fact by supplying the conclusory concept 'stole', by-passing the need to establish the legal elements of 'intention to permanently deprive' and 'dishonesty' which are the basis of the offence of theft.

4 *Imperfect syllogistic questions*   The method here involves persuading the suspect to accept the truth of a disputable or erroneous proposition, by inducing the suspect to accept that it logically follows from acceptance of other (unarguable) propositions which have already been agreed. This will occur, for example, where the suspect agrees that an act was done (not disputed) which led to a particular consequence (not disputed), and is persuaded to accept that guilt follows from these concessions (it often will not, without some further finding relating, e.g., to the suspect's state of mind).

These, and other styles of interrogation we illustrate below, have one other crucial property: they are almost never followed by 'neutral' questioning designed to elicit the suspect's own story and, indeed, are used in a context in which there are explicit efforts to suppress any attempt by the suspect to introduce exculpatory material into the interview. 'Confessions' obtained in this way are very often conclusive, resulting in a guilty plea or being otherwise unchallenged in court. Simple acceptance of the police assertion is regarded as *proof*. The following cases illustrate this process:

CC-A002 – The defendant was alleged to have damaged a mini-cab windscreen in the course of an argument with his girlfriend. Both had been drinking heavily and the defendant had to sleep off the effects of the drink before being fit to be interviewed. He said that, in the course of the row, he had swung his arm out 'and hit the windscreen and it broke'. The police then turned their attention to the question of *mens rea*:

Police: 'Did you intend to smash the windscreen?'
Defendant: 'No.'
Police: 'So you just swung your hand out in a *reckless* manner?' (emphasis supplied)
Defendant: 'Yes, that's it, just arguing.'
Police: 'Why did you hit the window in the first place?'

Defendant: 'Just arguing, *reckless*, it wasn't intentional to break it. . . .'
(emphasis supplied)

Here, therefore, the suggestion of recklessness is first implanted by the police as a favourable, exculpatory alternative to the defendant, who accepts it as such and then adopts it. Although recklessness is a term of art and part of the definition of the offence with which A002 was charged (criminal damage) it is clear that A002 was not using the term in the technical sense, but rather was using the term colloquially to support a plea that the breakage was *accidental*. Thus, in providing A002 with the terminology in which to press his excuse, the police construct a key element of the case. Having made this key strategic gain, the officer does not explore the matter further; to do so would be to run the risk of showing that A002 had used the term reckless in a sense quite different from that contemplated in law.

CC-A069 – Here the defendant was arrested on suspicion of shoplifting.
Police: 'How did you take it?'
Defendant: 'I just put it in my shopping bag'
Police: 'Then what did you do?'
Defendant: 'Walked out of the store.'
Police: 'So you stole the bag is that correct?'
Defendant: 'Yes.'

Case *CC-A069* is typical of a style of questioning that is common to much of police interrogation. Once the suspect has agreed to some act or acts, the police attribute the necessary state of mind and any other legal requirements of guilt by a 'question' which purports to *summarize* the legal effect of what the suspect has related: '*So* you stole . . .'. The suspect is being informed (incorrectly) of her *legal* position ('You are a thief') and the question form ('is that correct?') is effectively redundant.

CC-J45 – The defendant was arrested on suspicion of theft of chocolate. Under interrogation the crucial exchanges occurred as follows:
Police: 'What did you do in Smith's?'
Suspect: 'Took some chocolate.'
Police: 'How did you take it?'
Suspect: 'Put it in the shopping basket and then put it into the bag and then when we left put it into the trolley.'
Police: 'Did you pay for anything in Smith's?'
Suspect: 'No.'
Police: 'So you stole the chocolate, is that correct?'
Suspect: 'Yes.'

Here, the police introduce 'stole' without having established the legal elements which comprise stealing.

BW-A017 – This case arose out of a breach of the peace outside a disco, A017 allegedly being involved. The case illustrates a technique often employed by the police: putting an account of what happened and inviting its adoption. Even if, as here, this is resisted, it helps 'make a record' of the police reconstruction of reality. The concern of the police is *not* to extract a detailed account from the suspect of his movements, actions and motivations: these emerge, if at all, *despite* the style of questioning. The police appear to have constructed the case before the suspect is seen and are only interested in getting an acceptance or denial. They do not seek an alternative construction of events.

Police: 'At about 12.00 this morning you threw a stone at a doorman from the Flamenco Disco. Is that correct?'

Suspect: 'No.'

Police: 'You came to town tonight with a party for a stag night. One of that party was ejected from the disco, which resulted in stones and bottles being thrown at members of staff of the disco. Is that correct?'

Suspect: 'I went down to town, yes, with a stag party but I don't know of any bottles or anything being thrown.'

Police: 'After the person was ejected you also left the disco with the majority of the party, and ended up standing on the opposite side of the road to the disco. Is that correct?'

Suspect: 'I was walking past the disco but I wasn't just stood there. I was looking for the chap who had been ejected.'

Police: 'So you were there but didn't see anything being thrown?'

Suspect: 'I didn't see anything thrown.'

Police: 'You were seen to come from the direction of the car park. You stood in the road and lobbed a stone at the doorman standing on the steps. He saw you do this. He followed you over the road; he then saw a police officer, identified you to him, and that's how you were arrested. The doorman didn't lose sight of you at all. Are you going to tell the truth?'

Suspect: 'I'm telling the truth.'

The interview continued in the same manner, the suspect refusing to accept the police version of events, which, for the police, constituted the only 'truth' that was of interest to them.

The following case was one in which the police were convinced that the suspects in question were guilty of a criminal offence and they set out to secure a confession. Several strategies were tried in order to achieve this end but the principal (unsuccessful) strategy was an attempt to convince the suspects of their guilt by confronting them with 'logical' propositions. In this instance the suspects were too astute to fall into the trap, but suspects of lesser astuteness or resilience can easily succumb:

CC-*A074/A075/A076* – Three lads went into Pizza Hut, ordered a pizza each, and were served. A few minutes later, they went to the salad bar in the centre of the restaurant and helped themselves to salad. When they came to pay, they were asked for £8 and not £6 as they said they expected. They were told that, as the menu stated, salad is either an extra or a main meal and must be paid for. They disputed this on the basis that they did not know in advance that it had to be paid for. The police were called and the officer asked whether they had had salad and then told them 'You must pay up or you will be arrested'. The lads protested saying 'Will you listen to us, you've heard their side and not given us a chance'. They were then arrested and transported to the police station. At the interrogation, the police sought to obtain a confession – an admission to theft/deception. Throughout the interview of A074, the officer suggested in various ways that the three had had no intention of paying for the salad but this was adamantly denied. Then the officer tired of questioning and (unsuccessfully) sought to bring the interview to a close on his terms:

Police: 'I'm saying you three helped yourself to salad knowing it would have to be paid for but with no intention of paying for it because you didn't order it with your pizza. It has only become a misunderstanding since you realized the seriousness of your situation. The interview is terminated unless you have anything further to say.'

A074: 'Yes I have, that's wrong. We did not take the salad knowing it would have to be paid for. We took the salad thinking we were entitled to it.'

The interview of A076 sought to obtain an admission by getting agreement to a set of propositions relating to an 'obvious' theft and then putting to A076 that his situation was the same. Though this method of questioning is often successful, and almost succeeded here, it failed:

Police: 'What would you do if someone took something of yours without paying for it?'

A076: 'I wouldn't be very pleased about it, er, I don't know.'

Police: 'That would be stealing wouldn't it?'

A076: 'Yes.'

Police: 'So when you ate the salad and didn't pay for it that was also stealing, isn't it?'

A076: 'Yes, I suppose it is but it was unintentional. It wasn't intended to be that way.'

In this case, the police had become committed to a prosecution at the outset of the case and sought to secure a conviction through a confession, whereas the prosecutor (reviewing the file after the unproductive police efforts) saw this as a case where there was no criminal intent: 'it looked like a genuine mistake by three persons of blameless character.' In the result, the CPS advised against prosecution and no further action was taken.

The important point to appreciate is that 'confessions' which result from leading questions, or from the adoption of police-formulated statements of admission, or from the assimilation of information contained in police questions which was unknown to the suspect prior to the interview, or as a result of broken resistance to varying degrees of compulsion are not the consequence of deviant interviewing practices but are *systemic* products of standard forms of interrogation.

It follows that many of these practices are advertent and not the result of inadequacies of interrogation technique on the part of the police. Although little formal training in interviewing skills is provided within the police (but see Shepherd, 1986a, 1986b; Shepherd and Kite 1989a, 1989b), officers do acquire 'on the job' expertise, tricks of the trade handed down from officer to officer, and learn by experience what 'works' and what does not (Banton, 1964; Shepherd, 1984).

Officers, who drew attention to the absence of formal training, said that they had acquired interview techniques through on-the-job experience. However acquired, police deploy these skills consciously in order to maximize the chance of a confession or to put the suspect into an unfavourable light, as the following extract shows:

> *CC-J04* – This was a case of suspected theft in a store. The officer in charge of the case explained to us that stores had a routine for dealing with shoplifting cases. In this instance, the store detective, in the presence and hearing of the accused, 'walked in and said "I was on duty in the store, saw this individual in the store taking the shoes, leave the store without paying for them . . .". Depending on the store detective, I usually try and get them to say these people have *stolen* these things, but they are very wary about doing that. They seem to think that they shouldn't actually be alleging anything wrong and it's up to me to read their minds.'

Nor are the police alone in realizing that their role is creative. The Crown Prosecution Service, which claims to be independent of the police and espouses a 'Minister of Justice' position in the criminal justice system, is also aware of the creative nature of the police and the *threats* to a successful prosecution that the wrong sort of creativity might occasion. Thus, the CPS appreciates that the form of questions might assist the suspect, and is quick to intervene in such cases to limit damage for the future. Thus:

> *CC-A069* – In this case, cited above, the police engaged in construction; after the accused said that he walked out of the store, they said '*So* you stole the bag is that correct?' The CPS sought to ensure that the store detective did not in future provide the defence with a possible escape route, writing a memo to the police requesting them to proceed with the theft charge and asking them to advise the store detective not to say 'I believe you forgot to pay' when apprehending 'shoplifters' in the future.

Even where the suspect is uncooperative, police questioning is *purposive* rather than formalistic and token. It is only on rare occasions that the police will take an indication of silence or 'no comment' as a signal to end the interrogation. Questioning is still seen as useful if it can be used to convey to the court the police version of events, as the following case shows:

CE-A001 – A detective constable told us that some solicitors advised their clients to say 'no reply to all questions' but, where this occurred, the police continued to question.

Res:	'So you put questions to them?'
Police:	'Oh yes, we put the questions.'
Res:	'Why do you keep putting the questions if they say "no reply"?'
Police:	'Well, I think you're getting your case across a bit anyway. You're putting to them what you want to put because the questions you put are sometimes as good as the answers you get. And when it's read out in court, if you've put the right questions then you're sort of getting across to people what your suspicions are or what your evidence is, and it comes across better.'

Such an account may indeed be effective in putting across the police case to reviewers, CPS, defence lawyers and magistrates and juries, notwithstanding that such statements are technically inadmissible. In our sample, we had a number of such statements admitted into court without challenge.

Exculpatory statements

As we have seen, it does not follow that police questioning is always directed towards or successful in achieving an admission to the full offence charged. The police have a variety of motives in their dealings with arrested people and sometimes they are not interested in incriminating the suspect. This will be the case, for instance, where they wish to keep an existing informant 'out of the frame' or where they decide to 'downgrade' a complaint to a non-criminal incident. In such cases, *interrogation* is abandoned in favour of a style of questioning designed to assist the suspect's 'good' character or to minimise the nature of the suspect's behaviour. Thus:

CC-A078 – In this case, the police decided early on that this was essentially a 'domestic' arising out of an incident in which A078 twice punched his wife in the face with his fist. The police did not seek to side with the victim, adopting her story, but sought instead to give A078 every opportunity to reinforce his version:

Police:	'Lucinda said that you hit her once during the argument and then again after she had been out of the house, is that right?'
A078:	'No.'
Police:	'Where was she when you hit her?'
A078:	'I had hold of her and she fell on to the chair in the living room.'
Police:	'And that was the only time violence occurred during the argument, is that right?'
A078:	'Yeah.'

In general, however, police interrogation is concerned with securing evidence *against* the suspect. In the rhetoric of police professionalism this may be achieved in one of two ways. Either the suspect will provide a true confession or the suspect will give an untruthful account which can then be discredited by checking and testing it (Walkley, 1987). In this rhetoric, *whatever* the accused says under interrogation becomes a resource for the good detective. This, in turn, fuels concern over 'ambush' defences heard for the first time at trial which, it is claimed, the police are therefore not in a position to disprove, and lends legitimacy to proposals to weaken the right to silence in order to 'encourage the early disclosure of lines of defence' (Home Office, 1989b, para. 58). Suspects are thus depicted as intentionally withholding from the police information valuable to the case.

This picture misrepresents the reality of police interrogation. Whilst the police do make checks on accounts advanced by suspects, such checks tend to be confined to cases in which the police are genuinely unsure about whether to arrest and charge the suspect in the first place, and then are undertaken only where the matter may be checked out authoritatively with relatively little effort. In a very few situations, the police made further inquiries as a result of a clear and insistent account given by the suspect which was capable of being verified by resort to an identified individual. For instance, in *BK-A059* (discussed in Chapter 9), in which the suspect claimed that he had permission to be in possession of a beer glass taken from a pub, the police checked with the landlord and released the suspect once the story was confirmed.

The result is that whereas suspects are generally keen to proclaim their innocence and endeavour to furnish evidence in support of their claim, these attempts are routinely rebuffed by the police. For the interviewing officer the suspect is presumptively guilty and the purpose of the interview is to produce a confession. Lines of defence raised by the suspect are irrelevant red-herrings to be ignored or argued away. To show interest in the story which the suspect wishes to present is to demonstrate weakness of resolve in the battle of wills with the suspect. To permit material which contradicts guilt into the interview is to build weakness into the case and is the antithesis of constructing a case for the prosecution.

The primary means by which the interviewing officer controls the content of the interview is by controlling the focus, the agenda and the terminology of the interview. Once a charge has been chosen it becomes the organising matrix for all evidence collection and, in particular, the interview. The interview is not designed to elicit the suspect's own account of the incident, rather the suspect is invited to accede to the officer's view of the case. Where the suspect asserts innocence or introduces evidence which would support a defence, this is generally ignored.

> *CC-A043* – A043 was named as a person who was involved in disorder in a town centre on a Saturday evening following a football match. When arrested he told the police that he had spent the evening in a neighbouring town, had gone to the cinema and then returned home. He also named two people who were visiting his mother who could vouch for the fact that he had returned home at 9.50 p.m. and he also offered to describe what both films were about. The interviewer ignored his offer to describe the two films. A043 was charged with threatening behaviour. At trial no evidence was offered after it became apparent that the two named alibi witnesses would support his story.

It is routine police work *not* to follow up evidence raised by an accused which may support a defence. However, in pursuit of a strong case containing minimum contradictions the police may go further and suppress evidence tending to support the asserted defence (Devlin, 1979; McConville, 1987).

> *BK-A056* – V was found unconscious, bleeding and badly beaten outside a wine bar. A056 was apprehended close by, covered in blood. He admitted fighting V but claimed that throughout he was acting in self-defence. Although V refused to make a complaint the DI and Superintendent were very keen that A056 should be prosecuted because there was a problem with fighting after closing time which they wished to stamp out. In fact the officers dealing with the case thought that there was a fair chance that A056 might have been telling the truth, since V was well known to be violent and had a long record including assaults and causing grievous bodily harm. This information was not included in the file. The case was eventually dropped and no evidence offered when the accused elected Crown Court trial and indicated that he would plead not guilty.

In this case the overwhelming police objective was to be seen to be doing something about a crime which was particularly prevalent and was a cause of local concern. It was this objective, rather than a real assessment of the merits of the case which governed the selection and presentation of the evidence.

It would appear particularly important for the police to consider whether a suspect has raised a defence in cases which are considered suitable for caution. There are two reasons for this. First, a caution may be administered only if the individual admits guilt. Second, because the caution decision is wholly under the control of the police, there is no possibility of external review or challenge to the police determination that the suspect has confessed. The issue is important because the caution involves a determination of criminal guilt which may have consequences for the individual even where not dealt with by a court. Juvenile cautions are cited in court, and for all suspects a caution is recorded and the existence of earlier cautions influences later prosecution decisions.

This formal view of the caution is not internalized by the police. For the police the caution is essentially a 'let off' having few if any adverse consequences for the subject. From the police point of view the utility of the caution is in identifying individuals who will be suitable for prosecution should they re-offend, and as a means of warning a juvenile about undesirable conduct and associations. Thus, for the police there is no pressing need to apply rigorous standards of proof in caution cases, and the caution is seen as having utility not only for offenders but also for their associates or those on the periphery of crime. The consequence of this is that where cases are processed with a view to caution exculpatory remarks short of a flat claim to innocence are routinely ignored as being irrelevant to the caution decision.

> *AH-J33* – J33 had been named by another boy as having been involved with a group of children who had stolen a bicycle. In interview J33 described how the bicycle had been stolen by another boy who had then 'shown' it to him. J33 did not admit having ridden it or even having touched it. J33 was cautioned for the offence of taking a vehicle without consent.

CONCLUSION

Interrogation takes place in a social environment which increases the vulnerability of the suspect and maximizes the authority and control of the police. Confinement and isolation impose stresses which, whilst significant in themselves, are magnified by consciously manipulative devices such as bail-bargaining. *No* record can faithfully reproduce the environment which the suspect is required to confront; no system of contemporaneous notes can capture the suspect's predicament. But the *police record* is especially distortive, leaving out of account the critical social and environmental stimuli which influence the suspect's decision making. Whilst some of these cannot be adequately captured by any system of recording (written records, tape-recording or audio-visual), those features which are *designed* to influence are deliberately suppressed. All of this is enhanced by the form of questioning which seeks to manipulate the answers suspects can offer. Analysis of police interrogation records confirms that the relationship between interrogator and suspect is *dynamic* so that any confession is a product of the process of interaction. But it cannot properly be described as a *joint* product because the dynamic relationship uniquely favours the more powerful – the police. This is a classic demonstration of the general point that 'discourse produces an author, rather than the other way round' (Burton and Carlen, 1979, p. 34). The dramatic power imbalance between police and suspect enables the police to realign social relationships through words the suspect is induced to utter, thus maximising the legitimacy of the acts of low-level state officials. Interrogations are best understood therefore as social encounters fashioned to *confirm* and *legitimate* a police narrative.

In this sense they are similar to the trial – the event which interrogations traditionally lead up to and feed into, but which they increasingly *replace*. Indeed, the police seem to have learnt some of their interrogation styles from courtroom dramas. Thus in *CC-J45* the police were more concerned to put *their* version of events to the suspect – or, rather, to the hidden jury – than to elicit the suspect's version. Hence silence, as the officer in *CE-A001* said, is only a minor inconvenience since it does not prevent the police 'putting questions', which are actually assertions, to the suspect (cf. McKenzie and Irving, 1988).

And so it is hardly surprising that in *CC-A074* the officer sought to close the interview on his own terms (restating his case and saying 'the interview is terminated unless you have anything further to say'). The police are not interested in 'anything further', as the abandonment of the old practice of allowing suspects to prepare their own written statements shows. A written statement is, or can be, the suspect's story, on the suspect's terms. It is not just that statements from the suspect can be ambiguous or even exculpatory: they simply contain what *suspects* want to say, which is of no interest to the police (unless it is in their terms). As in court, witnesses and suspects are not given a free hand to tell their story.

5   Building the case: police records and non-interrogation evidence

The opportunities for case building are not confined to interrogation but infuse all aspects of police work. Although the police always complain about paperwork (Shapland and Hobbs, 1987) and claim that it restricts their 'real' function as crime-catchers, they are all too well aware that it is through paperwork (or its absence) that they are able to provide a controlled and selective presentation of their activites for external scrutiny. We have already seen how the interrogation process is depicted in police files, and the extent to which records of interrogation, though partial, assist in case building. In this chapter, we concentrate attention upon the use of police paperwork outside the interrogation in building cases and in insulating the police from external regulation. In the first section, we show how basic information gathered by the police may be reshaped and take on a different reality as it is processed within the police hierarchy. In the second section, we illustrate the capacity of the police, through control of key recording mechanisms, to validate their activities and insulate themselves from external review.

CREATING EVIDENCE OUTSIDE THE INTERROGATION

By their control over all aspects of pre-trial records and their dominance of police–citizen interactions, the police are able to control the extent to which 'the evidence' incriminates the suspect. In this process, the police act as moral arbiters, decide whether an incident is a crime or not, allocate responsibility for what happened and secure, so far as they can, that the evidence ties the suspect into the narrative that has been constructed. In this analysis, we see that the police are often not concerned to create desired relations but rather to realize them through official productions of knowledge. Police accounts and police records do not reflect the social relations which have occurred; rather they suppress alternative accounts and *resolve the situation* (Burton and Carlen, 1979,

p. 137). Records, which seek to reproduce legitimacy through the celebration of rational, democratic and consensual values, are always directed towards *closure*. The privileged status accorded police accounts generally ensures that closure takes place by suppressing and de-legitimating alternative accounts.

Warnings and cautions

It is sometimes thought that prosecution inevitably follows arrest or arrest and detention, but this is very far from the case. The police may detain an individual, as in drunkenness cases, with no intention of charging. Similarly, they may interview an individual on a speculative basis in the hope that incriminating evidence may be elicited, but that hope, as the police themselves know, may be very faint indeed. Even where an admission is secured, the circumstances of the offence, including its perceived seriousness, may persuade the police to take no further action or to administer a warning or caution. The control over the warning and caution system exercised by the police is absolute.

In situations covered by cautions, warnings and NFAs which comprise over 40 per cent of adult cases and over 60 per cent of juvenile cases the police can engage in unilateral construction. They are able to do this because the cautioning process is essentially *inquisitorial*. This process enables them to create any necessary pre-conditions, such as the 'consent' which the suspect is required to give prior to being cautioned. However, police power goes beyond this. On a deeper and more fundamental level, it enables the police to construct *criminality*. This is strikingly so in cases which are terminated by police-determined decisions such as giving the suspect a warning or administering an official caution. So complete is the police control of these interactions that the official account is often reported in terms of 'the facts' without any attempt to engage in the language of proof or 'evidence'. In these reports, the incident is clear, uncomplicated, exact and unproblematic. In the following case, for example, the police file incriminated the suspects even though proof of guilt was lacking:

CC-J05/J06/J07/J08 – After a window of an off-licence was broken, four juveniles went to see the shopowner and told him that they had broken it accidentally while, as they put it, 'pratting around'. They said that they had been engaged in horseplay and one had fallen against the window breaking it. When interrogated by the police, all four maintained that the window had been broken *accidentally* while larking around. Interrogation exchanges of the following kind:

Police: 'So you are saying it was an accident?'
J05:   'Yes.'

clearly show that the police fully understood the nature of the juveniles' story. The Crown Prosecution Service refused to take the juveniles to court in the absence of any evidence of the intention or recklessness which a charge of criminal damage requires.

The police decision-makers accepted that there was no evidence of intention, that recklessness would not be satisfied by proof that the boys were simply 'messing about' and that 'an admission or something like that' would be required. Discussing the case with the researcher, the Inspector said that in order to establish guilt: 'you would want more than just these facts that they were larking around'. Nevertheless, the police decided that the juveniles were 'guilty'. In line with this, and despite the fact that the formal requirements for a caution were absent (namely, an admission of responsibility), all four were *cautioned* and were thus officially given a 'record' which could be cited in court in the future.

One officer described how an 'admission' is sometimes established:

> 'Cautions are being used to ease workload. What you find is that if the custody officer is bogged down with cases, they start using the caution. Although it says so on the form the victim is not asked. . . . In some cases the defendant refuses to sign it but it's still used. I don't know whether it counts as a caution or not but if he won't sign it the custody officer will say "fuck off" and use it still. The only trouble is that we act as judge and jury in these cases.'

In some cases, indeed, the police are able to construct an official reality even where the evidence they obtain through investigation *contradicts* their own determination, as in the following example:

CC-J26/J27 – The defendants were arrested after a store detective alleged that J26 took ear-rings in a shop without paying. According to J26 and J27, J27 did not take anything, was not seen to be involved by the store detective but had been with J26 just before J26 was alleged to have taken the property in question. J26 said that J27 was not involved, and J27 maintained her innocence throughout. The officer in charge of the case was asked what the store detective said about J27's involvement:

Police: 'She just said she was with [J26]. She didn't take anything.'
Res: 'Did the store detective suspect [J27] knew what was going on?'
Police: 'Well, if they are together, they are always apprehended together or arrested together. . . .'
Res: 'Did they admit to being involved?'
Police: 'Well, the girl who took the ear-rings obviously did, but the other one didn't.'

Despite all of this, which was confirmed by witness statements and written records in the police files, both defendants were given police warnings. Indeed, the official report submitted by the officer in charge stated:

> '*Offenders* informally warned by Inspector [X], all criteria met' (emphasis supplied).

Even though the police believed that one of the parties was not involved (the case officer told us that 'at the end of the day I was satisfied that perhaps [J26's] friend didn't have anything to do with it') both individuals became designated by the police as offenders and might easily have been cautioned since the case officer had sought a caution on the basis that 'an informal warning is a waste of time'.

Although the administration of cautions and informal warnings without clear admissions of guilt contravenes official guidelines, these are not isolated aberrations (Sanders, 1988b).

The problem extends beyond cautioned cases to those in which no further action was taken.

> *AT-J09* – J09 and two others [X and Y] were arrested on suspicion of burglary after a witness said that she saw three children 'near' a door of a building from which property had been recently taken. The witness was taken to a nearby camp-site where she picked out X and Y as two of the children she had seen. Both X and Y were below the age of criminal responsibility. The police also arrested J09 who was seen leaving the site and the witness was shown J09 and asked if J09 was the other child: the witness said that he was.
>
> At the interview, all three children denied involvement in any offence. The witness identification of J09 also crumbled. As the officer in the case told us:
>
> > 'Although the [witness] said there was every chance it was [J09] she wouldn't swear by it. She is putting two and two together slightly. . . .'
>
> Without evidence, therefore, the police were forced to take no further action. However, for the purposes of police records there was a different account. The records stated that 'both persons under the age of criminal responsibility were responsible' and J09 'was eliminated due to insufficient evidence to connect him with the matter'. The police were not therefore prepared to consider any party innocent: two were designated as guilty, and J09 was not prosecuted simply because they could not *prove* guilt.

Such designations of guilt are not merely private slurs. As we shall see in Chapter 7, juvenile bureaux keep records of NFAs as well as cautions. A 'long record' may be made up entirely of informal warning and NFAs – with serious repercussions for any subsequent decisions about whether or not to prosecute.

Verbals and other unverified statements

Under the old system, in which the police, at some point after the interrogation had been concluded, produced a statement purporting to be a faithful record of what was said, it was well understood that there was at least some cross-fertilization between the words of the suspect and those of the police. The police, it was recognized, sometimes transformed the words used by the suspect into police argot. As Lord Devlin (1960) put the point:

> [S]tatements have sometimes been put in evidence which have been said to be the prisoner's own unaided work as taken down by the police officer and in

which the prisoner has recounted in the stately language of the police station (where, for example, people never eat but partake of refreshment and never quarrel but indulge in altercations) the tale of his misdeeds. (p. 39)

But stronger allegations were also made and from time to time it emerged that a suspect had been or was alleged to have been 'verballed'. Verballing was once regarded as something that could be talked about only in hushed tones but, more recently, its existence as a social phenomenon whatever its actual incidence has gained widespread acceptance (Morton, 1975; Justice, 1979; McConville and Baldwin, 1981). 'Verballing' occurs when a statement of admission is attributed to a suspect even though the suspect did not in fact make any such statement. Sometimes this is referred to as 'fabrication', sometimes as 'gilding the lily'. Occasionally verballing is established to have occurred; more usually it remains as an allegation with more or less suspicion attached to it.

If the PACE Act rules are complied with, any fabricated statement must occur outside the formal interrogation because formal interrogations are supposed to be recorded, in writing or on tape, contemporaneously. Typically this would have to be located in the suspect's home, on the street or in the police car on the way to the station (McConville and Morrell, 1983). The opportunities for this are, in fact, preserved by the PACE Act which does not render statements made in any of these situations inadmissible.

The problem of unverified police statements is not confined in fact to the false attribution of statements to the defendant but covers 'adjusting' evidence of what the officer witnessed. The constructive nature of such police evidence appears clearly from the following field note extract:

AT-A107 – A police officer asked us whether we knew what a 'verbal' was and whether we had encountered many. He explained by saying that for threatening behaviour the police would always say that women and children were present because this was needed to obtain a conviction. He then gave as an example: 'If some bloke called out "Pig" to me, I turn round and ask him what he said. If he says "Nothing" you leave it, but if he repeats it you've got to have him. You can't back down because then he'll think he can have the next PC who comes along.' He then added: 'If we know they're guilty, we make sure they are.' He illustrated this by saying that if he saw a car with a smashed window and a man walking down the street ahead of the car who dropped a radio cassette when he saw the police who, when apprehended, denied that he had been carrying the radio, he [the officer] would say in his evidence that he had seen the man smash the window and break in and take the radio. The man, he said, would inevitably say that he found the radio in the street, but, he added: 'That might be true but it would be 99 per cent certain that he'd broken in and taken it.'

One of the problems with unverified police statements is that it is not possible to determine with any confidence whether the statement was made or whether it is fabricated. Courts, placed in the position of having to decide such issues, have sometimes viewed the matter with scepticism. Thus, in *Thompson* [1893] 2 Q.B. 12, Cave J. stated:

'I would add that for my part I always suspect these confessions, which are supposed to be the offspring of penitence and remorse, and which nevertheless are repudiated by the prisoner at the trial. It is remarkable that it is of very rare occurrence for evidence of a confession to be given when the proof of the prisoner's guilt is otherwise clear and satisfactory; but when it is not clear and satisfactory, the prisoner is not infrequently alleged to have been seized with the desire borne of penitence and remorse to supplement it with a confession; a desire which vanishes as soon as he appears in a court of justice'. (p. 18)

Usually, however, courts have viewed challenges to such evidence with suspicion and modern courts are prepared to assume that the practice of verballing 'was probably a relic of the past' (*Vivian Parchment* [1989] Criminal Law Review, p. 290). What is true of courts is also true of prosecutors. There is, therefore, a general presumption of regularity about police evidence. Police officers come to a case without a stain on their character and, as witnesses, they have very high credibility. This can mean that even implausible police evidence can result in prosecutors accepting a charge and taking a defendant to court and it is only in an exceptional case that the defence can deconstruct the prosecution. The following case involved contested police evidence, the credibility of which became a central matter at trial.

AT-J22 – J22 was found sitting in a parked van owned by X, its quarterlight window having been broken, after a civilian witness had seen him and called the police. The police described J22 to us as a 'well-known miscreant, very arrogant, disrespectful. Snubs his nose at authority, his whole demeanour, manner. Not a very pleasant man.' J22 was eventually charged with criminal damage to the van and going equipped for theft (having been found with a spanner in his pocket). It was necessary, on the criminal damage charge, to show that J22 caused the damage deliberately or at least recklessly, neither of which would be established if he were too drunk to know what he was about. The state of J22's sobriety was to become a crucial aspect of the case.

When brought to the police station, J22 refused to be interviewed without his solicitor. On arrival at the station, the solicitor concluded that J22 (who appeared not to recognize the solicitor or acknowledge his presence) was unfit to be interviewed because of drink. Accordingly, the custody officer arranged for a divisional police surgeon to examine J22. The surgeon concluded that J22 was 'extremely drunk' and 'unfit to be interviewed'. J22 was thus released to be interviewed on another day.

Sometime after this, the arresting officers (apparently in ignorance of the determination of the divisional police surgeon) compiled their notebooks relating to the arrest. According to the arresting officers, J22 knew what he was doing and therefore fully intended his actions. Questions were said to have been put to J22 on the street and, according to Officer A's notebook: 'Through the questioning, [J22] was perfectly coherent and appeared to be in the best of health.'

This was supported by Officer B's notebook entry: '[J22] coherent at all times and appears in good health.'

These entries were highly unusual given that neither officer made *any* reference to whether J22 had been drinking or whether he was in any respect drunk.

The case eventually came to court, the Crown Prosecutor having allowed the case to proceed even though regarding the structure of the police evidence relating to J22's alleged coherent state on the street as fishy. Just before going into court, the police officers learned of the surgeon's report. Under cross-examination Officer A was asked to read out the notebook entry cited above and was then asked:

Defence solicitor:'Tell me, why did you add those words?'

Officer A: 'Because the gentleman had obviously been drinking.'

Defence solicitor:'Where is it in your notes that the accused had been drinking?'

Officer A: 'It's not, but I remember it distinctly.'

Defence solicitor:'So distinctly that you omitted it?'

Officer A: 'Yes.'

The defence attempted to get the officer to explain why there was no note of J22 drinking and of his attitude to the surgeon's clear-cut report:

Defence solicitor: 'What I am getting at is that . . . when he was arrested, my client smelt slightly of drink and two hours later my client was too drunk to be interviewed and needed a surgeon?'

Officer A: 'I suggest that he had been drinking heavily and that the effects didn't take place until two hours later.'

Defence solicitor: 'I have no need to make a greater fool of you than you are making of yourself. Thank you officer.'

The same saga was repeated with Officer B. When asked to read out from his notebook, Officer B stated that J22 *smelt of drink but was coherent at all times and appears to be in good health*.

Defence: 'Is this a usual practice to make such a note?'

Officer B: 'Yes.'

Defence: 'Why?'

Officer B: 'Obviously because he had been drinking but was not drunk.'

It was then pointed out to the officer that he had stated that his notebook recorded that J22 had been drinking:

Defence: 'Did you make a note in your notebook about the defendant being drunk?'

Officer B: 'No.'

Defence: 'I thought you just said in answer to a previous question that you had noted it in your book?'

Officer B: 'No, I did not. Sorry, I must have made a mistake – but I did remember it clearly.'

At the conclusion of this evidence, the defence submitted that there was no case to answer. When the court adjourned to consider the submission, the

Crown Prosecutor said to the defence solicitor that he was going to make a complaint about the officers' evidence. He added that he did not know the right course to take when a witness gives perjured evidence.

On returning, the Court held that there was no case to answer on the charge of criminal damage; and, at a later date, the prosecution discontinued the remaining charge, the CPS Reviewer explaining to us that 'the police constables' evidence in court lacked credibility ... and I doubted whether the officers would be believed.'

This is a striking example of the constructive potential of police evidence. The evidence might well have led to the conviction of the defendant through plea or verdict. What led to the case dismissal was the *careless* construction job done by the police, not their attempt to downplay the defendant's drunkenness. In general the police put together their evidence in a much more competent manner and thus better protect themselves and their cases from attack.

'Verballing' in particular and other discredited police evidence, because they represent obviously unfair or outrageous police behaviour, easily give rise to the 'bad apple' theory of policing. According to this, deviant practices in the police are characterized as caused by 'rogue' officers, the remedy for which is their removal from the force before they can contaminate the rest of the barrel. It must be understood, however, that this theory is unsatisfactory and inadequate. As is already apparent from our discussion of interrogation, whilst verballing, etc., may be an extreme form of behaviour, police work is *systemically* geared to the construction of evidence: the creation of evidence in one way or another is not a deviant police act but a standard form of production. The processes of production are more subtle and complex than 'verballing' suggests, and more easily overlooked, but they are all-pervasive.

The prosecution file: management and evaluation

The ability of the police to generate information and structure it in particular ways can also find expression in their control over the general management of the prosecution file. It is the police who are given responsibility for compiling the case dossier and, even where this is reviewed by the CPS, police influence permeates the process.

The police exercise considerable influence over the way in which an incident is viewed not only by the selection and creation of 'primary facts' but also by the way in which they evaluate facts. The characterization of primary facts ('A hit B' is reformulated as 'A viciously hit B') alters our *understanding* of the events in question, and the characterization of primary facts is a significant police power. It must be emphasized that this process of evaluation and re-evaluation usually occurs in police files as a case is reviewed internally not on the basis of the provision of new or additional information but on the basis of the reviewer's 'feelings', 'hunches' or 'prejudices'.

Police stereotypes, which are usually thought to find expression only in their stop-search and arrest decisions, inform every case evaluation decision. These stereotypes are not restricted to views about the suspect but also include views about whether the matter is properly criminal, whether the crime is 'rubbish' (not worth pursuing) and whether the victim deserved to be criminalized. Where files are being assessed within the police hierarchy, case construction is not usually dependent upon new information being received: the classification and re-classification of the case is finely calibrated in the minds of the social actor involved on the basis of their *views* of the information.

The creation of 'legitimate' facts begins with the police acceptance or rejection of accounts proffered by 'victims' or defendants. The following two contrasting cases illustrate some of the possibilities here. In the first the initial police decision that a prosecution was desirable became 'firmed up' as the case went through the review process, even though there were many features which might be thought to make it a 'domestic' in the eyes of the police and thus for them justifying action short of prosecution. In the second, every effort was made to characterize the case as a domestic, despite the existence of potentially aggravating features:

> *CE-A094* – A 10-year-old boy (V) was allegedly hit by the defendant, a 40-year-old neighbour. The defendant said that V had sworn at his daughter, that he had chased V and that V had injured himself falling. The initial police file referred to the defendant's assertion that V swore and added: 'There is no evidence to support this.' As the case progressed up the police hierarchy, the case became characterized as clear-cut and demanding only one course of action: 'An unprovoked attack by a 40-year-old on a 10-year-old boy. I suggest we proceed against [the defendant].' The police file was also incomplete in that it omitted to mention that 'the boy' (a description which conjures up an image of innocence) was, as the police told us in interview, 'a problem' schoolboy.

> *BK-A012* – The defendant was reported to be brandishing a shotgun at his home in the course of 'a domestic dispute'. He was said to have threatened his own life, not that of his wife but he was also said to have smashed the telephone after the wife tried to call the police. The police decided early on that they would not prosecute and sought to 'play down' the incident. The interview of the defendant, for example, was designed to minimise the incident and not to exaggerate it, as by the following question:
> *Police*:   'Isn't it really if you're honest with yourself . . . that you didn't really want to pull the trigger?'

As the police told us, they decided that the defendant was 'not a criminal' and they did not want, therefore, to consider firearms offences (the shotgun was loaded and the defendant had no certificate), criminal damage (of the telephone) or other offences (the defendant, who had previous criminal convictions for property offences and assault, told the police in interview that a few days earlier he had assaulted his wife: 'I lost my rag and hit her.').

Once an initial account of an incident has been rendered, the police exercise close control over its meaning and status by the way in which they assess the account and give it value. This is most clear in terms of their evaluation of facts or incidents, an evaluation that may be determinative of the way the case is disposed or at least will be influential in any later decisions (such as those by the CPS) that have to be made. Evaluation is an on-going task of classification and re-classification so that the shape and direction of the case may always be susceptible to change. Evaluations imbue facts with special qualities which take the case into or out of categories with legal consequences, as the following examples show:

BK-A056 – In this case, discussed also in Chapters 4 and 6, the defendant and another (V) had been involved in a fight. A056 admitted fighting but claimed that V had attacked him first and said that he acted only in self-defence. The arresting officer concluded that A056 should not be prosecuted because (i) V had a bad record for serious assaults and A056 did not; (ii) V would not make a complaint; (iii) there were no independent witnesses; and (iv) the only evidence was that of A056, and he claimed self-defence. On this basis the officer recommended that the matter be recorded as 'Detected – No Further Action'. However, as the matter proceeded up the police internal review hierarchy, the incident became transformed into a 'nasty assault' and prosecution was pressed because there was 'too much of this sort of thing going on and it must be stamped out'. However, the police were eventually forced to drop the matter and offer no evidence at court.

BW-A104 – The defendant took a shirt from a rack in a store, placed it in her own bag and walked out of the store without paying. A104 had no previous convictions and fell within the cautioning guidelines. The arresting officer recommended a caution: 'This appears to be out of character for [A104] and I would suggest consideration be given to cautioning her.'

This was supported by the custody officer. However, the course of the case was altered by a memorandum from the Inspector which read: 'Sir, this was a *deliberate* act of theft by [A104]. I suggest we proceed with summons' (emphasis supplied).

A summons was accordingly issued and, at court, A104 pleaded guilty and was fined.

CE-A069 – The defendant was apprehended stealing. She was in a position of trust and admitted stealing on previous occasions although the current incident was the first time she had been caught. The police decided, however, that this was suitable for a caution and constructed the case on this basis. Thus, the admission to prior thefts was downgraded as being 'minor' and 'would have gone undetected if she had not admitted' them. The file disclosed that the firm had also suffered other losses but these were not pursued as the police were 'satisfied she has no knowledge of these further items'.

Another way in which the police exercise influence over 'the facts' of a case is by the way in which they describe the case in their 'Summary of the Offence'. This is intended to be a short-form statement encapsulating the central features of the case, constructed for the benefit of superior officers and prosecutors. The influence of the summary increases where the reviewers rely upon it without reading the full file or without reading the full file carefully. Of course, this will be of little moment where there is a complete congruence between the summary and the key elements in the full file. In some cases, however, there are important discrepancies, as in the following example:

> *BK-J01/J02/J03/J04* – Four juveniles were arrested for shoplifting and, on questioning, three made full admissions. However, J04 denied taking anything but agreed that he was aware that the others were taking things. When asked what he would get out of it, he replied: 'Nothing'. The arresting officer's summary described all four as having made full admissions, and all four were prosecuted. Indeed, at court all pleaded guilty with the defence solicitor describing J04 as being 'somewhat on the periphery'.

This process of constituting and reconstituting 'the facts' is an ongoing and systemic feature of all police work and decisions taken at one point influence all other related decisions. Each aspect of the case-building process interacts with all other aspects.

PROTECTING THE POLICE FROM EXTERNAL REVIEW

It is sometimes thought that the police have limited potential to construct cases because they are in relationships of dependency with other social agencies such as the courts and, now, Crown Prosecutors. On this view, any attempted reconstruction of reality by the police is always susceptible to review and rectification by an organization higher in the hierarchy of credibility. This, it is said, helps account for the low regard in which prosecutors and courts are generally held by the police. It is the subordinate status of the police in the decision-making hierarchy which is said to explain their resentment towards prosecutors (who, in police terms, 'do not understand the realities of criminal behaviour' and who are 'too remote from the real world') who sometimes overturn police decisions to charge, and towards 'courts' when an accused is acquitted. In police ideology, it is always others who have the final say, never the police themselves.

This picture, however, needs considerable qualification for there are many situations, outside the interrogation room, in which the only legitimate account of reality is that of the police. In such instances, a 'case' is a product of unilateral construction. That is, in many situations the police are able to get the job done (to achieve the goals they set for themselves) precisely because they do not have to account to anyone in any real sense for the rules which purport to control and inform their behaviour. These rules are exclusively *police property*, and enable the police to engage in unilateral case construction.

We can best illustrate this unilateral case construction in relation to the ability of the police to create 'procedural compliance', to ensure that their actions are *ex facie* performed according to the rules and are, for all practical purposes, beyond attack. Police action, whatever its form, is largely self-validating. We discuss below two examples of the ways in which the police unilaterally construct procedural compliance: (i) in street encounters with citizens; and (ii) in custody records and other police files.

Street encounters with citizens

Record keeping, as a means of monitoring whether the police are carrying out their powers in terms of the law, is now seen as particularly important in relation to stop-search provisions. The power of stop-search gives officers almost complete autonomy over the way in which they exercise their authority. So long as the powers continue, a system of accurate record keeping, it is said, is the only practicable way in which the actions of the police in street encounters with citizens can be subject to any external scrutiny. The Royal Commission (1981), which continued and extended the stop-search power, did so only on the basis that there should be 'stringent controls' through a system of records. The proposals of the Royal Commission were set out as follows:

> The grounds for search should be given to the person stopped and searched and they should be recorded.... A copy of the record should be made available within a reasonable period on request by the person who has been searched. Supervising officers should have a specific duty to collect and scrutinise figures of searches and results. They should watch for signs that searches are being carried out at random, arbitrarily or in a discriminatory way. And HM Inspectors of Constabulary should give attention to this matter on their annual inspections of each force. Numbers of stops and searches should be contained in the chief constable's annual report, which will make the broad extent of the application of the powers subject to scrutiny by the police authority. (*Report*, 1981, para. 3.26)

The PACE Act, 1984, sought to give effect to these proposals by requiring that when a constable has carried out a stop-search under the Act, the officer *must* make a record of it in writing unless it is not practicable to do so. It should state:

(i)　the object of the search;
(ii)　the grounds for making it;
(iii)　the date and time when it was made;
(iv)　the place where it was made;
(v)　whether anything, and if so what, was found;
(vi)　whether any, and if so what, injury to a person or damage to property appears to the constable to have resulted from the search (s.3(6)).

Persons searched are entitled to ask for a copy of the record of search, provided they do so within twelve months of the date on which the search was made. By section 5 of the Act annual reports of chief constables (and the Commissioner of Police of the Metropolis) have to contain information about searches recorded under s.3.

This fairly elaborate system of checks has to be seen against a background of deep concern over the way in which the police have used their powers historically. The collected efforts of researchers clearly established that police actions were not based upon the reasonable suspicion requirement of the law nor were they random: rather, stop-search powers, anchored in police stereotypes, were used differentially against young, inner-city males, particularly young black males, especially those who were unemployed or economically marginal (Brogden, 1981; Tuck and Southgate, 1981; McConville, 1983; Willis, 1983; Policy Studies Institute, 1983; Southgate and Ekblom, 1984; Brogden, 1985; Dixon *et al.*, 1989). Suspicion was not individualized but directed against a person as a member of a group believed to possess deviant characteristics. The overwhelming majority of stop-searches were unproductive on any measure (Policy Studies Institute, 1983; McConville, 1983). The result, inevitably, as McConville (1983) pointed out, was poor police relations with large sections of the community and a deepening of police hostility and prejudice towards those on whom they focused suspicion.

Now we have already seen that the Act has not altered the basic criterion of stop-searches as they affect people in the street, the police continuing to displace reasonable suspicion in favour of crude stereotypes founded in age, gender, race and class. Still, it might be argued, the position after PACE may be a vast improvement if the Act succeeds in persuading the police to use their powers (albeit discriminately) with reduced frequency. Examination of the statistics before the Act and after does indeed appear to support the view that there has been a remarkable downturn in the use of stop-search powers. Prior to the PACE Act, stop-search was a favoured police strategy. Although there was no reliable systematic information on the frequency of use of the powers, figures supplied by the Metropolitan Police District to the Royal Commission (1981) showed that, in London alone, almost 500,000 stops were made each year. Since the police recorded fewer than half the stops made in London and only about one third of those made in the provinces (Willis, 1983; Policy Studies Institute, 1983), it is probable that nation-wide stop-searches were being carried out on over two million occasions each year prior to PACE. Stop-search was, therefore, the bedrock of police street operational strategy.

In contrast, official figures compiled since the implementation of the PACE Act suggest abandonment of stop-search as a front-line police strategy:

Table 8 Total national searches of persons or vehicles under s.1 of PACE, and resultant arrests

Year	Total stop-searches	Arrests	Arrests as proportion of stops
	n	*n*	%
1986–7	109,800	18,900	17.2
1987–8	118,200	19,600	16.6

Source: Home Office Statistical Bulletin 14/88, Table 1.

The figures in Table 8 seem to show, therefore, moderate use of the powers by the police, with a 'success' rate which lends some colour to a claim that the powers are used on the basis of reasonable suspicion.

Contrary to this official picture, we can state that the stop-search powers continue to be used as a front-line, routine police strategy, deployed against those who conform to police stereotypes, and that the image of procedural compliance put forward by the statistics is a wholesale distortion of police street practices. This contradiction exists because stop-search is essentially a *police* power, not a legal power, and because the rules purportedly 'regulating' the use of these powers are police property.

The police are able to project an image of procedural compliance because they possess an alternative power, unaffected by PACE, to stop-search individuals. This power allows the police to stop-search where the individual citizen 'consents'. The new statutory accounting system has encouraged officers to continue their former practices through 'consent' searches. Stop-searches are still made on the basis of discriminatory criteria and the police do not even have the problem of convincing anyone that there was 'reasonable suspicion'. The trick is to obtain 'consent' and police officers now devote their efforts to the construction of 'consent'. The following accounts of officers show how this is achieved through the use of social skills, bluffing and threats:

> *CE-A005*
> Police: 'Usually, when you inform somebody that you are going to
> search them or ask them, they might refuse or query it. Then
> you will say you have got a power first of all and will use it.
> Then they consent. So more often than not it's by consent at
> the end of the day, rather than under PACE. If you are good
> at it, you can talk to them and get their consent. . . . I don't
> think in fact that I've ever searched anybody under PACE.
> I've always got their consent because they don't want to be
> forcefully searched with a power of arrest. I tell people, "why
> make it difficult for yourself?"'

CE-A082 – A police officer explained to us that most of the public accepted having to be stopped and searched but 'it's just the minority will get a little uppitty and they'll start fighting and screaming and shouting'. Asked how this group are dealt with, he replied:

> Police: 'It's just your experience, you sort of, you know, if you get
> heavy, sometimes you may have to get heavy or sometimes try
> if you can talk them round a bit and have a chat. By the time
> you've finished they see your point of view.'
> Res: 'When you search somebody, do you try to do that with consent
> or do you actually use the power you've got under PACE?'
> Police: 'You do it with consent. I've never sort of had to use the powers
> under PACE so to speak. I mean usually you might have to
> pressure them a little, say "Do you want *me* to search you?
> Have you got something to hide then?" and they say "Oh,
> no!", "Well, let's have a look in your pockets", "O.K.", and
> they'll empty their pockets.'

'Consent', therefore, is a police construct. On many occasions, of course, individuals willingly submit to a stop-search, especially where they can see that there is a genuine investigation in progress and there is a need to eliminate them from enquiries. Assisting the police is understood by most people to be a social responsibility of every citizen. But this is premised on the basis that there is a *genuine*, well-grounded need to search individuals, for reasons already known to the citizen (as in well-publicized cases where the police are actively seeking perpetrators of some serious or notorious crime) or carefully explained by the officer (e.g. that a burglary has recently occurred in the immediate vicinity and the citizen appears to fit the description of the culprit). Since, however, the police wish to stop-search routinely in situations not covered by these scenarios and where consent might be withheld if the citizen knew the true motives of the police, submission and compliance are substituted for true consent (see also Freedman and Stenning, 1977; Ericson, 1981a). The police are not concerned to persuade the citizen of the *reasonableness* of their actions – which is hardly surprising since they know these to be often *unreasonable*. Instead, the police are concerned to persuade the individual of the *inevitability* of the stop-search, and to convince the individual that the alternative to 'consent' would be much worse.

The citizen is, therefore, subject to a Catch-22 in stop and search situations. Through ignorance of their legal position or through fear of police power even a reluctant citizen will permit a stop-search by 'consent'. Those who are more knowledgeable of their rights or are not intimidated by bluffs or threats and withhold consent will be deemed to have acted suspiciously and to have thus provided grounds for invoking the power in PACE. The point was neatly put by the officer in charge in *CC-J56*:

> 'It's better to search somebody by consent. . . . If they give their consent all well and good. If they don't give their consent, nine times out of ten they've got something to hide anyway and all the [PACE] forms will be filled out then.'

Thus, legality requires reliance upon either reasonable suspicion or consent, both problematic notions for the police. Consent is preferred because it does not normally require the officer to account for the stop-search to any superior, and a written record will be created only where the officer anticipates trouble (as by a complaint) and seeks to guard against it (see Smith and Gray, vol. IV, 1983, p. 236) or where the search has been successful, in which case it can be accounted for as having been undertaken on the basis of reasonable suspicion.

All of this reinforces the evidence in Chapter 2 that many stop-searches are made without 'reasonable suspicion'. In the experiences of citizens, however, this hardly matters: if there is no arrest the aggrieved citizen feels that there is little concrete basis to found a complaint, while, if there is, the evidence used to justify the arrest is also used to justify the initial stop-search. None of this would be possible without 'consent'. Yet 'consent' is itself capable of construction only because coercive powers are background realities which are available to an officer at will.

Custody records and other police files

In compiling custody records, refused charge books, search records and the like, the police have an unchallenged opportunity to construct 'reality'. This opportunity is utilised to convey an impressive sense of legality and rule-adherence on the part of the police as well as a single, unitary view of an event.

In some respects at least it must be made clear that certain types of inaccuracy in custody records are simply the result of work pressure. Thus, in busy stations or at busy times, staffing levels were such that it was difficult, if not impossible, to comply with the requirements of the PACE Act to undertake periodic reviews of prisoners in custody.

Many times, therefore, custody officers told us that it was not *possible* to comply with PACE in the full sense required, and superior officers usually understood their situation. It is hardly surprising, therefore, if custody records are sometimes the subject of 'creative accounting'. Times may be 'adjusted' and tasks which have not been performed logged as completed. Most superior officers looked at this 'drift' sympathetically. Supervisors generally sought to ensure that the custody record was immune from criticism (McKenzie *et al.*, 1990) and those who cracked down on records which disclosed defects in a critical tone were viewed with contempt by custody officers.

Although fixing the record in this way might be seen as functional, even harmless, the autonomy enjoyed by the custody officer also provides the opportunity for serious distortion. This is especially so in relation to their responsibilities for informing suspects of their right to have someone told of their arrest and their right of access to legal advice. Mastery over the records here provides a cover for failure of duty, trickery and deceit.

One example in relation to custody records will suffice to show how the police are able to choose to construct reality and to portray themselves as rule-bound:

Field Note Extract (Area AT)
*Research notes:*I was sitting in the charge office working on custody records when a young man was brought in under arrest. The custody officer, who had been chatting to me, went over to the other desk:
Custody Officer:'What's he done?'
Constable: 'He's in for breaking a window of a Mercedes.'
Custody Officer:'Just outside?'
Constable: 'No, over [x] Road.'
Custody Officer
(to arrestee): 'Have you done it before?'
Arrestee: 'What?'

Constable: 'He used a spark plug, threw it at a distance so he wouldn't be near when it broke.'
Custody Officer
(smiling): 'You've done it before, haven't you?'
Arrestee: 'No.'

The custody officer then filled in the custody record, asking the arrestee for his personal details (name, age, address). The arrestee was then searched and no property was found on him. The custody record was then placed in front of him and, pointing to the custody record, the custody officer barked out: 'Sign here, here and here'. The arrestee signed in all three places and was then put in a cell. He was not given any notice of his rights, nor told of his rights.

I asked to see the custody sheet later after the custody officer had left the room to go to the front desk. An inspection of the custody record showed that the custody officer had ordered the arrestee to sign the boxes relating to his rights: the boxes had been completed by the custody officer to indicate that he did not want a solicitor or anyone notified that he was being held. The arrestee did not read any part of the form – he signed immediately when asked.

This, like the other occasions observed, demonstrates how records create a self-serving reality whose connection with what happened is tenuous at best. According to the records, suspects were nearly always scrupulously told of the right to have someone outside informed that they were being held in custody; according to the records, suspects were told they could have a solicitor. As we know from our research and that of Sanders *et al.* (1989), in a substantial minority of cases this did not conform to the realities of the charge room. In fact, Sanders and Bridges (1990) found that in 7.6 per cent of all cases observed, the custody record declared rights to have been provided in accordance with the Code when they had not been.

In like manner, those occasions which resulted in a refused charge, some of which were no doubt accompanied by conflict and bitter recrimination and some of which had been initiated by precipitous or illegal police action, were solemnly recorded for posterity as having concluded satisfactorily: 'Suspect showed no signs of resentment. Police action correct.'

In circumstances of this kind, what the police choose to record *is* reality and not merely a representation of reality. The police decide what they wish to record and what they wish to omit. No independent person is present to provide a second view, an alternative perspective. The suspect's voice is not heard. Once created the reality constructed is verified by the very existence of the record: the police narrative becomes for all practical purposes a source of indisputable accuracy.

CONCLUSION

In the rhetoric of police professionalism, 'paperwork' is an obstacle to 'real' policing, an unnecessary bureaucratic demand placed upon officers preventing them from being out on the streets thief-taking and suppressing other forms of criminality. In this way, officers have historically created distance between those engaged in active policing and those engaged in supervision and management. However, a more significant effect of this contempt of paperwork tradition has been to divert attention away from a central police activity by depicting it as trivial, marginal and unworthy of notice.

Far from being marginal practices, mastery of paperwork and the ability to manipulate the 'paper reality' (Goffman, 1961) are core police skills, study of which is essential to an understanding of policing. The ability of the police to create a convincing paper record is a necessary part of successful case construction. Cases against individuals or about their involvement or non-involvement in alleged criminal incidents *are* cases made out on paper, subject to assessment on paper and, for the most part, decided upon paper. Police records generally conceived are designed to present a picture of police compliance with rules and procedures and their fair treatment of suspects; they are not intended to disclose police operational practices. And so, for example, police coercive behaviour towards citizens in street encounters leading to stop-searches or towards official suspects upon whom the police decide to inflict a caution is sanitized and disguised by the construction of 'consent'. The low visibility of policing is thus in great measure a deliberately created construct of police officers rather than an environmental attribute of their work setting (cf. Chatterton, 1983). Every feature of policing which enters the official domain is grounded in and based upon a paper reality crafted to authenticate and legitimate the police version of events, and to insulate police action from critical review.

6 Grading and sorting the suspect population

Having analysed the initial processing of suspects in the police station we now turn to what happens to that suspect population and why. 'What happens' in each case, in formal legal terms, is the decision to prosecute, caution or take no further action (NFA). It might be thought that the police would prosecute as often as they could. This might follow if each arrest related to a specific case of alleged crime or disorder which the arresting officer was concerned to punish or suppress. But this would be to misunderstand the nature of policing.

As is clear from Chapter 2, evidence sufficient to arrest need not be sufficient to prosecute and does not always even satisfy the requirement of reasonable suspicion. Indeed, the 'reasonable suspicion' rule in arrest does not significantly control discretion: it is vague and manipulable, and low visibility discretion is hardly controllable anyway. Even where 'reasonable suspicion' does operate meaningfully the evidence that creates the suspicion need not be legally admissible. It follows that in many perfectly lawful arrests there will be no basis for prosecution unless more evidence – e.g. a confession – is secured following arrest. A sorting process at the police station, in which the expectation would be that many arrests would lead to no further action, is therefore inevitable.

As we have seen, the reasons for arrest are to be found in police working rules rather than in offence seriousness or evidential strength *per se*. For example, the police prioritize their work, and aim to maximize their 'quality' work. The police can use certain suspects in order to catch bigger fish. The purpose of arrest is sometimes therefore to lay the foundation for bigger and better cases. In these circumstances it would be wrong to expect the police always to prosecute; indeed the deal with a particular suspect may be to exchange information for prosecution immunity. Similarly, the long-term aim of order maintenance may be served by displays of authority in particular localities.

According to this perspective, then, grading and sorting is not a one-track line geared to finding the evidence to support a prosecution; it is a multi-track network where the destination of the case depends as much on the policing goals of the officers in the case and on the context of the case as on the evidence that is available. Nevertheless, the state has in recent years subjected the grading and sorting process to control criteria which are legal and formalistic, rather than police-defined. These criteria, which relate to evidential sufficiency and whether it is in the public interest to prosecute will be outlined first.

THE INSTITUTIONAL FRAMEWORK

At one time arrest was the culmination of the criminal investigation, not the start of it. Arrest was primarily a mechanism by which the prosecution process was initiated (Bevan and Lidstone, 1985). Upon arrest the issue for the charge sergeant was whether to agree or to refuse to charge. If there was sufficient evidence a charge would follow automatically.

Evidential standards

When the Judges' Rules were revised in 1964 it was formally recognized that, in reality, many arrests were made without sufficient evidence to charge and that much investigation was done while suspects were in police custody. The Rules therefore legitimized police detention prior to charge, the aim of which was to secure the necessary additional evidence primarily through interrogation. None the less, the legitimacy of that detention, and the arrest preceding it, was uncertain regarding suspects who were not charged. Hence a respected ex-Chief Constable wrote in 1972 that:

> If an arrest has been made on *prima facie* evidence of guilt the police feel that the safest course is to justify action in court; there is then less danger of liability for unlawful arrest and detention. (Wilcox, 1972, pp. 106–7)

There are no national figures of refused charges prior to PACE, but – extrapolating from Steer's (1980) research – it is likely that the majority of arrestees were charged (see 'The pattern of police dispositions' below). The low evidential threshold which probably applied as a result of this led, in the Royal Commission's opinion, to large numbers of weak cases being prosecuted (RCCP, *Report*, 1981). This threshold and the control exercised by charge sergeants certainly did not appear to inhibit police charging (Sanders, 1985a). Consequently the police were encouraged, in the Attorney-General's Guidelines in 1983, to move from requiring a *prima facie* case to requiring a more demanding 'reasonable prospect of conviction'. This change would be expected to create more refused charges if it was effective. Arrest and detention with no further action was clearly legitimized by PACE 1984 which created specific grounds for detention which were not linked to the eventual police disposition (see Chapter 3). PACE also replaced charge sergeants with 'custody officers' (also usually sergeants). According to Code of Practice C, investigating officers should bring a suspect 'before the custody officer who shall then be responsible for considering whether or not he should be charged' (para 17.1).

When the CPS was introduced one of its tasks was identified as the policing of an amended evidential threshold:

> The Crown Prosecution Service does not support the proposition that a bare prima facie case is enough, but rather will apply the test of whether there is a realistic prospect of conviction. (CPS Code, para 4)

It is the job of the CPS, in each case, to assess whether the standard has been adhered to and – if not – to secure more evidence from the police or drop the case.

Police cautioning

The development of police cautioning also stimulated efforts to control charge practices. Although cautioning has for a long time been available to the police, its real development came in the 1970s and 1980s. Specifically intended mainly for juveniles as a result of the Children and Young Persons Act 1969 (Ditchfield, 1976), cautioning gradually grew also in adult cases. The scope for abuse as well as inconsistency was obvious (Steer, 1980; Laycock and Tarling, 1985). Control was sought in part through national guidelines. The Attorney-General's Guidelines included 'public interest' criteria, and revised Home Office Guidelines echoed them (Home Office, 1985).

The guidelines distinguish between adults and juveniles. In juvenile cases the police should ensure 'that prosecution does not occur unless it is absolutely necessary' (para 1). Even formal cautions are to be avoided if 'an informal word of advice or warning' would suffice (para 3). There are certain pre-conditions: there must be sufficient evidence (as discussed above); the juvenile must admit the offence; and the parents or guardian must consent. If these pre-conditions are met, cautions are urged if 'the offence is not serious and the offender's record is not serious'. Two or more cautions for a particular offender are not ruled out, but otherwise little guidance is given on the meaning of 'serious' (para 6). When further consideration is needed, additional factors are the interests of the victim, the offender's character and family circumstances and whether the offender was part of a group.

The guidelines for adult cases are even more ambiguous. Although 'prosecution should only take place where . . . the public interest requires it' (para 1) – suggesting a presumption against prosecution – 'unlike the case of juveniles, there is no general presumption that cautioning will be the normal course' (para 1). None the less, cautioning is not regarded here as an exceptional disposition requiring particular justification.

Certain groups are identified as being particularly worthy of caution: elderly, infirm, emotionally or mentally disturbed or young (17–20-year-old) adults. Otherwise, the pre-conditions and criteria for adult cautions are virtually identical to those for juveniles. In particular, 'the fact of a previous caution or conviction does not remove the possibility of a course of action other than prosecution . . .' (para 6).

Also, if 'prosecution is deemed not to be required in the public interest, it will often be appropriate to take no further action . . .' (para 7). Thus in both adult and juvenile cases if the offender refuses to accept a caution or to admit the offence, no further action rather than prosecution should be considered. Offence seriousness is defined to some extent in para 4: 'prosecution may not be appropriate where . . . the probable penalty on conviction would only be a conditional or absolute discharge . . .'. Finally, the guidelines urge the police to caution drunks, up to a normal maximum of three cautions per month.

The Code for Crown Prosecutors reiterates Home Office policy, restating the principle that prosecution should occur only when 'required in the public interest' (para 7). Crown Prosecutors should 'strive to ensure that the spirit of the Home Office Cautioning Guidelines is observed' (para 8), and the 'public interest' criteria which follow therefore mirror the Home Office criteria.

THE PATTERN OF POLICE DISPOSITIONS

The Attorney-General's Guidelines and Home Office Guidelines have undoubtedly influenced police dispositions. Cautioned indictable offenders, as a percentage of all offenders cautioned or found guilty, rose from 20 per cent in 1982 to 23 per cent in 1984 and to 28 per cent in 1986 and 1988. The equivalent figures for adult males (the largest single group) were 4 per cent, 5 per cent, 10 per cent, and 13 per cent respectively. For juvenile males aged 14 to 17 the comparable figures were 38 per cent, 45 per cent, 55 per cent, and 60 per cent. The presumption in favour of cautioning now clearly operates in juvenile, but not adult, cases. The greatest percentage increases have been for adult males, but only because so few were cautioned before 1983 (Home Office, 1989a).

Not too much should be read into these figures. Just because there are now proportionately more cautions than in 1982 it does not follow that the likelihood of a suspect being prosecuted is reduced. It is equally likely that offenders are now being cautioned where previously no formal action would have been taken. The phenomenon of 'net widening' has been discussed extensively elsewhere (Pratt, 1986, 1989; Sanders, 1988b), but suffice to say here that the Home Office Circular which contains the guidelines explicitly warns against it:

> 'Net widening': the guidelines make clear the danger that a formal caution may be used and the juvenile thus brought within the fringes of the criminal justice system when less formal action might have been more appropriate. (para 7)

It follows that to truly assess changes in the pattern of police dispositions we need to monitor changes in NFAs too. There are no national figures for NFA, but these would, in any event, be unreliable because of other changes in police practices following PACE and the unreliability of police custody records (Sanders *et al.*, 1989, App. II). For our current purposes, it is sufficient to note that cases which were cautioned in our sample (collected in 1986 and 1987) could, if dealt with some years before, have been either prosecuted, refused charge, reported for summons and then NFA, or dealt with informally on the street. Police discretion is such that the great bulk of minor offences – i.e. the great bulk of all offences – could justifiably be disposed of in any of these ways.

Table 9 compares the national caution rate in 1987 (which was very similar to that of 1988) with that of our sample. The caution rates in our sample are generally a little lower than the national rates, but not dramatically. Only our caution rate for adult summary offences was greatly different, probably because our sample included so many drunks

Table 9 Offenders cautioned as a percentage of all found guilty or cautioned

	1987 National statistics *		*Research sample*	
	Juvenile	*Adult*	*Juvenile*	*Adult*
Indictable offences	69.6	13.7	57.3	10.7
Summary offences (excluding motoring)	71.99	14.0	64.3	55.6

* *Source:* Criminal Statistics 1987, Table 5.10

(now habitually cautioned). Leaving aside this anomalous figure, the juvenile cases suggest a non-prosecution presumption while the adult cases suggest the opposite.

A different perspective on these figures is provided if we analyse *overall* police dispositions. We can look both at police dispositions immediately following detention and at final dispositions. In our research sample only 41.2 per cent of adults were charged initially (and 8.3 per cent of juveniles), the rest being immediately cautioned, refused charge or bailed or reported for later decisions. There are no national figures with which to check the representativeness of these figures. However, two recent studies provide a point of comparison. In Brown's (1989) study of custody records in 32 police stations for one month in 1987 he found that 55 per cent of adults were charged initially, 23 per cent were bailed or reported, 11 per cent were NFA and 8 per cent immediately cautioned. Sanders *et al.* (1989) analysed the custody records of ten police stations for 15 days each in 1988 and produced similar results. Brown provides no figures for juveniles, but Sanders *et al.* found that 18 per cent of juveniles were charged, 47.4 per cent were bailed or reported, 13.5 per cent NFA and 8.7 per cent cautions. The high percentage of juveniles who are bailed or reported is a direct result of the 'welfare ideology' in juvenile justice. More of these cases are routed through juvenile bureaux or their equivalent (discussed in Chapter 7).

The pattern of final dispositions in our sample is displayed in Table 10. Little over one half of all arrested adults were prosecuted, 14 per cent were cautioned, but over one quarter were NFA. In a similar proportion of juvenile cases no further action was taken, and prosecutions and cautions totalled around 35 per cent each. The different ratios of prosecutions to cautions in Table 10 as compared to Table 9 is because Table 9 excludes not guilty verdicts. There are no national figures with which to compare ours, and neither Brown (1989)

Table 10 Final police dispositions in research sample

	Adults		Juveniles	
	n	%	n	%
Prosecution	415	58.4	125	35.0
Caution	100	14.0	127	35.6
Informal warning	2	0.3	8	2.2
No further action	184	25.9	86	24.1
Other non-prosecution (e.g. TIC)	10	1.4	11	3.1
No information	9	–	3	–
Total	720	100.0	360	100.0

nor Sanders *et al.* (1989) tracked the eventual dispositions. However, Steer (1980, Table 4.1) examined dispositions in a random sample of arrests in Oxford in 1974. He found that only 8.3 per cent were NFA (with a further 5.1 per cent NFA 'detected'), and only 9.1 per cent were cautioned. The great majority – 77.5 per cent – were prosecuted. This suggests that, as expected, the police are more willing to NFA post-PACE than they were prior to PACE. Whether this means that they used to prosecute more often, or to arrest less often, is not ascertainable.

In around one quarter of all cases now, arrests appear non-productive. The reality, to which we now turn, is, however, not this straightforward.

GRADING AND SORTING CRITERIA

Chapter 2 analysed the sift which the police make when on the streets and Chapter 3 discussed the (non-functioning) sift that should occur on reception into the station. This section analyses the sift that follows the detention 'decision', in an attempt to understand how the disposition patterns discussed earlier are constructed and to understand the relevance, if any, of the official criteria.

Grading and sorting can be seen as a form of private trial. Suspects are grossly disadvantaged by the closed world of the secret trial, yet the 'real' trial takes place as if there had been no such trial first. There are two consequences of this. First, the outcome (charge, NFA, etc.) is of immense importance to suspects, since this is almost their last chance of extricating themselves. Second, and related to that, the process of grading and sorting continues the construction, or de-construction, of a case – making police objectives all the more likely to be achieved at any subsequent public trial. For court trials look only at certain issues and certain evidence – as set up by the police. The defence is a defence to the prosecution case. That case is a construction. We will see that it is the police's own informal working rules (what Ericson, 1981a, 1981b, calls their 'recipe rules'), not the official criteria in the guidelines, which construct the case and which therefore produce police determinations of guilt and innocence.

Police have no wish to pursue the arrested suspect

Why do the police arrest people against whom they do not wish or intend to proceed?

Arrest results from concerns other than policing concerns

Often this will be when the arrest was made only because of the desire of the victim. When victims later decide they do not wish to prosecute, or simply display uncertainty, the police will usually happily NFA. Businesses, for instance, are often more interested in getting their money back than in prosecution. Thus, in *BK-A014*, where the suspect presented a cheque which bounced, the arresting officer explained: 'we did a deal. He had £10 in his possession and agreed to take it down to the garage.' Hence no further action was taken against A014. The influence of compensation over the prosecution/NFA decision has been observed before (Sanders, 1988b) but does not feature in the official criteria. Other financial considerations also influence businesses:

> *AT-A005/A006* – Two individuals were asked to leave a restaurant. The police were called after, it was alleged, A005 had threatened the manager with a bottle. According to the police, this was 'openly admitted' by A005, but the case was soon NFAed. The arresting officer asked the manager 'what he wanted to do.... I got the impression that [the manager] regarded this sort of thing as an occupational hazard.... And also purely financial considerations come into it; sometimes obviously if they've been involved in a court case once they know that it does involve quite a lot of time, so I'm sure that plays on people's minds sometimes.'

'Domestics' are classically categorized like this. Non-prosecution is usually justified by the actual or predicted withdrawal of the complaint by the victim. As Sanders (1988a) showed, this is actually common in non-domestic cases too. Moreover, withdrawal of the complaint did not preclude prosecution in Sanders' study when the police wished to prosecute (usually where 'Order' and 'Authority' were at issue). So, in *BW-A118*, a 'domestic' discussed in Chapter 2, the AO only reluctantly arrested A118 for criminal damage. When the victim withdrew the complaint, no further action was taken even though the custody officer admitted that the defendant could have been charged with breach of the peace offences. Similarly, in *AT-A005/A006* (above) the Inspector in charge of the case said: 'I've known cases where the police have initiated criminal proceedings themselves even though the victim has not been willing to go to court ... but those are very rare.' Here is an example from a different police force area:

> *BK-A056/A057* – After a fight the two protagonists on one side were arrested. The injured parties did not wish to prosecute but, according to the arresting officer: 'We're prepared to take the prosecution on even if we haven't got a complaint ... where you've got a serious assault I think it's our duty to pursue it really and it may well be that [V] is reluctant to make a complaint because he's going to get a good hiding so you can't sort of just push it to one side on that basis.'

But the issue is the upholding of Order and Authority, rather than just undermining 'domestics'. So the police have little interest in merely 'interpersonal' violence (Sanders, 1988a). Thus *BW-A059/A060* (discussed in Chapter 2) and *AT-A005/A006* – neither 'domestics' – were NFAed, unlike *BK-A056/A057*.

Even victims who do not change their minds may none the less have too little social standing to persuade the police to prosecute when they do not want to. Again the 'domestic' is the classic example:

> *CC-A052* – The defendant, who had been drinking, was found in a public place shouting and threatening his girlfriend. According to the arresting officer, he ignored police 'advice', became 'threatening towards the police . . . abusive and started fighting with police officers and had to be arrested for his behaviour'. The defendant, he said, had already struck his girlfriend before the police arrived on the scene: 'she had injuries, she had a swollen face, I believe she had a black eye, and she was in a very distressed situation'. In the course of a struggle the officer said that the defendant fought with the police and damaged the police vehicle. The 'offences', as seen by the officer, included 'drunk and disorderly', 'definitely breach of the peace', 'maybe assault police' and 'maybe attempt criminal damage'. The defendant, who was well known to the police with a criminal record of violence, was NFAed. This 'domestic' incident was, according to the custody officer: 'just a flash in the pan . . . would have calmed down on its own. . . . When he stood in front of me [A052] was quite reasonable.'

'Domestics' are just one type of interpersonal violence which, if there are no public order or other police-significant considerations, will be liable to be brushed aside by the police (see *CE-A039* below). Also the general principle applies in non-violent cases. In *CE-A015*, V alleged that A015 had stolen his ladders, although there was no other evidence of this. The arresting officer explained to the researcher: 'I basically arrested him and interviewed him just to get something down on paper really.' The officer did not expect to secure any evidence, and did not care sufficiently to try to construct it. This case, like many other NFAs, was an arrest that the police never expected to be 'successful'.

Further examples are provided by drunks. As we have seen, drunks are not automatically – or even usually – arrested. When they are arrested it is because of public complaints, where they are a danger to themselves or just to get the 'figures'. In the absence of other policing goals (e.g. submission to authority) these goals are satisfied *by the arrest itself*. Hence virtually all suspects arrested for simple drunkenness are cautioned, as are most 'drunk and disorderlies'. The homogeneity of police response reflects not just the existence of Home Office policy towards this end, but the simple lack of purpose in prosecuting as far as the police are concerned:

'The best thing was to get him off the street since he wasn't in a fit state to be on the street. So the power of arrest was used rather than wanting to bring any charges against him – rather than wanting him to be punished.' (Arresting Officer in *CE-A039*)

Innocence

Sometimes the police are not convinced of the suspect's innocence but they are sufficiently unsure of guilt to NFA. Or, as in this case, the major offence is not sustainable and the minor offence is relatively trivial:

> *CC-A092/A093* – The defendants were found with three packets of stolen cigarettes. They were arrested on suspicion of burglary, but there had been no burglaries near where they were found. The police concluded that they had knowingly bought them from a burglar, which is a less serious offence. According to the arresting officer: 'They knew that they were stolen by the price . . . I don't think it would have been worthwhile pursuing what we had got.' No further action was taken.

The police are less concerned about arrests with negative outcomes if *someone* can be charged. What concerns the police is how many *cases* are 'detected' – if, in order to detect one case, the police arrested and NFAed six suspects this would cause them little concern.

> *AT-A018* – Joint tenants of an off-licence were arrested on suspicion of theft after an audit revealed deficiencies in takings of several thousand pounds. A018 said that her partner had taken money from the till over a period of time with her knowledge, while her partner said that A018 was responsible for some of the 'borrowing' and that, in any event, he was not responsible for all of the losses. After interview, A018 was NFAed, and her partner was charged. The officer in the case said: 'I wasn't absolutely satisfied she was telling the truth. It was a balance. . . . There was an element in what she said of sour grapes and I have to say that if she hadn't actually taken the money, there wasn't much doubt that she'd enjoyed the benefits. . . . I'm happy that we couldn't have done anything else; I'm not happy that we got to the bottom of it.'

Sometimes the police are genuinely convinced of someone's innocence after interrogation and are happy to release them even if the case as a whole remains unsolved:

> *AT-A011* – The police, acting under a search warrant, searched a flat in which they found a small piece of cannabis resin and stolen credit cards. At the time of this search, two individuals (including A011) were present in the flat though neither lived there. No further action was taken against A011 and the police explained that 'It was only after the interview it was clear that he had nothing to do with the questionable property in the house, the drugs or the credit cards or any other [items].'

It is likely that the large numbers of NFAs where even the police accept the suspect's innocence are due to the legitimization of detention without charge. Arrests are made in circumstances which at one time would have been dealt with at the scene of the arrest or at the suspect's home – leading to NFA without arrest rather than, as now, NFA following arrest.

Social justice/cautionability

In some cases the police recognize the case as suitable for caution and the purpose of the arrest is to establish the grounds for caution and/or to satisfy the expectations of the offence victim. This is typically the case with young children arrested for shoplifting. In other cases the factors which make the case suitable for NFA or caution emerge only after arrest. We would emphasise that the 'emergence' of cautionability factors is not simply a process of discovery but normally involves an element of construction. Thus, in *AT-J53/J54* two youths were found with some lead on a roof. As there were no previous convictions a caution was on the cards. But the youths refused to admit criminal liability. The families were middle class, one of the youths attended a private school and it was therefore no surprise to find the Juvenile Bureau officer say that 'this offence appeared to me to be out of character'. The arresting officer's recommendation to prosecute was overruled and no further action was taken against either juvenile.

These considerations can apply to offence types as well as to suspect types. Drunks are one example; possession of small amounts of 'soft' drugs another. In area AH for instance many suspects arrested for the latter reason were cautioned in accordance with the Home Office Guidelines. The police arrest in part to ascertain whether the individual is 'suitable' for caution (in terms of previous convictions, warrants, etc.) and in part to see what information an interrogation might produce.

Workload

We have seen that this is a factor in the stop-search/arrest decision. It can also arise at the sorting stage. An officer who is overburdened with paperwork and/or a court appearance the next day may not bother arresting where otherwise an arrest would have been made. But if an instant caution is anticipated with virtually no paperwork involved, the officer may get the credit for the arrest without the effort of prosecution.

> *AT-A015* – A015 was instantly cautioned at the station for drunkenness. The Inspector was not consulted about this.
> *Res*: 'Did you consider any other charge, such as breach of the peace?'

AO: 'No! If I had I'd have had to go to court next morning and I
               didn't want to do that!'

Sometimes the officer feels obliged to arrest, but does not let the case
interfere with her personal time. Squaring this circle – a case too serious
to caution informally on the street, but which can be formally cautioned
– requires a process noted earlier: construction 'downwards' of a case
from 'serious' to 'trivial':

> *CE-A039* – The suspect was arrested after entering V's garden. The 'facts'
> were related to the custody officer. According to this version, A039 was drunk
> and had threatened V with a half brick. On this basis, the custody officer told
> the constable to prepare a file and charge A039. The constable, however, was
> shortly to go off duty. Accordingly, in the words of the custody officer, the
> constable 'related a slightly amended version of the facts to the Inspector
> before he went off duty' in order that A039 be cautioned.

Protecting informants

We cannot say how much reliance is placed upon informants by the
police but in one force area the use of informants was a recurrent theme.
When the police mentioned to us the informant system we expressed
surprise.

Res: 'I didn't know that.'
Police: 'Oh yes, there are financial rewards.'
Res: 'But aren't these for terrorist offences and very serious things?'
Police: 'No. Just ordinary crime. There are facilities within the police
            force for informants. We never disclose the identity of an
            informant. The reward could be a packet of fags, could be a
            box of chocs for his wife.'

Other officers confirmed this general picture with 'regular informants'
being paid 'very small sums of money, a few pounds' with the prospect
of more substantial sums upon successful convictions at court. The use
of informants, however, places obligations upon the police to deal
'fairly' with informants and creates tensions between the desire to
control crime committed by the informant and the need to keep the
informant out on the streets to incriminate others. This tension can lead
to NFA or a caution:

> *BK-A114* – The suspect had an extensive criminal record and was alleged to
> have stolen money from a fellow lodger. He admitted that he had taken the
> money which he said was owed to him, a statement the police took to be an
> admission of 'theft' even though A114 returned the money and V, it was said,
> did not wish to proceed. The true reason for not proceeding, however, was, as
> the arresting officer told us in interview, 'in view of the fact he [A114] could be
> useful to us' in his capacity as a police informant. This was not revealed to
> senior officers, who treated the case as one where V withdrew the complaint.

Police wish to, but do not, pursue the suspect

The following is an example of a case where the police did not think it worth trying to proceed even though they suspected that A033 was guilty.

> *BK-A033* – There was a theft from a domestic meter involving a sum of £3 but no sign of a break in to the home. A033, who was V's nephew, was a former lodger who had keys. He was arrested and detained purely to make the interrogation more effective because the police had no actual evidence against him. But A033 had an alibi. The custody officer said: 'A story could have been arranged but there's nothing you can do – without the evidence you can't charge.'

Whether the police do, or do not, pursue the suspect in more important cases often depends on more than just whether they judge there to be sufficient evidence. In *BK-A110*, discussed in Chapter 2, there was, again, no evidence. But this case was pursued after the initial sift (the suspect was released on bail and then re-interviewed, although eventually no further action was taken). Cases like this which are dropped reluctantly by the police often stem from arrests made on the basis of pure personality or criminal record.

The police accept the logic of their stop-search and arrest practices – that if arrests are made on the grounds of hunch, instinct and the hope that confessions will be forthcoming there is bound to be a fairly high wastage (NFA) rate. But they realize that in the medium term this approach often pays off in terms of intelligence gathering and detections and that incremental benefits accrue as certain suspects are 'logged in' to the collators' quasi-formal filing systems and officers' mental filing systems.

A very different kind of case is presented when prosecution could embarrass the police:

> *AT-J13* – The police raided an unlicensed party at a shebeen. J13 was arrested for threatening behaviour. According to the Inspector 'certain officers ... acted against the wishes of the people supervising the raid. That is to say, the matter could have been dealt with in some other way ... I think he [J13] had been put under a bit of pressure ... he was spoken to in derogatory terms, being coloured etc.'. The case was NFA in the end because (according to the Inspector's memo) 'it might prove embarrassing to the police in the future' if they were prosecuted. The Inspector told us: 'I was approached by the senior officers from [AT] saying if it was in my power – and they weren't exerting any influence at all – to deal with it in any other way than juvenile court ... they would be very content.' Also the shebeen was now licensed and 'if we enlist their help [J13 and his associates] ... we'll probably be able to control it.'

Without dismissing the control factor here (policing issues taking precedence over legalistic prosecution guidelines), misconduct was the major issue. Had the case been brought to court 'there were certain things that [J13] would have said which may well have jeopardised, if you like, the case of the more serious offences (disclosed by the raid)'. The Inspector reluctantly NFAed J13 who was in breach of a conditional discharge for similar offences – which in itself would have 'normally' guaranteed prosecution.

Police wish to pursue the suspect and do so

This category may suggest that a 'prosecution at all costs' ethos prevails. This is undoubtedly true of cases where police working rules point towards strict enforcement. The maintenance of Order and Authority is one such rule:

> *CE-J26/J27/J28* – There was a disturbance at a children's home, which included four children getting into a scuffle with one of the resident social workers, who was kicked or tripped. The staff at the home held a meeting and decided that the children involved should be prosecuted in order to re-establish authority at the home. Three children were arrested and charged with s.47 assault before all the evidence had been collected and without going through juvenile procedures 'because of the breakdown in order at the Home' (Arresting Officer).
>
> *Res*:   'Did you consider caution?'
> *AO*:   'No, not at all, because I thought that the breakdown of order which caused the incident was too serious to have let go.'
>
> The AO agreed in interview that the injury was, in itself, minor and said that s.47 was 'probably the lowest charge . . . anything below that would probably come under common assault, which is a private matter really'. The prosecutor reduced the charge to common assault because she said there was no evidence for a s.47 assault charge.

Prosecutions can sometimes satisfy other policing objectives. In *AH-A050* there was a fight outside a club, notorious for minor disorder. The arresting officer said that A050 would normally have been cautioned for his part in the fight but 'the reason he was charged was because we are objecting to the licence at [the club] . . . and the more charges we've got the better'.

Cautionability

Prosecution guidelines seem to envisage a hierarchical structure of thinking – is this an offence? is there the evidence? is there any need to prosecute? is the suspect suitable for caution? This might be the thought process of a detached decision maker, but not that of an involved one.

As we have seen, when officers have policing reasons for not prosecuting they construct their cases to justify those decisions. But because policing culture creates a presumption in favour of prosecution, police officers simply prosecute with little thought about how to justify it. Official guidelines may seem to demand reasons but they are too remote to infuse 'routine' decision making. Thus, despite the presumption against prosecution in the guidelines and Code, and their apparent cautionability, the following cases – representative of many in all areas – seem to have been prosecuted without a second thought.

> *CC-A088* – A woman with no previous convictions ran into financial difficulties and sold a hire TV. The arresting officer did not consider a caution because of 'a) the value and b) I think the company has got certain rights . . . [and] she was not forthcoming as where the property was anyway. So far as I'm concerned if she's going to do that then I think she deserves to go to court, regardless of financial circumstances or anything . . . we ought to follow it through with regard to the punishment.' The officer predicted a conditional discharge, making the case cautionable (although she was in fact put on probation).

> *AT-A069* – The defendant, a middle-aged woman, had damaged a door and was charged with criminal damage. According to the police: 'The case was cut and dried. She caused the damage and had admitted it. . . . She has no criminal record at all. She was mentally unbalanced slightly.'

We should note here not just the failures to consider prosecution guidelines, but the overriding precedence given to the wishes of the victim, retribution and information provision. This was not a random, individualized phenomenon depending on the personalities of the police and prosecutors involved; it was patterned. Adult shopliftings, for instance, were habitually prosecuted:

> *BK-A011* – The arresting officer appeared not to have considered the possibility of a caution in this simple shoplifting. When asked, he looked uncomfortable, said that the manager wanted prosecution, and said, 'it's a serious offence anyway – theft'.

Nor is police culture undermined by the legalistic values of the CPS, as Chapter 7 will show. The differences between cases which were, and were not, charged did not relate to the criteria set out in official guidelines; more freqently, they concerned the factors outlined in this and earlier chapters. For these concerns, unlike official prosecution criteria, relate to policing priorities. Hence the police perception of the suspect is as important at this stage as at the arrest stage:

> *BK-A085* – A085 was a youth with previous convictions. He had picked up a Mars bar in a shop and broken a piece off. When the police charged the defendant, they were asked whether a caution was considered: 'If it had been threepence halfpenny we would have charged.' Asked why, the police

described the defendant as a 'toe-rag' who had been suspected of shoplifting on several occasions but never caught.

In other cases, the defendant may create a negative image by refusing to conform to police authority or by being 'awkward'. Consequently she may be placed into a different police category than her behaviour would normally warrant. Thus:

> *AT-A089* – The defendant had no previous convictions and was arrested for being drunk in a public place. The arresting officer, who had not recommended that he be charged, said that A089 had been getting on the custody officer's nerves – 'mouthy' (shouting whilst he was dealing with another prisoner) but not physically aggressive. After the arresting officer left, A089 was charged with being drunk and disorderly. The custody officer was initially reluctant to explain his decisions but made it clear that A089 had upset him:
>
> | | |
> |---|---|
> | *Res*: | 'What was the disorderly behaviour?' |
> | *Officer*: | 'I can't remember.' |
> | *Res*: | 'Was it in the police station?' |
> | *Officer*: | 'No, it was out on the street because it has got to be in a public place.' |
> | *Res*: | 'Why was he charged?' |
> | *Officer*: | 'To be perfectly frank, you make your decision on what you see in front of you. If he gives you a hard time, say verbally, then you think "Oh yeah, he's obviously given the PC a hard time on the street and he's obviously of a disorderly nature and therefore we'll send him to court". That's how I decide.' |

Placating significant victims, another generally important policing concern, is important in this context too. The power of local businesses was identified in Chapter 2. Employers are particularly influential victims:

> *CE-A060/A061* – Two shop employees took items from the shop without paying. Neither had previous convictions and, according to the police, the offences would never have come to light other than by admission. When asked about missing items, both made admissions. The Detective Constable in charge of the case visited the store to suggest that both defendants should be cautioned. However, he told us, the shop security officer was a 'harsh man' who 'saw everything in black and white' and wanted A060 prosecuted. Although the DC said that the decision lay with him, he cautioned A061 and charged A060 because of the wishes of the shop.

This case highlights inconsistency in cautioning which again shows the greater importance of police organization and culture than of official guidelines. Where A061 was cautioned despite being in a position of trust (he was an assistant manager), *CE-A014* – from the same force – was prosecuted despite there being no breach of trust and A014's theft being worth £2 as compared to £15. For the DC in charge of A061 this was a trivial case, but for a member of a shoplifting squad, as in A014, prosecution was his *raison d'être*. So the working rules operating in the two cases were different, and the non-directive official guidelines allow this apparent inconsistency to flourish.

Failure to consider, or be consistent about, official guidelines is particularly evident, and not surprising, when we consider the *instant* nature of so many of these decisions. Instant decisions are inevitably more prone to routinization than are decisions on files. They are also more vulnerable to emotion. As the custody officer put it in *AT-J53/J54* (discussed earlier):

'when someone sits and looks at it in a file coldly the next morning it probably gives them a slightly different picture to what I see – the toe rag coming in f'ing and blinding at all and sundry . . . straight away you think "well, yeah, OK, here we go", perhaps an independent says "no, no, NFA".'

Evidential sufficiency

Official guidelines on evidential sufficiency also take second place to police priorities. Although it may appear counterproductive to charge where the evidence is weak or lacking, this is not how the police often see things. First, failure in the courts does not render prosecution pointless (Sanders, 1985a). Second, 'weakness' and 'strength' are not fixed in time. Weak cases are often charged in the hope that the defendant will plead guilty, that the evidence will strengthen or that the defendant will be convicted anyway. As we shall see in Chapter 8, outcomes in court are very difficult to predict. Third, some officers simply see prosecuting the 'obviously' guilty as their mission in life, no matter how inadmissible their personal belief in guilt is. The following case is representative of many others from all of our areas, indicating that the guidelines have done little or nothing to change police charge practices since Sanders' (1985a) research in the early 1980s.

CC-A023 – This case arose out of a fight between over 30 youths. A023 was standing on the edge of the fight, shouting. He was told to move on, and when he refused to do so he was arrested for obstruction. According to the custody officer: 'he was on his own street, which I thought quite justifiable. . . . I thought he [the arresting officer] might be stretching the point to justify an obstruction.' According to one of the other officers involved, officers from another sub-division had arrested 'precipitately' and 'without any prior knowledge of why they were arresting him'. Once the arrest was made, however, the arrest had to be justified and thereafter it became, in his words, 'a case of getting a shoe horn to fit the charges', so A023 was charged with threatening behaviour.

CHOICE OF CHARGE

In the great majority of cases the decision about the appropriate charge is made following interview while the suspect is still in custody. At this stage there will rarely be a written file, and certainly not a full file. The custody officer has formal responsibility for the decision which is made after discussion with the officer in the case. In cases of perceived difficulty a C.I.D. officer, the duty inspector or other senior officer may be involved. Some suspects are reported for summons or released on bail pending return at a specified date to the police station. This allows senior officers, and even the CPS, to be involved. In fact, it is usual only where further evidence is to be sought (e.g. for drug offences dependent upon a chemical analysis), or for juveniles and elderly people, where the police may take account of the Home Office Guidelines. It is rare for suspects to be reported or bailed in order to give fuller consideration to the appropriate charge.

Thus charges are usually chosen by relatively junior officers, without long consideration, on the basis of incomplete information. This reinforces the system's rhetoric that charge selection is generally straightforward, even mechanistic, and that incorrect or inappropriate charges may be weeded out in the process of case review by the prosecutor. But this misrepresents the significance of the initial choice of charge. Rather than being an assessment of a case which already exists, the choice of charge is itself part of the process by which the case is constructed. Once chosen, the charge itself becomes the organising matrix round which the case is built, and which governs the creation, selection, interpretation and presentation of the evidence.

> CE-A113 – Police put A113 under surveillance because they suspected that he was selling drugs from his car. When A113 tried to evade the police he was arrested and his car was searched. No drugs were found, but a bat, with flowers painted on it was found. The police wished to charge A113 because they remained convinced that he was a drug dealer. The following is an extract from the interview between the officer and A113:
>
> PC: 'I would describe this as a truncheon. Would you agree?'
> A113:   'No comment.'
> PC: 'Do you agree that it has no use other than as a weapon?'
> A113:   'No comment.'
>
> Discussing the case with us, the PC said: 'I imagine he does have a defence. If he had said that his mother had brought it back from Torremolinos, from a street seller in Spain. I mean, my mother brought one back for me from Spain. It's got decorations on it.'

Although the police recognized the bat as a cheap, commonly available souvenir, for the purposes of the case it became a truncheon. The 'facts' were presented so as to fit the charge, immunizing the case from effective review until the defendant pleaded not guilty and the bat was produced in court, because the defence was not apparent in the file as reviewed by the CPS.

A major factor governing choice of charge and cutting across strictly legal considerations is the police evaluation of the worth of the case. Thus, in *CE-A113* considered above, it was important for the police to find a suitably serious charge both in order to justify their actions in chasing and arresting A113, and because they believed him to be a regular drug dealer whom they had been keen to catch: 'It was as though we were charging him with the offensive weapon because we didn't get any drugs. To get something at the end of the day' (arresting officer).

Equally, a less serious charge may follow where the offence rates low in police values.

CE-A036 – The defendant was alleged to have chased and beaten an eight-month pregnant woman with whom he had previously had a relationship. She suffered a broken nose, cut lip and bruising. For the arresting officer the affair was a 'domestic' and warranted only a charge of assault occasioning actual bodily harm. When interviewed, he justified not choosing a more serious charge by stating that 'There's got to be intent. He meant to hit her but not necessarily to do that amount of damage.'

However, the interrogation was short, the defendant's assertion that he hit the woman once only with the back of his hand went unchallenged and no question was asked as to his intent. It seems, then, that the case was constructed from the outset with the lesser charge in mind.

Even when the police feel strongly about a case and desire harsh punishment for the offender, as in the following case, they will not choose the highest possible charge unless there are strong *policing* reasons to do so.

AT-A024 – A young man had followed a female foreign student on to a bus late at night. When she got off he followed her, then chased and grabbed her and fondled her breasts under her clothing. He then tried to pull her across a road towards a dark alley, but was apprehended by police officers. She said that 'I understood that he wanted to rape me. He said that he did not want to hurt me, but just wanted to have sexual intercourse.' The officers believed that this was A024's motive, and considered this a particularly serious offence. After consulting detectives A024 was charged with the lesser offence of indecent assault because, according to the police, his actions were 'consistent' with his story that he merely intended to fondle the woman.

Whilst the rationale for charging only the lesser offence may appear to be logical in itself, it is inconsistent with other police decisions. The police do not restrict the level of charge to the offender's view of the facts when policing imperatives suggest higher or different charges, as is obvious from the cases discussed earlier in this section.

There are other reasons for lesser charges than those which might be sustainable on the evidence:

> *BK-A095* – The defendant entered a domestic garage and stole some food from a freezer. The police recognized that this amounted to burglary, but because the defendant was a police informant who supplied information in the course of interview they were able to 'view it more leniently'. A095 was charged with theft. The detective involved in the case explained that this was a significant benefit to the defendant: 'He's quite happy with the theft charge. He's on a suspended sentence. If he's charged with burglary he'll certainly go down; if he's charged with theft, he may get away with it.'

In the above case the working rule which overrode formal legal considerations as to choice of charge was that informants should be cultivated and encouraged. Charges become commodities, to be bartered for information.

Our approach to case construction makes notions of 'overcharging' and 'full-charging' (McCabe and Purves, 1972; Baldwin and McConville, 1977) difficult to sustain in this context. To talk of 'overcharging' implies that there is a single reality which demands a single charge, anything in excess of which is beyond the proper or appropriate charge. This misses the point that evidence is malleable and that cases are constructed so that any charge selected will appear plausible. Whilst no-one will be charged with murder where the victim survives a personal attack, a case may be constructed in such circumstances so that the charge chosen is defensible; but that charge could be anything from attempted murder, s.18 wounding with intent, s.20 unlawful wounding, s.47 assault; or the case could be not proceeded with on the basis that it was a 'domestic'.

THE ROLE OF THE CUSTODY OFFICER

The ideology of the Royal Commission and of PACE is that the police should have the powers they claimed to need but only if the exercise of those powers is genuinely controlled and supervized. Great faith was placed in internal procedures – record keeping, time limits and, of course, the custody officer (CO). The Commission believed that rules would be better enforced 'by contemporaneous controls and good supervision than by review often long after the event' (RCCP, *Report*, 1981, pp. 110–11). The need for routine controls is set out by the CO in *BW-A118*, and then the CO in *AT-J33* sets out the need for control in more unusual circumstances:

> *BW-A118* – 'The officer on the case is looking to prove the case, which is what

he is paid for and we wouldn't want it any other way. He's all fired up to do just that and that's what his job is. A custody officer's job is to stand back perhaps, to look at a wider situation, to appraise the situation in a wider light and to try to make a rational decision, one step removed from intimately being involved . . . nine times out of ten the evidence is there because police officers only arrest if the evidence is there. The odd occasions where perhaps it's not so clear-cut well then you have to do what you think.'

AT-J33 – 'Some bloke [an arresting officer] will come in and he's "gilded the lily", as the term is, and you know full well he's gilded the lily but he's so dead straight when he's talking to you you believe it's gospel, but I know him – you know [laughs] – I can read between the lines as well and see what's happening.'

In reality, as we saw in Chapter 3, most custody officers do not ensure the accuracy of records or the provision to suspects of their legal rights. This chapter shows their failure to enforce prosecution criteria. We now need to examine why and how the disjunction between reality and rhetoric comes about.

Enforcing the guidelines: evidential sufficiency

In deciding whether or not to charge, the CO should apply both the evidential standards and 'public interest' tests in the Attorney-General's Guidelines. It is, in fact, rare for a CO to apply any officially contemplated test at all. The following case is the only exception which we could locate in the whole sample, and even this decision was based on 'common sense' rather than any specific guidelines:

BK-A093 – A fight broke out outside a hospital out-patient unit. Three men were arrested. A093 was a friend of the other two and was trying to separate them when the police arrived. The CO NFAed A093: 'My questions were initiated by [A093] having said something to me himself. Obviously I would go along with what the arresting officers have to say. I think they would agree with me that he was acting in good faith . . . it would seem a bit rough to do him for it when he was only trying to keep his mates from being locked up.'

COs usually accept that if officers in charge want to charge that is their prerogative:

CE-A007 – The defendant, who had no previous convictions, was arrested for theft of expensive radio equipment. He denied having criminal intent. We asked whether the CO asked the arresting officer or A007 any questions.
CO:　　　　'Not at all. I accept that [the officer's] got no cause to be telling lies and the other chap has.'

So it was not just in this case that the CO decided to charge – it was her *policy*. She refused to make an evidential decision on the grounds that the word of the officer could not be doubted (even though the dispute in the case was not about objective facts which required the choice of one story over another).

Custody officers rubber stamp non-prosecution decisions too. In *AT-A005/A006* (discussed on p. 106) the CO made it clear that if the arresting officer wanted to NFA a case because it was not worth further effort that was 'fine' by him. No evidential (or public interest) justifications were required. In *AH-A032* the CO said that the CID 'told him' not to charge the defendant. Another revealing remark was made by the arresting officer in *CC-A078*:

> '. . . in the absence of a complainant's statement I bailed him [A078] to see me a few days later, and – well, the custody sergeant bailed him but I approached the custody sergeant with that in view. But it was his decision.'

The arresting officer in *CC-A062* made no attempt to hide the nature of the process:

Res: 'Do you . . . put the story before the CO?'
AO: 'No. Perhaps by the book you do in terms of what's laid down in procedural guidelines – "the custody officer will decide" sort of thing – but in practice it's different. He trusts your judgment and you know from experience what you're going to do. If I say "I'm going to charge" I know the CO will agree so you just go ahead and do it . . . technically the CO has to make sure there is evidence for a charge but there again if he spent all day doing that he'd never get anything done so he knows who he can rely on. If it was a complicated case or a sensitive one it might be different, he'd actually go through it.'

As the arresting officer in *CC-A062* suggested, and as many other officers confirmed, the exact role of the custody officer in any one case depends on a number of factors: her opinion of the officer in charge, how busy she is, the nature of the case. These may be practical policing criteria, but none of them relate to the official guidelines. The problem with using the nature of the case as a criterion is that only close enquiry can reveal the nature of the case: otherwise COs have to rely on superficialities which reveal nothing about criminal intent, emotional problems and so forth. Even when a custody officer takes a closer interest this may be inadequate to permit a proper review of the evidence. Thus in *CC-A061* the arresting officer described a typical discussion of a case with a custody officer. Custody officer: 'Did he cough then?' to which the arresting officer would answer: 'Yes, no problem.' The value of enquiry at this level is illuminated by our research finding that officers would frequently understand there to have been a confession in cases where the suspect admitted presence at the scene of the crime but no involvement (e.g. *AH-J33*), or knowledge of the crime without participation (e.g. *CC-J33*), or strongly asserted a defence such as self defence or lack of intent (e.g. *AT-J52*).

Enforcing the guidelines: 'public interest'

It follows from what has gone before that COs very rarely inquire into the 'public interest' aspects of cases either. If an officer in charge wishes to caution, the CO usually assumes that the pre-conditions and criteria are satisfied, and if the officer does not suggest it the CO will rarely think of it. In part this is because the police rarely see cautions as being appropriate for 'normal' adults:

> *BW-A010* – A010 was arrested for deception. We asked why he was charged. 'We cannot caution an adult for theft by deception.... The only time cautions come into play is if it's an elderly person or they are suffering from ill health or something like that' (CO). In this case, though, the CO had no idea what A010's state of health was.

The CO in *BW-A066* similarly said that cautioning is 'designed to safeguard the 60-year-old with a dickey heart and persons who have no previous convictions'. But when we asked whether the defendant had previous convictions the CO replied: 'I don't know'. As we shall see later, the same CO had a different attitude towards *BW-A104* because of class differences, showing that – as in all aspects of policing – the absence of real controls over discretion allows patterns of bias to emerge. In CE-A007 (see p. 119) the CO, asked about the possibility of a caution, was forthright:

> 'I'd made up my mind that the chap was going to be charged when he first stood in front of me.... With an adult thieving, I never do consider a caution. It's a deliberate act. They know the rules, they should play by them.'

As with evidential standards, there is a policy (albeit not conscious) of ignoring the guidelines except when they can be used to justify what the police want to do for other reasons. Even when they believe a caution is appropriate, custody officers do not usually feel that this is for them to decide.

The ideology of independence and the realities of policing

The ideology of the custody officer as independent rests on three assumptions. First, that custody officers can insulate themselves from general policing concerns. Many of the cases we have discussed show that this assumption cannot be supported. Another example is *CC-A023*. In this case, the custody officer told us: 'I was of the opinion that the obstruct police was very thin . . . so shall we say I increased the reason for arrest from obstructing the police to include s.4 of the Public Order Act as well.'

The second assumption is that custody officers will not be influenced by demeanour, manner, dress and so forth. In fact, as many earlier examples show, custody officers are as influenced by the perceived 'moral character' of suspects as are arresting officers. The 'public interest' criteria do, of course, require custody officers to make character judgments, although not, presumably, on the basis of these superficialities.

The third assumption is that the information on which to make independent decisions is available. Yet as we have seen, custody officers usually do not know whether suspects have emotional or physical problems, have fully confessed or even whether they have previous convictions. The assumption also becomes invalid if the person whose recommendation is being scrutinized supplies the information and controls its quality and quantity. Like the CPS, the custody officer is dependent for information on officers down the line. Thus in *AT-A005/A006* the custody officer believed that there was no independent witness to the alleged assault. In fact, the arresting officer told us, the assault had been confirmed by someone else. But he neither told the custody officer this nor did he write it in his report. The case was 'constructed down' and the custody officer inevitably agreed with the arresting officer. Conversely, in *AT-J59* the custody officer, whose heart, he told us, might 'have melted' had he known of the death of the suspect's mother prior to the incident in question, was never given the chance to thaw, for he was not given this information by the arresting officer.

The problem was neatly summarized by the custody officer in *AT-J13*, in which J13 was arrested for threatening behaviour. When we asked what the evidence was, he replied: 'I'm dependent completely on what the officer says happened.'

CONCLUSION

The main theme of this book is to understand the policing imperatives which underlie police prosecution decisions. This chapter has shown that the informal rules which lead to arrest continue to influence decision making in the police station. Policing imperatives do not always lead to prosecution. When it is in the interests of the police they will caution or NFA. But it is rare for them not to charge if they really want to do so. What they want often reflects economic interests.

This chapter has also shown *how* the police manage to take the decisions which they want – through control over information and procedure and the enlistment of a 'cop culture' that elevates experience over going 'by the book'. A corollary of this is that both official guidelines and the institution of the custody officer are ineffective in constraining the police. We have seen that guidelines – particularly regarding cautioning – are often not even considered by decision makers. When cautions are issued, to adults at any rate, this is often for reasons completely outside the guidelines, such as the 'buying' of informants or prosecution witnesses.

The official guidelines contain several different criteria, set out in no order of priority. Many cases contain some elements which are favourable to caution, and others which are not. This makes it easy to justify any decision, and to dismiss any alternative. Thus whether drunks are prosecuted or not can depend on the individual's sexuality or demeanour, yet any decision can be justified by 'legitimate' criteria. The same is true of, for instance, 'seriousness' in theft and of the wishes of the victim. Thus victim withdrawal is used to justify non-prosecution when that is the result desired by the police, but when they want to prosecute they ignore the views of the victim.

One result of all this is a pattern of class bias. We have already noted how demeanour is as important to custody officers as it is to officers on the street, and saw in Chapter 2 how demeanour is related to class. Hence the woman arrested for shoplifting in *BW-A104* was reported for summons with a caution recommendation because, according to the custody officer:

> 'She was . . . not – I hesitate to say this – the type of client we are normally used to dealing with. . . . She was basically a lady of good character . . . it really was a one-off and she was a very clean tidy lady.'

The connection is sometimes more direct, especially when officers know individuals and/or their families:

> *BW-A006* – A006 was arrested for theft of a purse [discussed earlier in this chapter]. The arresting officer said that she was reported for summons because there was insufficient evidence to charge. We asked him whether he had considered NFA: 'No, because I think that she probably done it . . . I have to admit because of her background. She's come from a family who are in and out of here.'

The result is a tendency to caution and take no further action against the middle classes and to prosecute working-class suspects (Silver, 1967; Quinney, 1977; Shearing, 1981; Sanders, 1985b). Again, the ambiguity and absence of prioritization in the guidelines allow such decision making to take place in a virtually uncontrolled manner.

7 Reviewing the case for the prosecution

All cases which are either charged or reported for summons are subject to review both within the police and by the Crown Prosecution Service. Since the CPS was superimposed upon the pre-existing police system rather than replacing any part of it, there is considerable duplication and overlap of functions. For both organizations the grounds of review are the same and involve consideration of whether the public interest is best served by prosecution or some other disposal, whether the evidence establishes a realistic prospect of conviction and whether the proposed charge is appropriate in law. Although the CPS, like the police reviewer, is isolated from operational policing, the prosecutor may seek to influence the investigation process by requesting that specific further enquiries be made. However, certain functions are exclusively the preserve of one or other organization. The police have total control over which cases enter the system and only the police caution or informally warn an offender. In juvenile cases it is the job of the police to solicit the views of other agencies with responsibility for the welfare of children. On the other hand, the CPS has responsibility for the conduct of the case in court, may drop or amend charges and has ultimate veto of prosecution.

All forces have instituted special procedures to enable agencies with responsibility for the welfare of children to take part in the juvenile decision-making process. The official purpose of these juvenile liaison procedures is to ensure that public interest factors including the welfare of the child are considered on an individual basis. The police are under a statutory duty to notify Social Services if they are going to prosecute a juvenile (s.5(8) Children and Young Persons Act, 1969). The systems in operation vary considerably (Tutt and Giller, 1983; Wilkinson and Evans, 1990), ranging from permanent multi-agency bureaux as pioneered by Northampton (Bowden and Stevens, 1986; Davis *et al.*, 1989), to less elaborate systems in which the views of the other agencies are solicited by post or telephone. In the forces which we researched, one force relied upon home visits conducted by specialist police officers to obtain information about the circumstances of juvenile suspects, with the views of the other agencies obtained by post or telephone. One force considered juvenile cases at a regular juvenile liaison meeting convened by the police and attended by representatives of Social Services and the Probation Service. In the third force a specialist juvenile liaison officer collected information and views from the other agencies, with the option of convening a 'panel' in the event of persistent disagreement about a particular case.

Conventional explanations for the development of the CPS and juvenile liaison procedures can be traced to the argument that the traditional police role and skills in investigating crime are incompatible with the objectivity required in prosecution and the need to take a broader view when applying public policy criteria to prosecution decisions (Morris and Giller, 1987). Under this view, CPS and juvenile liaison provide effective scrutiny of earlier police decisions because the individuals involved are independent of the police and operate according to the skills and values of their own professions.

Another interpretation is that such agencies and procedures are simply doing the state's job for it more efficiently than previously, albeit in a 'welfare disguise' – whether by 'winning by appearing to lose' in the case of the CPS (de Gama, 1988) or by adopting a 'corporatist approach' in the case of juvenile liaison (Pratt, 1986, 1989). Corporatism refers, in Pratt's words, to the tendencies found in advanced welfare societies

> whereby the capacity for conflict and disruption is reduced by means of the centralization of policy, increased government intervention, and the co-option of various professional and interest groups into a collective whole with homogenous aims and objectives. (Pratt, 1989, citing Unger, 1976)

Under corporatism, the legal process takes on the form of bureaucratic-administrative law, blurring the boundary between the public and private realms, and increasingly concerned to develop routinized criteria in order to enable dispositions to be effected according to an extra-judicial tariff in the most efficient manner. We shall argue, especially in relation to juvenile liaison bureaux, that this corporatist tendency is apparent in the dominant position occupied by the police in all decisions, in the co-option of other professionals into police ideologies and in the routinization of extra-judicial decision making.

As we described in earlier chapters, constructing the case is not simply an exercise in collecting together and marshalling all relevant information. Rather the selection, creation and presentation of the evidence is geared towards the objective which the police seek to achieve, and effectively dominates later review procedures. Because the police expect case review and understand the ground rules which govern it, they can anticipate it. Thus, the 'seriousness' of an offence may be manipulated by description: an attack may be 'vicious', 'unprovoked' or 'premeditated'; a shop theft may be 'motivated by pure greed'; a suspected shoplifter may have 'looked round furtively'; emphasis on the suspect's own words may be used to convey the officer's view of the case, as by stressing that a shoplifter said 'it just seemed easy' thereby perhaps negating a doubt the reviewer might have about the offence being rooted in forgetfulness, illness or stress. Construction by omission is equally significant. Thus in one case (*CC-A069*, discussed in Chapter 4) a store detective had suggested to a suspect that she had forgotten to pay. This was criticized by the CPS reviewer who requested the police to advise the store detective not to make such suggestions when questioning shoplifters in future. Case construction may also be a means of co-opting non-police reviewers into police ideology and values or may convey a more general message about local policing imperatives. Thus, the offence in question may be 'rife' in that part of town, the suspect may be described as a 'football hooligan'.

The rhetoric of prosecution decision making emphasizes objectivity, impartiality and individualization. Police influence over a case is said to be confined to the investigation and case preparation stages with ultimate decision making by the prosecutor applying rigorous tests of public interest and evidential sufficiency. The reality is a system of routinized decion making embodying an overwhelming propensity to prosecute, bolstered by the presumption that earlier decisions were properly made and should not be overturned. The system is dominated throughout its stages by the interests and values of the police, with the CPS playing an essentially subordinate and reactive role.

THE PROPENSITY TO PROSECUTE

Public interest considerations

Both the Code and the guidelines proclaim a presumption against prosecution, yet the systems of review by the police and by the CPS exhibit a strong presumption in favour of prosecution. This is particularly marked where the suspect has already been charged by the police. In these cases the presumption is bolstered by a further consideration that a decision to overturn a subordinate officer's decision might be seen as disloyal or damaging to morale.

> *CC-A014* – This was a case of minor shoplifting by a 17-year-old. The decision-making inspector told the researcher that had the case come to him as a report for summons he would have cautioned. However, since A014 had been charged: 'We have to support the bobby. To offer no evidence would be a slap on the wrist for the arresting officer.'

However, the presumption in favour of prosecution also operates in relation to cases which have been reported rather than charged and hence have been previously identified as cases in which the decision is not clear cut.

> *CC-A011* – A young woman was alleged to have stolen a T-shirt from a shop. Because she did not admit the offence the options were either charge or NFA. However, the case was reported because of doubts about the strength of the evidence. The decision to prosecute was made by the CPS reviewer. She explained her decision: 'I start from the basis that they should be prosecuted if the evidence is there. I might change my mind if it's some old lady nicking a packet of crisps. But with this one there is no choice – it was a deliberate theft in cahoots with someone else and a person who denies it. You just can't let that one go.'
>
> *Res*: 'Does it make any difference that she has no previous convictions?'
>
> *CPS*: 'Previous convictions? That would not influence us at all.'

The presumption in favour of prosecution is manifest in the limitations which case reviewers see as attaching to their role. Thus, both police and CPS reviewers assert that their function is confined to checking for evidential sufficiency and that they are not required to consider issues of policy. A corollary of this is that reviewers commonly assert that their function is to decide between prosecution or non-prosecution and that caution is *not* an option.

Even in cases in which the reviewer acknowledges that the public interest should be considered, the relevant facts are susceptible to construction and interpretation in a way which justifies the prior presumption in favour of prosecution.

> *CC-A020* – This case concerned an 18-year-old who did odd jobs for cash at an auction house. He took £57 from the petty cash box which he admitted when challenged. He was charged following arrest. The decision-making Inspector explained to the researcher that there were two reasons why it was in the public interest to prosecute. First, A020 was not a juvenile but was a young adult; secondly, it was a case of employee theft.

The case illustrates the essential malleability of criteria and the way this may be exploited as an aid to case construction. The significance of A020 being a 'young adult' was that he was no longer a juvenile. The guideline which requires consideration of a caution for juveniles was apparently interpreted as mandating prosecution without such consideration for a young adult, although this is clearly contradicted by the adult guidelines. The prosecution decision was further justified by describing the youth's casual relationship with the auction house as one of employment.

In the great majority of cases there will be little material apart from the suspect's age and evidence of her degree of involvement which might prompt the reviewer to consider whether as a matter of policy prosecution is appropriate. This is a consequence of the manner in which police files are constructed, emphasizing evidence suggestive of guilt whilst ignoring or obscuring matters which the police consider irrelevant, such as the alleged offender's circumstances, any excuse offered for her conduct or the context in which the offence took place.

> *AT-A098* – A 20-year-old mother of an 18-month-old child was caught taking nappies from Woolworths without payment. On arrest she had no money in her possession and told the police that she needed the nappies for her baby. The custody officer told a researcher that a caution was out of the question because she had previously been 'arrested'. Her file disclosed convictions for minor theft, committed while she was a juvenile, the most recent being four years previously. The CPS approved the charge. In court it was disclosed by the defence that she was a single parent, in severe debt, who received no financial help from the father of the child. In discussion, the CPS said that, as the defendant was an adult, the CPS would not expect such information to be provided by the police: arrangements to transmit such information existed only for juvenile cases (despite comparable provisions in the Code for public interest factors in adult and juvenile cases).

Even in relation to juveniles, in the majority of cases significant evidence of the suspect's circumstances will not be found on the file. This is so notwithstanding the procedures for liaising with the caring agencies in relation to juvenile decision making. This finding is borne out by research on CPS handling of juvenile cases by Gelsthorpe and Giller who report: 'In the majority of cases the police provide sufficient technical information (i.e. evidence of the offence) and there is little (if any) reference to secondary material. In routine cases there is little in the way of "character assessment"' (Gelsthorpe and Giller, 1990). There are two reasons for this absence of 'secondary material' on juvenile files. First, and much to the annoyance of designated juvenile liaison officers, the juvenile liaison procedure is not activated where juveniles are charged immediately following arrest (35.4 per cent of our juvenile prosecutions). Second, the involvement of the caring agencies does not guarantee that information about a child's background will be made available. The provision of such information often depends upon quite arbitrary factors such as whether or not the child is already known to the Social Services or whether a member of the child's family has had dealings with the Probation Service, rather than being provided as a matter of course by proactive, independent caring agencies.

Where the file does contain information which could suggest that the case is suitable for caution or NFA on policy grounds, this is frequently not considered by reviewers for *any* purpose on the basis that it is irrelevant to the question of whether there is sufficient evidence. Similarly, if the file hints at such information, reviewers rarely seek clarification or return the file to the investigating officer asking that the matter be explored further.

Background information is however commonly included in the file where it provides a positive reason why the police would wish to prosecute.

> *BW-A083* – A youth of 18 took a bulb from the civic Christmas tree. When chased and apprehended he dropped and smashed the bulb. He was charged with theft. The police file noted the general problem of interference with the town's Christmas decorations and contained the following minute: 'It would be nice if publicity could be given to the matter with a view to deterring others from acting in the same manner.'

Where reviewers do acknowledge that it is part of their function to consider policy issues they may assert that these are relevant only to fixed categories of case. A corollary of this is that many reviewers operate on the basis of fixed notions as to what sorts of cases and what categories of offender may be cautioned.

> *CC-A014* – A 17-year-old unemployed youth with no criminal record stole a can of hair bleach, and was prosecuted. Commenting on the case the CPS reviewer said that it was so commonplace that there was nothing which would make him consider not prosecuting and that he did not consider £1.95 to be *de minimis*. He added that in shoplifting cases people over 65 and menopausal women were the main ones he looked at with a view to caution. [In this case, the DPP decided that we could not quote the prosecution directly.]

Where reviewers deny that policy issues or cautioning must be considered, this is frequently on the basis that these issues are relevant only to a different stage in the decision-making process. Thus, in *CC-J33* the prosecutor who had been designated the 'juvenile specialist' for his office denied that the CPS had any role in relation to caution, telling us that the matter would have been decided by the police with or without a panel.

> *CC-A064* – A freelance salesman had been arrested and charged with obstructing the highway by selling cheap jewellery from a suitcase in the town

centre. The custody officer explained to researchers that A064 had been charged because he was 'making an awful lot of money' and that from the point of view of local traders who paid rates, he was 'trading on your patch'. These factors were not set out in the prosecution file. A researcher asked the CPS reviewer why the case had been considered suitable for prosecution. He replied that the officer in the case was a city centre bobby and he presumed therefore that he would not have picked him up without a reason. [In this case the DPP decided that we could not quote the prosecution directly.]

Perhaps paradoxically, the presumption in favour of prosecution is particularly manifest in cases in which either a recommendation has been made to caution or NFA on policy grounds or where the ultimate decision is to caution or NFA.

AT-A101 – The defendant in this case had noticed a badly damaged car parked in the same spot over a period of four days. He was seen removing some spare parts from it and arrested. In interview he maintained that he thought the car had been abandoned. In fact the car had been stolen and crashed, and at the relevant time belonged to an insurance company. A101 was charged with theft but the case was dropped by the prosecutor partly on the basis of lack of evidence of intent, and partly on the policy ground that a conviction would be disproportionate to the gravity of what was done in view of the effect which it might have on his career. Both the PC and Inspector who had dealt with the case were outraged at this result. The Inspector wrote a long critical note to the prosecutor in which he pointed out that: 'He was a comparatively well paid young man, motivated by pure greed which abrogated any clemency under the Attorney-General's Guidelines.'

In the rhetoric of criminal justice both prosecution and caution are seen as being positive means of dealing with crime. Both are geared towards achieving the objectives of the criminal justice process in deterring further offences, in protecting the public, in bringing home to the offender the wrongfulness of the relevant conduct and in educating the offender in the social values embodied in the criminal law. In offering two main positive responses to offending, the criminal justice process acknowledges the 'double effect' of prosecution. Whereas its purpose is the achievement of the positive goals of the criminal justice process, it may also have negative consequences, such as disproportionately stigmatizing the offender or causing the offender to identify herself as a criminal. Where the negative consequences of prosecution outweigh its positive benefits, caution or NFA is the appropriate response.

The rhetoric of the criminal justice process also acknowledges that less formal actions such as NFA and informal warning may also be appropriate responses to crime. This is particularly so where a prosecution would be inappropriate because its harmful consequences would outweigh its benefits, but where a caution cannot be administered, typically because the alleged offender does not admit the offence. In these cases, once a judgment has been made that prosecution is not appropriate the only proper alternative to caution is NFA.

This rhetorical position does not inform routine prosecution decision making. A caution is seen as having no positive utility in its own right but as merely amounting to a 'let off'. Any notion that caution is an appropriate means of mitigating the law's response is rejected as a usurpation of a function which properly belongs to the courts. Where cautions are administered, i.e. to juveniles, this is not usually seen as fulfilling a proper goal of police work but rather as an antagonistic external restraint. In juvenile cases, if cautioning is viewed as having any utility it is in providing a necessary stepping stone to an eventual court appearance in the event of further offending.

The tariff

The presumption in favour of prosecution is a particular expression of the desire to achieve a result which legitimates police action in the case. As we discussed in Chapter 6, in cases where there is insufficient evidence to either charge or report, a number of alternative disposals are acceptable to the police. Similarly, where a case is reviewed after having been charged or reported, where the evidence is too weak to charge the reviewer may choose alternative disposals which reward police work with a positive result and legitimate earlier police actions in the case. For reviewers the range of alternative courses of action is seen as a *tariff* with prosecution for a serious offence at the top, followed by, in descending order, prosecution for a less serious offence, binding over, caution, NFA or dropping the case where it has previously been charged. The presumption is always in favour of the response highest on the tariff which is possible in the circumstances.

> *CC-A016* – A016 was arrested following a 'surveillance' operation in a public lavatory, in the course of which he had allegedly offered to masturbate a PC. A016 was reported for persistently importuning for an immoral purpose in a public place. The CPS reviewer wrote on the file: 'In view of the fact that it is a weak case go for bind over.' When asked about this decision the reviewer acknowledged on the file that the essential elements of the offence could not be established because there was no evidence of persistence. Nevertheless, the reviewer suggested that the prosecution seek a bind over. When asked why, the reviewer indicated to us that there was no question of letting the matter drop without some penalty regardless of the absence of evidence. [Here, the DPP decided that we could not quote the prosecutor directly.]

In relation to juvenile cases two-thirds of alleged offences are dealt with other than by prosecution, i.e. by detected NFA, informal warning, immediate caution or report followed by caution (see Table 10 in Chapter 6). This might be taken to suggest that the presumption in favour of prosecution does not operate in relation to juvenile cases, and that, in accordance with welfarist ideology, police and CPS procedures permit systematic consideration of policy factors and the individualization of decision making. This is not so. Consistent with the corporatist perspective, juvenile decision making is routinized not individualized, and informed by privately generated criteria expressed in terms of local tariffs rather than by welfare concerns. In relation to minor crimes the presumption in favour of prosecution is in effect *deferred*, according to local practice, until the juvenile has first received either one or two cautions. For the police, who are suspicious of large segments of the public sphere (such as courts), the juvenile caution is seen as a form of *private conviction*, which is a necessary step on the road to eventual public conviction by the courts. In relation to more serious cases the presumption operates as for adults.

> *Area BK Field Notes*: A researcher attended a juvenile liaison meeting. A number of cases were dealt with in a routine fashion. The juvenile liaison officer read a brief account of the case and related the child's record if any. A piece of paper was then circulated, upon which each participant wrote something. The juvenile liaison officer then moved on to the next case without comment. When the researcher asked what was happening, it was explained that the paper recorded the recommendations of each participant. There was no discussion because in each case the child's record clearly indicated either caution or prosecution and this was recognized by all participants.

Our study confirms the findings of other researchers that previous record is the dominant factor in determining whether a juvenile will be prosecuted or cautioned in non-serious cases (Landau, 1981; Mott, 1983) and that juveniles who re-offend having been cautioned once are far less likely to be cautioned than first offenders (Laycock and Tarling, 1985). In our sample of juveniles with one previous caution who were either cautioned or prosecuted, 17 were cautioned and 16 prosecuted. Among juveniles who had two or more previous cautions (but no previous convictions) who were either cautioned or prosecuted, one was cautioned and 14 prosecuted. Thus, once a juvenile has received two cautions, further offending is very unlikely to be dealt with by caution, whatever the juvenile's personal circumstances. This finding is supported by Table 11 which shows that of 115 cautioned, only eight had previously received two or more cautions or had been convicted.

Thus, contrary to the welfare ideology, relatively high rates of cautioning are not indicative of individualized decision making. Rather they indicate an acceptance of a certain overall level of cautioning for

Table 11 Previous records of juveniles cautioned

	n	%
No criminal record at all	83	71.6
No formal record/'known' to police	7	6.0
Cautioned once	18	15.5
Cautioned twice or more	2	1.7
One conviction	3	2.6
Two or more convictions	3	2.6
Not known	11	–
Total	127	100.0

juvenile offenders and the operation of a tariff system, leading to eventual prosecution and court appearance which operates in spite of the individual characteristics of the offender and in spite of the policy considerations spelt out in the official guidelines.

THE DOMINANCE OF POLICE INTERESTS AND VALUES

The rhetoric of the criminal justice system emphasizes that non-police agencies are introduced into the vetting and reviewing system in order to import skills other than police skills, values other than police values and in some cases to introduce or seek information beyond the scope of normal police investigation. Thus, the Crown prosecutor brings to bear her lawyer's skills and an objectivity arising from her independence from the police and absence of previous involvement in the case. The agencies involved in juvenile cases draw upon their expertise in dealing with the broader problems of children and their families. But this rhetoric ignores the strategic importance of police control over initiating prosecutions and constructing the case file; and obscures the extent to which the police dominate prosecution decision making by anticipating and pre-empting review and by co-option of other actors into police ideology.

Control through case construction

Junior police officers are able to anticipate and in some cases dictate later review decisions by senior officers and prosecutors by skilful case construction. The scope for construction is enhanced where proof of an offence depends upon a qualitative assessment. This is typically the case with offences under the Public Order Act 1986 which may involve proving that behaviour was 'threatening', 'abusive' or 'insulting' or that others were likely to be caused 'alarm', 'harassment' or 'distress' by such behaviour; or that such behaviour would be likely to put reasonably firm persons in fear. In the large number of cases in our sample in which it was alleged that a public order offence was committed in the presence of police officers, the key evidence was supplied by that officer's characterization of the suspect's behaviour and the assessment of its effects on other people. Because the officer anticipates review of the case for evidential sufficiency and having to prove the offence in court, the relevant behaviour of the accused is described in the exact terms of the offence. Generally evidence of this sort is inscrutable short of cross-examination in court.

Techniques of case construction are particularly significant in obtaining 'confessions'. The term 'confession' suggests a spontaneous coherent account of events in which culpability is admitted. In reality 'confessions' are abstracted from interviews, built round a framework of police questions, wholly focused by the police interviewer, with no opportunity given to the suspect to determine the course or substance of the interview. In this environment the police control not only the scope of enquiry but also may supply the terminology from which the confession is constructed. The interviewer will normally be careful to avoid giving the suspect a direct opportunity to deny the offence, and will eschew lines of questioning which might provide the suspect with an opportunity to exculpate herself. The consequence of these techniques is an unbalanced interview which obscures any weaknesses in the case, thereby pre-empting later review.

> BK-J01/J02/J03/J04 – In this case (discussed in Chapter 5) four boys had been arrested for shoplifting. J04 initially denied taking anything, but then agreed to the proposition that he was aware that the others were taking things, and the proposition that he was with the others when they took things. When asked what he would have got out of it he said 'nothing'. The file describes all four boys as having made full admissions. The decision to prosecute was made by the superintendent (following a recommendation from the juvenile liaison panel), and endorsed by the prosecutor.

In this case, once the suspect had denied actually taking anything, the interviewer was careful to confine questions to matters which J04 would have had difficulty denying, whilst avoiding questions going to the root of liability which might have allowed J04 to deny that he had either assisted or encouraged the thefts.

Case files are constructed at two levels. The first level of construction involves choosing what evidence is collected and what questions are asked of suspects and witnesses. The second level of construction occurs when the officer involved prepares the case summary which is normally the first document found in the case file. The summary becomes the official account of the case which may be displaced only if later reviewers choose to test the officer's summary against the more detailed evidence which it purports to summarize. Thus, in *BK-J04* the officer who prepared the file was able to influence the reviewer's approach to the file by a case summary which described J04's answers as amounting to a full admission.

In some contexts the officer's summary becomes the definitive account of the case on which later decisions are based. On the evidence of our research, this is the case with juvenile liaison, in which the only source of information about the case on which the other agencies base their recommendations is the summary. It is also true generally of cases which are processed with a view to caution. Where a caution is the proposed outcome, senior officers are content to rely on the summary: first, because they view a caution as a 'let off'; second, because they know that the decision to caution is conclusive and will not be subject to further scrutiny by either prosecutors or defence lawyers. Where this occurs the reviewing function on grounds of evidential sufficiency is in effect abdicated to the officer in the case.

In line with the findings of earlier research (Steer, 1980; Sanders, 1988b), cautioning where a full confession had not been made occurred in all six force sub-divisions in which we conducted the research. Of 127 juveniles who were cautioned, 22 (17.3 per cent) had not made a full confession. Some 100 adults received cautions. Of these a group of 76 involving mainly drunkenness offences was not interviewed. Of the 24 adults who were cautioned following interview, three (12.5 per cent) had not confessed.

The control which junior officers exercise over evidence collection and the presentation of the case also permits characterization of the suspect or the circumstances of the crime in a way which indicates the disposal of the case favoured by the officer dealing with it.

CE-A094 – Following an altercation between two school children, the father of one of them (A094) became involved and assaulted the other child, a 10-year-old boy. The file contained evidence of the altercation. The officer dealing with the case reported it for summons. Discussing the case with a researcher, the officer mentioned that enquiries had revealed that the boy was known at school as a trouble maker who picked on other children. The officer felt that A094 should be prosecuted. The file contained no mention of the boy's history. In the summary the case was described as an 'Unprovoked attack by a 37-year-old man on a 10-year-old boy'. A094 was prosecuted for occasioning actual bodily harm and eventually pleaded guilty to common assault following a plea bargain at pre-trial review.

The key technique of construction in this case was omission. This technique has been noted by Moody and Tombs, describing their research on Scottish procurators fiscal, who quote one prosecutor as saying: 'the police can withold information. They usually don't do it deliberately but they can do it because they decide that the fiscal doesn't want to know that or doesn't need to know that' (Moody and Tombs, 1982, pp. 47–8). As Sanders has argued: 'When the police (usually junior officers) decide that someone should be prosecuted, those officers rarely consider that prosecutors need to know anything pointing another way' (Sanders, 1988b), a position that has been confirmed by other writers (Elliman, 1990).

Control through exploiting malleable criteria

According to the rhetoric of criminal justice, the guidelines on cautioning and the complementary code for Crown Prosecutors provide external criteria by which the appropriate disposal for a particular case may be determined. Because prosecution is the natural response of the police to crime, in constructing the case file their ten- dency is to collect evidence of the crime and to eschew other information which might inform the decision as to whether or not a prosecution is desirable in the public interest. The result is that for the majority of cases there is nothing apart from purely formal information such as age and sex, which might trigger the application of relevant guidelines (Sanders 1985a, 1988; Gelsthorpe and Giller, 1990).

This is not to say however, that the guidelines have no impact on the process of case construction and prosecution decision making. Examination of case files and discussions with officers indicate a broad awareness of the factors which militate for or against prosecution. However, for the police the relevance of these public interest factors is not in providing external criteria against which cases are to be judged. Rather, these public interest factors provide a resource upon which officers preparing or reviewing cases can draw as means of justifying the decision or recommendation made and of achieving the favoured outcome. The informal working rules of the police provide the reason for a particular decision, the formal guidelines provide the justification. The use of public interest factors as resources of construction is enhanced in two respects. First, whether or not relevant information appears on the file is almost entirely within the discretion of the officer preparing the case. Second, the public interest factors relate to abstract and essentially malleable concepts dependent upon an interpretation of events.

BK-J26 – An argument between two schoolgirls led to J26 hitting the other girl in the face, breaking her nose and her spectacles. The PC dealing with the case described it as a fight betwen two schoolgirls with one coming off the worse and that the victim would not have reported it if J26 had offered compensation for the spectacles. On this basis the PC recommended caution despite the fact that J26 had been cautioned once previously.

In this case the evidence on file indicated that J26 had been taunting the other girl and then hit her. However, having decided to caution the PC was able to construct the case as trivial by describing the incident as a fight *between* the two girls.

> *AH-J35* – A boy had taken some jackets from an unlocked factory. The PC who dealt with the case told researchers that he was impressed by the boy's pleasant personality and frankness and recommended a caution. In his recommendation, the PC wrote: 'The family are strict and will punish him for offence if cautioned.' Actually, this statement was at odds with the boy's interview on file in which he had said that his mother had suggested he go to the factory and take a jacket.

The PC recognized that a factor which may determine cautionabilty is whether the child would be deterred from future offending by a caution and that the attitude of the parents is considered relevant to this issue. The reference to the family being strict was thus a means of anticipating the later review and justifying the caution recommendation.

Subordination of juvenile liaison procedures to police values

In the welfare model of criminal justice for juveniles, the involvement of social workers, probation officers and educationalists in the decision-making process evidences a substantial shift of responsibility for decision making away from the police. Although this may be true of some multi-agency bureaux (Davies *et al.*, 1989) in other cases the juvenile procedures are set up by the police to service their existing decision- making procedures, are controlled by the police and are dominated by police values.

The guidelines recommend that consultation is appropriate for all juvenile cases, but the police exercise a pre-emptive function by deciding that some cases should be prosecuted without reference to the special procedures (Landau, 1981). In our sample, 45 cases (35.4 per cent of juvenile prosecutions) fell into this category. The primary reasons for steering a case past the juvenile procedures are that to the police the case for prosecution is so clear that reference to the juvenile bureau would be a waste of time, that the informal working rules of the police dictate a prosecution or that prosecution serves a parallel interest in bureaucratic convenience.

CC-J23/J25 – Three youths were disturbed attempting to break into a roller-skate shop by the manager who had been sleeping on the premises. One of the youths was cornered by the manager and allegedly stabbed him in the arm with the knife which he had been using to remove putty from the window. The two who were not responsible for the stabbing immediately went to the police station and gave themselves up. All three were charged following arrest. This decision was explained by the PC on the basis of the seriousness of the offence (the stabbing): 'Not all have had previous cautions but once we charge, we charge them all.'

As this case demonstrates, the police tend to make decisions about 'the case' thus usurping any possibility of individualized decision making. The factors which determined the immediate charge were the seriousness of the stabbing (although only one youth was involved in this) and the convenience in having all offenders dealt with in the same way in a single file. As the following case illustrates, the latter factor may equally operate to pre-empt juvenile liaison in cases where a caution should clearly have been considered.

BK-J23/J24 – Twins aged 15 were reported on suspicion of theft. J23 had two previous cautions and at the time of arrest was awaiting trial on other charges. The file was passed to the senior decision maker who marked it: 'To juvenile liaison with a view to proceedings'. In fact the juvenile liaison officer did not put the case before the liaison panel. This was explained in a minute on the file from the JLO: 'One of the juveniles is presently being processed by us for a series of other offences, the case is adjourned to court. Obviously there is little point in liaising the file with Social Services.' Both were prosecuted.

The power of immediate charge permits the decision to initiate proceedings to be made purely on an officer's personal view of the case or suspect, without any consideration whatsoever of the guidelines. Curiously, this may involve a judgment by the officer on issues such as the child's attitude to a caution or likelihood of re-offending: precisely the sorts of issues which juvenile liaison is set up to consider.

It is arguably necessary to preserve the power to charge suspects (including juveniles) immediately in order that dangerous suspects or those likely to abscond may be kept in custody and brought to court on the following day. It is however apparent that the power of immediate charge is used for a much wider category of suspect. Indeed of the 45 juveniles in our sample who were charged immediately following arrest only five (16.7 per cent) were refused bail from the police station.

Pre-emption of the juvenile procedure may also occur in cases which are actually considered by the juvenile bureau. This arises where senior officers have recommended prosecution before referring the file to the juvenile bureau.

BK-J28/J29 and *BK-A045* – J28 and J29 were suspected of stealing a bicycle.

J28 had a previous conviction for using threatening words or behaviour and J29 had a previous caution for theft. The DI marked the case for prosecution before sending the file to juvenile liaison. At the juvenile liaison meeting the representative of Social Services had recommended cautions for the two juveniles. The file was then returned to the DI who reported to the Superintendent as follows: 'It would appear that all have been involved in other similar matters where bikes have been stolen and cannibalized although we are not in a position to prove this. This offence is becoming very prevalent to [Xtown] and although Social Services ask for a caution, I feel the youths should go to court.' The Superintendent endorsed the recommendation to prosecute.

In this case the relevant police working rule was that prosecution is a high priority for those suspected of regular criminal activity. The case demonstrates that where there is a conflict between the estimation of the public interest made by other agencies and the police working rules, the latter determine the ultimate decision. Where juvenile procedures are operated the police maintain their dominant role, by reserving the power to disregard and overrule any recommendation from the liaison procedure, and by exercising control over the discourse of the procedure.

Because the juvenile procedures which we observed operated on the basis of a tariff which was understood and accepted by all participants, disputes as to the outcome of cases were rare. However, where disputes did arise, senior decision-making officers had no compunction about overruling the liaison recommendation without any attempt to address the arguments which had been raised.

The general rule that the senior officer's decision was not open to question was subject to a practical exception in force C. In this force, there was provision for convening a 'panel' at the request of Social Services where their caution recommendation was overruled by the senior officer. Although the ultimate decision remained that of the senior officer, in cases in our sample a threat by Social Services to call for a panel was sufficient to ensure a caution in cases where the senior officer would have otherwise prosecuted. The senior officer explained that he took this course because he considered a panel as a 'waste of time'. Another police working rule therefore – to spend only as much time on a case as the police believed it deserved – came into operation in such cases.

The discourse of juvenile liaison

The function of juvenile liaison is supposed to be to consider the most appropriate disposal in the public interest. This entails taking into consideration the juvenile's 'previous character and family circumstances' (Guideline 10(ii)(c)) as well as issues relating to the seriousness of the offence and the juvenile's particular role. Although this is not articulated in the guidelines, the purpose of involving other agencies is to introduce information about the juvenile's circumstances as well as to ensure active consideration of such information. Where home visits are conducted, the purpose is to collect information about the child's background and attitude.

Many cases are considered without any information other than that contained in the police file (see also Gelsthorpe and Giller, 1990). Where the views of the local Education Welfare service are sought these are frequently informative as to the child's schooi record and general character. Although there is an obligation on the police to give advance notice to Social Services that a juvenile is under consideration for prosecution, the Social Services do not make enquiries particularly for the purpose of juvenile liaison. Thus, in most cases the input of Social Services, whether by post or in liaison meetings, is confined to a view of the 'proper' disposition of the case, based on the information provided by the police. It is unusual for the other agencies to press for a caution in cases in which, according to the informal tariff, the juvenile was due to be prosecuted. However, social workers or probation officers would intervene to enforce the tariff.

Information may be forthcoming however if, by chance, the child or its family is already a client of Social Services. Thus in one of the few cases in which personal circumstances were discussed at a liaison meeting the juvenile was already subject to a supervision order. By chance the probation officer present was her supervisor. He was able to report that she appeared to be doing well and pointed out that a prosecution might adversely affect the programme of supervision.

Home visits could be a more certain means of providing information about the child. However, although officers conducting the visits may collect quite detailed information about other members of the family and the physical environment of the home, no officer whom we interviewed was able to explain the relevance of this information to the decision in hand. Officers were also careful to describe the juvenile's demeanour and apparent attitude to the police, the offence and the possibility of caution. Although such information is more clearly relevant, it is in the form of a snapshot of the child on a single day in potentially stressful circumstances. As such it is not a reliable basis for decision making. It was also apparent that in a number of cases the home visit was simply an extension of the investigation, as in the following case.

AT-J48 – A boy lent his jacket to a friend. The police later searched the friend and a small quantity of drugs was found in the pocket. J48 denied any involvement in interview. Although there was no real evidence against J48 a home visit was conducted. The officer's report of the visit indicates that it was little more than a re-run of the earlier inconclusive interview conducted in the police station.

In the exceptional case which is subject to substantial discussion at a juvenile liaison meeting, the terms of the discussion are effectively dictated by the absence of information apart from that in the police file. Where substantial discussion does occur this normally involves social workers and probation officers engaging in debate on typically police issues relating to proof and law (such as whether damage was intended) or to the degree of involvement of the juvenile.

Juvenile liaison is essentially a *police* process. Its case work is determined by the police and its recommendations are subject to ultimate police veto. Its primary function is to operate a tariff in which discretion operates within limited parameters and subject to police leave. Its determinative values are essentially bureaucratic and impersonal rather than discretionary and individualized. Juvenile liaison does not share responsibility for decision making between the police and other agencies or import welfare ideologies into the decision-making process. Rather, juvenile liaison simply involves the co-option of other agencies within a police-dominated system.

THE SUBORDINATE POSITION OF THE CPS

The major issue in the political and legal debate which surrounded the setting up of the CPS was whether it was right in principle that a body independent of the police should take over responsibility for prosecuting (White, 1986). The principle championed by those who favoured an independent prosecution service was of separation of the functions of investigation and prosecution. The image of the proposed prosecution service conjured by both sides of the debate was of a body which would *displace* the police from their central role in prosecution decision making and relegate the police to a subservient role in investigating crime and preparing cases for the new prosecution service.

The reality is of a Crown Prosecution Service which is in many respects subordinate to the police. The police retain total control over many key decisions, such as decisions to take no further action, informally warn or caution. The police also decide whether or not to consult the CPS prior to making their initial charge/caution/NFA decision. This is important because prior to the establishment of the CPS it was recognized that it was easier for prosecutors to NFA or caution a case prior to its being charged than afterwards (Mansfield and Peay, 1987). In other words, 'prosecution momentum' was best avoided if the police consulted with prosecutors before charging. They rarely did this prior to the establishment of the CPS (McConville and Baldwin, 1981; Sanders, 1986) and they rarely do it now. In our sample, of the 711 cases in which prosecution decisions were taken after the inception of the CPS, advice was sought in just 51 cases. Advice was *not* sought, then, in 93 per cent of cases. Moreover, force C accounted for most of the advice sought (n = 48 cases). However, this force was unusual in that it had previously used its prosecuting solicitors' department in this way, and so was simply continuing a pre-existing practice.

CPS defers to the police on matters of policy

A prominent argument which was voiced (particularly by police representatives) against the creation of an independent prosecution service prior to 1985 was that the prosecutor would have insufficient grasp of local conditions and problems to determine questions of prosecution policy (West, 1986). The key to this argument is that the public interest in this context is double edged. Nationally recognized interests which might militate against prosecutions for trivial crimes or particular categories of offender must be balanced against particular local interests bearing on the question of whether prosecution is desirable for particular types of crime, or in particular areas or for particular individuals.

This argument was resolved in favour of vesting ultimate power to drop cases on public interest grounds with the CPS subject to a procedure by which the police can contest particular decisions with which they disagree, and subject also to regular high-level consultation between the police and the CPS on general matters of policy. The theory underlying the present arrangements is that notions of public interest in relation to prosecutions should be developed nationally and applied with some degree of consistency throughout the country. It is appropriate for national policy to be varied to take account of local conditions, but this should be done by the CPS who vet the claims of the local police in a detached manner and who can balance particular local interests against national policy.

In reality prosecutors almost invariably defer to the police on questions of policy and public interest on the basis that the close involvement of the police with the community makes them the best arbiters of local needs. In many cases this deference to the police view of the public interest is expressed in an uncritical acceptance of the police decision, on the basis that if the police have decided to proceed in a particular case, they must have had a good reason for doing so (see *CC-A064*, discussed above).

Another illustration of prosecutorial deference to the police is found in the following case.

> *CC-A108* – A woman of 36 was charged with criminal damage to a small window at a probation office. She explained to the PC who interviewed her that she had broken the window in frustration when the staff at the office had refused to help her to find accommodation. She further explained that she needed accommodation because she had left her previous flat after her landlord tried to rape her. She gave fairly full details of this incident but the interviewing officer made no attempt to follow up the rape allegation and concentrated on securing an admission to the damage charge. The prosecutor who reviewed the case simply endorsed the decision to charge. When interviewed about the decision by the researcher, the prosecutor replied that she had left it as far as the police had taken it. When further asked whether it was her role to ask the police to investigate another crime disclosed by the file, she replied that she thought that she should have done.

Under the guidelines, a factor suggesting non-prosecution in the public interest is that the offence was committed at a time of great stress. In this case the defendant's allegation of a recent attempted rape apparently had no bearing on what to the prosecutor was a routine prosecution decision. In adopting the police decision to prosecute, the prosecutor also simply adopted the interviewing officer's summary dismissal of the rape allegation. The case also emphasizes the CPS role in processing police cases, rather than as an independent decision maker. The allegation of damage presented by the police was prosecuted, whereas the failure to investigate the allegation of attempted rape was not even queried by the CPS for that would be to trespass on police prerogatives.

The CPS is fortified in its uncritical acceptance of some prosecution decisions by related beliefs that police review procedures (including juvenile bureaux) are the proper settings for consideration of policy, that such consideration will have been given in every case and that for the prosecutor to vet the case on policy grounds would be to duplicate and usurp a police function.

Prosecuting weak cases on policy grounds

In theory the CPS should consider questions of evidence and policy separately and should not proceed with a case unless there is sufficient evidence *and* it is in the public interest to do so. In practice the CPS often allows what it sees as a strong policy reason for prosecuting to override any perceived evidential weakness. In particular, the CPS is amenable to prosecuting cases which it recognizes as evidentially weak where to do so serves some police imperative.

> CC-A027 – A man of 26 had been present at the scene of public disorder in the town centre in the evening following a football match. He was alleged to have shouted abuse at officers conducting arrests and was himself arrested for being drunk and disorderly. The CPS reviewer described the evidence as looking a bit thin. He further explained that what probably happened was that the police had arrested A027 and after the event asked themselves what to charge him with. He said that he thought that the arrest had been made simply to remove A027 from the street. The prosecutor then explained that the centre of this town on Friday and Saturday nights could be an intimidating place and that the police regularly drafted in large numbers of officers but still found it difficult to keep order. The reviewer instructed the police to proceed as charged, but also asked the police if there were any further witness statements. In court A027 pleaded not guilty and was acquitted. [In this case the DPP decided that we could not quote the prosecutor directly.]

An example of a case where the CPS endorsed a prosecution in spite of acknowledged evidential weakness was given to us by a senior Crown prosecutor as an example of a case which he described as being worth a special effort. A PC had pursued a driver whom he suspected of reckless driving. When he lost the suspect in rush hour traffic, the PC who had recognized the driver went and waited outside his house. When the suspect arrived home the PC tried to reach through his car window to grab his ignition keys. In response the suspect wound up the window trapping the PC's hand. The PC smashed the car window and the suspect then retreated to his house. Police reinforcements arrived and smashed down his front door but the suspect barricaded himself into a bedroom. After a siege lasting some hours the suspect was persuaded to come out by a Superintendent. The suspect was charged with reckless driving and assault on a PC in the execution of his duty. The senior Crown prosecutor who reviewed the case pointed out to a researcher the evidential difficulties with both charges. The reckless driving charge was not substantiated by the PC's evidence on file, and, at the time of the assault, the PC had not been in the execution of his duty since he had no legal power to detain the suspect. The senior prosecutor then explained that the suspect had made complaints about every officer involved in the case including the Superintendent. He said that he had known the Superintendent for 15 years and you could not get a straighter copper, adding that this was a case in which the police obviously needed to be supported. (In this case, the DPP decided that we could not quote the prosecutor directly.) When asked what outcome he expected he said that he expected that the charges would be dropped if the suspect withdrew his complaints.

In cases like these it is self-evident to prosecutors that the necessity to support the police requires prosecution despite obvious flaws in these cases.

Dropping cases for insufficient evidence

For the CPS the fact that a large number of cases are dropped for insufficient evidence prior to trial both justifies their existence as an organization and is an indicator of their independence of the police. However, this simplistic equation misrepresents both the significance of dropped cases and the working relationship between CPS and the police. Under the Prosecution of Offences Act the CPS must take over all prosecutions initiated by the police and only the CPS has a power to abort the case. Thus, the dropping of a case simply indicates that its weakness has been recognized at some point between charge and trial, but does not illuminate the relative roles of police and CPS.

Although cases do occur in which the CPS drops a case for insufficient evidence where the police wish to proceed, such cases are rare. In a larger group of cases (discussed in the next section) the decision to drop is essentially a reaction to some defence initiative and either reflects a recognition that the case is hopeless or is designed to secure an acceptable result (such as plea to lesser charge or bind over) whilst avoiding trial. Apart from this group, the typical model for dropping cases is one of agreement between police and CPS, normally with the evidential weakness having been identified initially by the police. In relation to adult cases, in two of the three CPS regions which we studied we found that in all cases except one the recommendation to drop on evidential grounds emanated from the police. In these cases the CPS simply adopted the police view and the dropping of the case followed as a formality.

AH-A099 – The defendant was a visitor to this country who was charged with taking paid employment as a mini-cab driver in breach of his landing conditions. The Inspector who reviewed the case described it as: 'a complete dog's dinner. There is no evidence.' In particular certain necessary documents had not been obtained from the immigration authorities. The CPS offered no evidence in court.

In the third CPS region, in seven cases a decision to drop or not proceed with a case was initiated by the CPS, seven cases being dropped or not prosecuted on the prompting of the police. The degree of rigour which some prosecutors in this region demonstrated was encouraged by local police practice involving greater use of the report for summons procedure and of the facility to seek CPS advice prior to the charge decision.

CE-A011 – Some doors had been stolen of a type which was manufactured solely for a particular house builder. A011 was found in possession of one of the doors. In interview he said that he had bought it from a man in a pub for £20. A011 was reported and the file was passed to CPS for advice.

Crown Prosecutor (on file): 'There is no evidence of theft of the door. A trial of the handling alternative is unlikely to succeed in view of the explanation given in interview and the price paid.'

Significant CPS decisions are reactive

The CPS is charged to weed out cases which are evidentially weak or which it is not in the public interest to prosecute. Official accounts locate these functions in the 'case review' – the stage at which the file is read critically by a prosecutor, soon after the file is received by CPS, enabling key decisions to be made promptly in the interests of economy, efficiency and justice. Figures indicating that, in 1987–8, 7.5 per cent of cases were dropped prior to full hearing (National Audit Office, 1989) might be taken to indicate the rigour of the review process. However, this view is contradicted by an examination of the course of individual cases. In many instances where cases are dropped for evidential weakness or where charges are amended this occurs at a much later stage in the process and as a result of prompting by the defence.

The review, where it actually occurs before first court appearance, is a cursory examination of the file, conducted on the basis of a presumption of propriety, the normal consequence of which is endorsement of the prior police decision in the case. Indeed in the environment in which the prosecutor operates there is no incentive to perform the review rigorously. Dropping cases on grounds of weakness will antagonize the police and may lose a successful conviction, since, as all participants in the system understand, the great majority of cases, weak or strong, are disposed of by guilty pleas. If, on the other hand, there is a weakness in the case which the defence intend to exploit, a decision to drop it, or amend the charges or drop charges in return for a bind over, may always be made once the defence have signalled their intent to contest the case, as in the following case.

AT-A063 – The defendant was charged with criminal damage to a hotel and malicious wounding of a member of the hotel staff. Both incidents occurred on the same evening and from the outset it was assumed that the same person had been responsible for both incidents. A063 was arrested and charged on the basis of a description given by the victim of the wounding who later identified him. At the fourth court appearance, the criminal damage charge was dropped after the defence had pointed out to the prosecutor that there was no evidence whatsoever to link A063 to the offence.

CONCLUSION

In the welfarist rhetoric of the criminal justice process, no individual is charged until after the case has been thoroughly reviewed, not only within the police but also ultimately by an independent and impartial prosecuting agency divorced from the investigatory functions of the police. This review process, it is claimed, operates to overcome the danger that 'case commitment' by arresting and case officers may lead to unjustified charging, and, generally, to ensure that individuals are brought to court only where there is a realistic prospect of conviction on the basis of the evidence and where it is also in the public interest to deal with the matter by way of prosecution. The special position of juveniles has led to the creation of juvenile liaison bodies where representatives of the caring agencies can give further impetus to non-prosecution by bringing to the forefront non-police values and ideologies.

In reality, the system of review is corporatist in nature: marked by continued police dominance of decision making, a propensity to prosecute, extra-judicial tariffs, routinization rather than individualized judgment and the broad rejection of public interest criteria. Police dominance is primarily secured by their control over how cases are constructed, a function which enables them to anticipate and thus control review. Although the police have been required to involve other agencies in decision making, this has been done within police structures (juvenile liaison bureaux) and on police terms but surrounded by a welfarist rhetoric which masks a structure whose objectives appear to be the opposite of its rubric (Pratt, 1989; Cohen, 1985). The CPS, far from being an independent agency, is a police-dependent body, confining review to evidence-sufficiency questions, eschewing public interest criteria, utilizing the contradictory and malleable nature of the principles in the codes to further narrowly conceived objectives and, at its worst, adopting an uncritical support-the-police mandate.

8 Acquittals and convictions

We have seen that case construction by the police is generally (although not invariably) geared towards producing strong cases – that is, convictions. We have also seen that the CPS role is (except where 'public interest' factors arise) to prosecute strong cases and to eliminate weak cases (by either strengthening or rejecting them). It follows that an obvious test of police and CPS effectiveness is the conviction rate. This is the criterion against which these agencies commonly judge themselves. The CPS Annual Reports, for instance, point to 'dismissal rates' (i.e. the percentage of not guilty pleas ending in acquittal) as one indicator of their performance (CPS, 1989, para 1.1.7), as does the National Audit Office (1989, p. 11). The CPS considers that a more useful test is 'judgment quality'. This measures the percentage of cases in which it is held by the courts that there is no case to answer.

We may note here in passing that 'high' acquittal rates are sometimes attributed to factors outside police and prosecutorial control – unscrupulous defence lawyers, jury perversity and so forth (Mark, 1973; Sanders, 1979; Baldwin and McConville, 1979a). Some legal and institutional changes have followed in consequence of this debate, such as majority verdicts and the abolition of the peremptory jury challenge by the defence, despite the absence of real evidence supporting these characterizations of defence lawyers or juries in even a small minority of cases (Zander, 1974; Vennard and Riley, 1988; Gobert, 1989). We shall briefly touch on these issues when we look at the acquittals in our sample.

Rather than accepting Sir Robert Mark's argument, the Royal Commission saw 'weak' cases as the major problem underlying acquittals. The guidelines, Codes and CPS itself were all established with a view to their reduction. In one sense we accept the Royal Commission's characterization of the problem as one of technical efficiency on the part of police and prosecutors. The higher the level of acquittals the more weak cases there are that could be eliminated. However, we adopt the perspective of Kitsuse and Cicourel (1963). Many years ago they urged criminologists to take official crime statistics seriously, although not as guides to any 'real' level of, or trend in, crime that might exist: instead they pointed out that 'rates can be viewed as indices of organizational processes rather than as indices of the incidence of certain forms of behaviour' (p. 137).

So, rather than seeing 'weakness' and 'strength' as objective attributes of cases, we see these qualities as products of the police construction process which we documented in earlier chapters. High conviction rates, in this light, may not be matters of congratulation for a justice system, but a sign of disturbingly effective case construction. By the same reasoning, acquittals may not be 'failures' of prosecution, but predictable and predicted outcomes. The ensuing pattern of acquittals and convictions may not be a product of 'strength', 'weakness', 'adversarial tactics', 'jury perversity' or any other conventional problems. It is more likely that these patterns are a product of the norms which shape initial prosecution decision making, which in turn are shaped by the informal working rules of the police.

In this chapter we explore these issues by first looking at the distribution of acquittals and convictions. Then we look at the impact of working rules and institutional forms upon outcomes in court. Finally we draw the threads together in an attempt to assess the 'meaning' of acquittal and conviction rates.

THE DISTRIBUTION OF ACQUITTALS AND CONVICTIONS

National statistics of acquittal and conviction are collected and collated in different ways by different bodies, making them impossible to interpret precisely (Baldwin and McConville, 1978a). However, the different sources are broadly consistent with each other. Table 12 shows results for magistrates' courts in 1987/8.

Table 12 Outcomes of cases disposed of in magistrates' courts, 1987-8

Outcome	n	%	
Guilty plea	978,761	78.9 ⎫	87.1%
Convicted after trial	101,159	8.2 ⎭	
Not guilty (incl. discontinuances)	159,920	12.9	
Total	1,239,840	100.0	

Source: National Audit Office (1989), Table 1. Table 12 excludes cases written off and cases committed to Crown Court.

Overall, 87.1 per cent of all defendants were found guilty on all or some of their charges. Most of these pleaded guilty. Considerably over half of those who pleaded not guilty were acquitted. The figures for the Crown Court are broadly similar (LCD, 1988, Table 6.8). Our own figures are similar, confirming that our sample is broadly representative of criminal cases in general in this respect (Table 13).

In our sample, 84 per cent of adults and 74 per cent of juveniles were found guilty. Again, rather more than half of all those who pleaded not guilty were acquitted, but over three-quarters of all defendants plead guilty to all or some charges (Tables 14 and 15).

Table 13 Outcome of cases in research sample

Outcome	Adult n	%	Juvenile n	%
Guilty	307	84.1	93	74.4
Not guilty (incl. discontinuances)	58	15.9	32	25.6
No result (e. g. not prosecuted)	308	–	234	–
Not known	47	–	1	–
Total	720	100.0	360	100.0

Table 14 Research sample cases according to plea

Plea	Adult n	%	Juvenile n	%
Guilty	280	76.7	86	68.8
Not guilty (incl. discontinuances)	85	23.3	39	31.2
No plea	304	–	234	–
Not known	51	–	1	–
Total	720	100.0	360	100.0

Table 15 Outcome of contested cases in research sample

Outcome	Adult n	%	Juvenile n	%
Guilty	25	30.1	7	17.9
Not guilty (incl. discontinuances)	58	69.9	32	82.1
Not known	2	–	0	–
Total	85	100.0	39	100.0

Conviction and acquittal rates vary between different police forces, CPS areas and court centres (National Audit Office, 1989, Table 2). In our sample the rates varied between forces too, but the numbers involved are too small to be statistically significant. Despite these variations, nationally and in our study, the overall pattern remains the same everywhere: the overwhelming majority of defendants plead guilty. And they do so in the magistrates' or juvenile courts rather than go to Crown Court. Only 23.6 per cent of our adult, and 2.5 per cent of our juvenile, cases were heard in the Crown Court. Moreover, most of the Crown Court cases were guilty pleas anyway, and those that were not were usually dropped before they came before a jury. Thus Baldwin and McConville's (1979a, p. 7) observation that trial by jury – the epitome of the Due Process Model – is used by less than 10 per cent of all defendants remains true today.

Both nationally and in our sample most acquittals (including discontinuances) were through cases being dropped: of the 58 adult acquittals, 12 followed trial and 46 were dropped; of the 32 juvenile acquittals, 10 followed trial and 22 were dropped. For as long as is documented, the prosecution has dropped cases when it did not wish to fight a full trial. Although traditionally cases could be dropped only with the permission of a judge or magistrate, this last vestige of judicial control was usually a rubber stamp exercise. The legal form adopted was that no evidence was offered or the charge was withdrawn (the two forms being effectively identical). If prosecutors wanted to do this prior to the establishment of the CPS, they had also to secure the permission of the police as part of the solicitor–client relationship. The Prosecution of Offences Act, 1985 (POOA), gave the CPS the right to do as it wishes, subject to the views of the court.

The POOA also introduced, in the form of the 'discontinuance', a new way of dropping cases. This itself takes two forms. First, under s.23(4) (statutory uncharging) the CPS may discontinue any case without reference to the court if it does so prior to the charge sheet/information being sent to court. The defendant is simply 'uncharged' as if s/he had never been charged in the first place. Procedurally, this is the easiest way to drop a case because the case is not listed and no-one need appear in court in respect of it. Since most institutions adopt the easiest way possible to achieve their goals, one might expect 'uncharging' to be a popular procedure. Yet in our sample *not one case* was dropped in this fashion (nationally, no figures are available). The reason for this is that it relies on the CPS being sent the papers by the police in time to invoke s.23(4), which they almost never do.

Second, the CPS may discontinue cases under s.23(3) at any time while the case is still before the magistrates. No permission is needed, but it is not, legally, an acquittal; in theory, the police could re-charge any suspect whose case is discontinued. In our sample, out of the 68 dropped cases there were just 11 (16.2 per cent) discontinuances. In practice, neither the police nor the CPS distinguish between discontinuance and other ways in which cases are dropped, and hereafter they will all be treated together as dropped cases even though official statistics treat discontinuances separately.

EXPLAINING COURT RESULTS

Conviction is the normal result of a court case. But 'normal' in what sense? It is normal in so far as it is usual, and normal in that it is usually expected. However, although expectations are commonly shaped by experience, in reality many contests in court end in acquittal. In our own sample 70 per cent of adult not guilty pleas in fact ended in total acquittal. It is true that the system produces large numbers of guilty pleas (77 per cent of the adults in our sample), but these are failures to fight the case in the first place. Conviction is usual only as a result of our guilty plea system.

Legal structures centred around Crime Control (as distinct from Due Process) are often used to explain the guilty plea system (McBarnet, 1981). For instance, case mortality in pre-prosecution stages, as we have seen, is very high. Decisions about guilt and innocence are made by the police *before* cases get to court. However, just because the police decide that a person is guilty and should be prosecuted, it does not necessarily follow that cases which do go to trial will result in conviction. Pre-trial decision making may be seen by the *police* as an alternative to court decision making, but there is no reason why defendants and their lawyers should comply with this Crime Control perspective. Paradoxically, much of the system operates on Crime Control values even though the applicable legal rules do not require this – despite McBarnet's (1981) assertions that Crime Control processes are structured by Crime Control rules. It is no longer true, for instance, that the right to advice is unclear and malleable. It is unambiguous, yet still used rarely (Sanders *et al.*, 1989). It is now clear whether or not persons 'helping police with their enquiries' are arrested or not, yet many are in reality in a legal limbo (MacKenzie *et al.*, 1990). Much police practice is driven by Crime Control values when this is simply either not required by, or is even in breach of, the applicable legal rules. The rules do not force defendants and their lawyers to opt in to Crime Control but they do. Two reasons are commonly adduced to explain this, but neither is satisfactory.

First, there is the argument that most defendants are guilty anyway. Whether this is true or not (rather, whether this is a meaningful claim or not) is irrelevant. The rhetoric of Due Process insists on the right of defendants to require the prosecution to prove its case beyond reasonable doubt before a guilty verdict can be entered. Regardless of what the defendant may or may not have done or said, the defendant is entitled to a declaration of innocence in the absence of proof by the prosecution. This is clear from the Bar Code of Conduct (1989, para 24.2): 'a barrister must endeavour to protect his client from conviction except by a competent tribunal and upon legally admissible evidence sufficient to support a conviction'. Even when defendants confess, barristers are 'entitled to test the evidence given by each individual witness, and to argue that the evidence taken as a whole is insufficient to amount to proof' (*ibid*, Annex 7). If a defendant has a chance of acquittal through lawful means why is this so infrequently taken? If innocent, it is surprising that the defendant does not assert innocence; and if guilty the defendant would not be expected to suffer moral compunction about being 'wrongfully' acquitted and 'wasting' the state's time and money. Defendants have a right; why do they habitually fail to exercise it?

Second, it is argued that since sentences for conviction after trial are more severe than those for a guilty plea, the 'sentencing discount' (Baldwin and McConville, 1978b) deters many suspects from pleading not guilty. This explains why defendants who expect conviction plead guilty, but it does not, of course, explain why most defendants expect to be convicted in the first place.

It is impossible to determine empirically whether cases in which there is a guilty plea would have resulted in a guilty verdict if they had been contested. However, generally this would depend upon the effectiveness of case construction – the more effective the construction, the more likely it would be that guilt would be 'proved'. Similarly, it is failures of construction which underlie acquittals. For we are not arguing that the police have total power to construct cases in any way they wish. Much of the time they do not have that power, nor would they choose to exercise it even if they did. Thus some cases are NFA, while others are constructed weakly for conviction or even not for conviction at all. Many cases therefore fail, while many more are bargained over.

While the police do not possess absolute power, they do – in most cases – have more power than any other individual or institution in the criminal justice system. This power is at its height in the early stages of a case when the suspect is in the police station. Case 'outcome' should be understood as more than just acquittal and conviction at court. The grading and sorting process discussed in Chapter 6 also produces outcomes. Cautions are forms of conviction, as are some NFAs, used to decide whether or not to prosecute (see previous chapter). Some NFAs, on the other hand, are forms of acquittal. In neither case is the outcome publicly announced, so the police are not required to justify it or have it reviewed or vetted by non-police agencies. The normal rules of evidence and procedure therefore do not apply, despite the rhetoric of the guidelines about evidential standards for cautions. The police exercise almost complete power over these outcomes regardless of the evidence.

As time and the case proceed the hold of the police weakens. Some features of cases, such as defence corroboration, are completely beyond their control (Baldwin and McConville, 1979a). Sometimes they are beyond the control of the defendant as well – as when the defendant becomes unfit to plead because of mental illness (*CE-A031*), or prosecution witnesses fail to appear in court (*AT-J03*) or do not 'come up to proof' (see *BK-A067* below, and McConville and Baldwin, 1981, ch. 3). Some cases are beyond the ability or willingness of the police to create strong constructions from the start, but are prosecuted anyway.

The impact of informal working rules

We saw in Chapter 6 that prosecution decisions are structured in part by evidential considerations, but also by informal police working rules. In the previous chapter we saw how the CPS and other review agencies are largely carried along by these rules, regardless of evidential considerations. The result is often case weakness. Whilst this is not always evident at first to police reviewers or to prosecutors, at other times it is obvious to just about all the participants. Those evidential problems can be fundamentally damaging to the case or merely problematic.

In this section we discuss three informal working rules in terms of their impact on case strength. The first relates to the use by the police of prosecution procedures to assert their authority, rather than merely to enforce the law after rational assessment of evidence. Linked with this is the policy of the CPS to support the police in this endeavour. Whilst the public rhetoric presents the relationship between police and CPS as conflictual, in reality their day to day working ideologies are marked by harmony. Thus in the following case there was never sufficient evidence, as the police reviewer also recognized, but it was prosecuted to support police authority:

CC-A085/A086/A087 – Three lads were involved in a disturbance, as a result of which, *inter alia*, two were charged with public order offences. The DMU (police decision-making unit) wrote to the CPS concerning the only independent witness: 'The witness [H] looks like a better witness for the defence than the prosecution.' The CPS none the less continued the prosecution even though the police themselves said that there was not sufficient evidence to justify the charge.

The second working rule relates to negative police assessments of particular suspects and their distaste for particular offences. Again the police tend to let their sentiments dominate their prosecution decisions. This is apparent from the following two cases:

> *BW-A098* – A098 was charged, with others, with deception (presenting a forged cheque). His fingerprint was on the cheque but he had an innocent explanation for this. There was no evidence that he had written or presented it. The CPS reviewer wrote to the police that 'the fact his thumb print appears on one cheque doesn't prove he presented it'. In her opinion 'there wasn't a prima facie case' without more evidence. As extra evidence was not available the case was discontinued.

> *CC-A074/A075/A076* – In this case (discussed in Chapter 4) three defendants took salad openly from a restaurant salad bar, and offered to pay what they considered – wrongly – to be the correct amount. 'I am not happy with the evidence . . . you may wish the complaint to be dealt with as a civil debt only' (DMU to CPS). CPS agreed, and dropped the cases.

In *BW-A098* the police claimed that the defendant was part of a criminal 'firm' and that they knew that firm's 'modus operandi (m.o.)'. They therefore wanted him dealt with in any way possible. And in *CC-A074/A075/A076* the arresting officers found the defendants' attitude 'arrogant' and their refusal to admit they were wrong infuriated them.

It is clear from this that case 'weakness' and 'strength' are not fixed passive quantities: the police play an active role in constructing that weakness and strength. Confessions are the most frequently constructed evidence, and it was the refusal of the defendants to confess in *CC-A074/A075/A076* which both undermined the case and so infuriated the police. Similarly, there was no confession evidence in this case:

> *BK-A100* – A100 was charged with unlawful sexual intercourse and indecent assault on two young girls. Medical opinion after a brief, if cursory, examination of the girls at the police station appeared to support the charges, but medical evidence provided by a paediatrician nominated by the defence totally undermined this opinion, which was then withdrawn by the police doctor. By then, 'it was embarrassing, [A100] in custody for four months and our case had gone . . . we couldn't prove anything . . . I asked DS [X] to put it to [A100's] solicitor that we'd drop the USI and just go on the indecent assault and would his client plead to this. Well he's come back and said 'no' so we've no alternative but to offer no evidence.' (DI)

Clearly the police were not shaken in their belief in the defendant's guilt simply because the evidence had completely changed. They still tried for a conviction regardless. The DI told us 'it could affect the girls for the rest of their lives. I tend to believe them but I could be wrong. . . . If he did it he's had some punishment. If he did it, of course, it's not enough. But it's some.'

The third working rule is that the police do not put equal resources into all cases. Cases about which the police are relatively unconcerned, but which they prosecute anyway, are often constructed less strongly than others. Sometimes this is because the police simply could not construct them more strongly or could not negotiate the obstacles in the way of doing so. But, as Shapland and Vagg (1987) also note, often the police simply do not pursue all the possible – or even all the obvious – lines of enquiry in these cases. Where informal norms, such as we examined above, are not operative there is less motivation for the police to create strong constructions. They want prosecution and conviction, but not at great cost to themselves. But weak cases are not automatically dropped, and are in any event rarely dropped quickly, because cases gather a momentum once started: there are institutional obstacles to reversing decisions to prosecute that do not exist at the point of decision about whether or not to initiate proceedings (McConville and Baldwin, 1981; Sanders, 1985a, 1986).

Evidential weakness is the constant complaint of the CPS, and has been a consistent feature of British criminal justice. Cases where the police could have investigated more completely or with more care (albeit with no certainty that it would strengthen the case) sometimes come to public attention – as in the *Confait* case (Fisher 1977) where the police attempted to negate an alibi rather than to reassess the case in the light of countervailing evidence; and *Madden*'s case (*Guardian*, 9 March 1981) where a man was charged with theft of a toy after the police omitted to question the shop from which Madden had made the purchase and for which he had a receipt.

Even where the police do secure more evidence after cajoling by the CPS it is often difficult to retrieve the situation.

> *BW-A013* – A013 was charged with stealing a jacket. Her co-accused [X] pleaded guilty. CPS wrote to the police that 'on the evidence you have submitted, without a witness statement from [X], we cannot prove the case. . . .' A statement was obtained, but, as the defence solicitor pointed out to the magistrates, conviction largely on the evidence of a co-accused is dangerous. A013 was acquitted. This did not surprise the prosecutor: 'The evidence was a bit thin, but I think there was a case to answer.'

As cases proceed, police control lessens and their constructional power declines. Even so, prosecution momentum makes prosecutors reluctant to let go even when acquittal is imminent. In the above case the prosecutor did not claim that there was a realistic prospect of conviction – merely that 'there was a case to answer'. This was the common refrain prior to the introduction of the CPS (McConville and Baldwin, 1981; Sanders, 1985a, 1986), but one which the CPS was supposed to have eliminated through its power to discontinue in the absence of a 'realistic prospect of conviction'.

Why weak cases are prosecuted

The prosecution of weak cases appears to have certain obvious disadvantages: conviction rates are lowered, prosecuting authorities are exposed to criticism and occasionally made to look foolish, scarce resources are tied up and civil actions for malicious prosecution are risked. Even if the policing advantages of prosecution outweigh these disadvantages in some cases it is not self-evident that *so many* cases with these potential disadvantages are prosecuted with advantage to the police and CPS. Moreover, how have the police managed to sustain this strategy since the creation of the CPS, which was introduced expressly to eliminate these practices?

In part, the answer lies with the very existence of the CPS. The CPS, and not the police, are now responsible for what happens in court. The police do not suffer when cases fail. Prior to the creation of the CPS, the police were responsible, although that did not deter them from 'policy' prosecutions which were doomed to fail (Zander, 1974; McCabe and Purves, 1972; McConville and Baldwin, 1981; Sanders, 1985a). But now the CPS is a shield behind which the police can shelter.

The police used to sustain their policy, and the CPS continue to do so, in part because of a second cluster of reasons: a guilty verdict, a guilty plea or a face saving compromise in the form of a plea bargain. These outcomes are far more common than absolutely unconditional vindication for the defendant, despite that result in many of the cases discussed in the previous section. In our sample, 87 per cent of adults pleaded guilty, were found guilty, or were bound over. In the following case there was no more evidence than in most of the cases in the previous section:

> *CC-A084/A085/A086* – Three lads were involved in a disturbance. Two were charged with assaulting police officers and obstruction, but claimed that there was just a general mêlée. The prosecution solicitor would have dropped the charges in exchange for a bind over but was 'under strict instructions from CPS to run it'. Officers and CPS all described it as a typical assault case of one

person's word against another's, but 'I don't think there's quite enough to justify the assault' (interviewing officer). In the event, there were convictions on all charges.

In *BW-A023* (drunk and disorderly) our notes of interview with the prosecutor read:

> 'he told me that the evidence of disorderly behaviour was not so well made out as the drunkenness element and that drunk and incapable would perhaps have been the better charge. He explained lamely that he hadn't been the one who had reviewed the case. . . . He might have considered discontinuing the charge of drunk and disorderly against A023 if A023 had pleaded not guilty.'

Since A023 pleaded guilty the issue did not arise. Had that prosecutor reviewed the case the result might still have been the same: certainly other research has also found that the absence of strong evidence was no bar to prosecutors accepting guilty pleas, even when they knew that they would drop the case in the event of a not guilty plea (McBarnet, 1981, p. 71). Thus, in *BW-A002/J02* the CPS asked the police for additional evidence because of the weakness of the case. However, no more evidence was produced, but the defendants pleaded guilty to all the charges anyway. Even these reactions, however, required some review of the file. As we know from the previous chapter, genuine reviews are rare (before first appearance, at any rate):

> *AT-A055* – A055 was charged with theft. He was bailed to appear in court the next day, and pleaded guilty. In interview we asked the prosecutor what he thought of the police case and he told us that he had not had time to read the file as the suspect had been arrested only the day before. He added that it did not matter since he was pleading guilty anyway. [In this case, the DPP decided that we could not quote the prosecutor directly.]

Yet para 4 of the Code for Crown Prosecutors provides:

> When considering the institution or continuation of criminal proceedings the first question to be determined is the sufficiency of the evidence. A prosecution should not be started or continued unless the Crown Prosecutor is satisfied that there is admissible, substantial and reliable evidence that a criminal offence known to the law has been committed by an identifiable person.

In *BW-A083* (theft of light bulb, discussed in Chapter 7), A083 was prosecuted in order to deter others in similar circumstances. The CPS instruction was 'if not guilty plea consult with defence – a binding over and payment of 50p compensation as an alternative means of disposing of this case'. But the defendant pleaded guilty, so the bargain was never suggested. In the following case fate produced a different result:

> *CC-A019* – A019 was charged with a public order offence allegedly committed in a police station waiting room with no members of the public present (see

Chapter 7). This presented legal difficulties, and the police reviewer told the CPS: 'I am not happy with the charge and I would be prepared to accept a bind over.' The CPS secured the agreement of the defence solicitor to this. Unknown to anyone else, and because of a communication problem within the CPS, another prosecutor was also dealing with the file. She decided independently to drop the case. We asked her if a bind over was appropriate, and she said that it was not.

The defendant was saved from a disadvantageous bargain in that case not by his solicitor – who was prepared to agree to an inappropriate disposition – but by a prosecutor. What that prosecutor did not know was that the defendant had complained against the conduct of the police in that incident, which probably accounts for the keenness of the police and, initially, the CPS to secure the bind over.

Strong cases usually lead to prosecution and conviction. The corollary – that weak cases lead to NFA or acquittal – is not true. Weak cases usually lead to compromises or even straight guilty pleas. This finding is supported elsewhere in the literature. Thus, in Baldwin and McConville's (1977, p. 74) sample of late guilty pleaders, acquittal was judged, on the basis of the prosecution case papers, to have been likely or possible in some 21 per cent of the cases, and Moody and Tombs (1982, p. 307) also found 'bargaining' over charges which the prosecution could not prove.

The fact of the charge – however justified it may or may not have been in the first place – gives the police and CPS in most cases sufficient bargaining power when they want to secure guilty pleas. Prosecution *evidence* is not usually needed. In *BK-A054*, where the defendant was charged with attempted criminal damage as a result of letting air out of a police car tyre, the charge simply did not fit the facts howsoever they could be constructed. But the police were determined to charge with something. It was dropped at the second court appearance, and a bind over ordered. Again the police and CPS secured a compromise.

We observed earlier that the police frequently fail to gather evidence on even obvious issues. Sometimes they care little about the prosecution and are perhaps over-confident about the strength of what evidence they do have. Sometimes they are unwilling to investigate the defendant's story in case it strengthens the defendant's account. Yet in *BK-A054* the police went to great lengths to secure evidence in what has to be regarded as an exceptionally trivial case. They secured a written report from their maintenance department which, they hoped, would substantiate the 'attempt damage' charge. Thus, police constructional effort – police allocation of priorities regarding evidence gathering – is not determined by case seriousness, availability of other evidence and so forth. Rather, it is a product of their informal norms, in this case response to an attack on their authority.

The institution of the CPS and the 'realistic prospect of conviction' test has not eliminated weak cases from court, and the CPS does not automatically drop these cases. The detriments from an expected acquittal or failed case are insufficient to deter the CPS from going forward with prosecutions. A case which is dropped cannot turn into a conviction; it is irrevocably lost. A case which is continued has the chance of conviction:

> *AH-A020* – A020 was arrested for possession of drugs, but the police also found items in his car which they considered could be 'offensive weapons': a baseball bat, a broken billiard cue, a broken flick knife and so forth. He had explanations for having all these, and pleaded not guilty. Prosecution counsel said the case was 'very weak'. There was, for instance, a poor interrogation by the police who 'never checked [A020's] story' (i.e. to test it). Prosecution counsel asked us rhetorically why there are acquittals, and answered that the police do not investigate thoroughly, 'and it is no use their complaining about acquittals back in their canteens'. But the jury convicted A020.

The fact is that many verdicts are simply impossible to predict. In any of these contested cases the accounts would have been equally plausible (and made the same points) if the verdicts had been reversed. So while it is true that in many failed cases the police could have done more to 'firm up' the case, this is also true of many 'successful' cases. In other words, it would often be, from the police point of view, wasted effort. Absolutely hopeless cases for trial are actually fairly rare, although there are examples from all of our police force areas. Poor raw material is more usually either NFAed (as discussed in Chapter 6) or constructed in ways which 'firm them up'. Those which 'slip through the net' rarely seem to slip through in reality but are pushed through in full knowledge of the weakness because the offence/offender embodies a police priority.

The police-dependent nature of outcome

Major weaknesses in cases which get to court, where this occurs, are frequently a product of inadequate police investigation. In one over-heard argument between a prosecutor and a Detective Constable (DC), the DC wanted to know why a case had been dropped; the prosecutor said that a crucial interview had not been done (*AT-A055* above). The DC wanted to 'give it a run' anyway, but the prosecutor refused, saying that the DC had better 'conduct your investigations properly in future if you want a conviction'.

The lack of preparation in many cases means that it often becomes apparent to the police themselves that the case is weak. Occasionally the officer in charge recognizes this:

> *AT-A003* – V was assaulted whilst in his car, which was then damaged. He saw the group of men who did it, followed them home, and then called the police. He identified A003 in his home (a lodging house) as one of those responsible, but afterwards he was not sure. The officer in charge was convinced it was *NOT* him. But because 'the victim had positively identified him we had to charge'. The officer continued to ask questions of witnesses afterwards, though, and requested that the case be dropped. CPS agreed at the second court hearing.

This case illustrates two points: that some cases fail because the police decide that they should; and that those same, and many other, cases fail because the police initially failed to investigate as thoroughly as they could have. Better investigation would not always resolve ambiguities, but it would sometimes have either produced stronger cases which would be more likely to have led to convictions or weaker cases that would not have been prosecuted in the first place.

The net result is that, much of the time, *both convictions and acquittals are products of the police*. Even where, as rarely happens, the defence produce new evidence (as in *CC-J47/J48*) this is evidence which the police could have produced for themselves but did not.

This does not account for all acquittals by any means, but, in many cases which resulted in acquittal, the same plausible explanation was given at trial as at interrogation or the evidence was intrinsically ambiguous. In many cases, failure could have been, and sometimes was, predicted at the outset. This was McConville and Baldwin's (1981, p. 61) conclusion too, where over 84 per cent of the cases which were identified as being weak at the committal stage ended in acquittal. Very few acquittals are attributable to lack of police powers or procedural hurdles – although we shall see that inadmissibility of confession evidence accounts for some. In most cases it is usually just a question of who is believed by police/magistrates/jury. And, *on the evidence*, it could be anyone.

CPS independence and the Code of Practice

We saw in the previous chapter that the CPS rarely sees itself exercising a 'public interest' role by dropping 'policy weak' cases, but that it is rather more vigorous regarding evidential weakness. None the less, confrontations between police and CPS are quite rare. This is not because problem cases are rare, but because the structurally weak position of the CPS leads it to avoid confrontation. As previous sections have shown, police capacity to construct cases and establish prosecution momentum constrains the CPS, but room to manoeuvre does often remain.

Although the CPS drops many more cases than many critics expected (Sanders, 1986), they could still drop more than they do. Indeed, we saw in Chapter 7 that when cases are dropped it is usually at the instigation of the police. Instead the CPS usually hopes to secure guilty pleas, plea bargain or ask for more evidence, as in *BW-A098*. The prosecutor in that case commented that 'we have to do the police's work for them. . . . If we sent every file back which we should, we'd never get any cases to court.' More important, this would ruin the fragile relationship the CPS has with the police *and* make their conviction statistics worse. Why do this when a straight guilty plea or a bargain can be wrested from a compliant defence solicitor?

> *BK-A104/A117* – Two young men were arrested for shoplifting after they had allegedly run away. According to the DI (prior to charge) the identification evidence was very poor. Prosecution none the less proceeded. Four months later the CPS wrote on the file 'He had done it, it's a matter of proving it. I was going to ask for an adjournment for the police to find some more evidence.' He did not do so because the defence solicitor intimated guilty pleas. When not guilty pleas were in fact entered the case was dropped.

Given the reluctance of CPS to harm their relationship with the police it is at first sight surprising to find as many cases dropped as there are. Prior to the Prosecution of Offences Act prosecuting solicitors were certainly reluctant to drop cases. However, there is no doubt that the CPS is now more ready to drop cases on evidential grounds than was previously the case. Contrast most of the cases in this chapter with those cited by Sanders (1985a, 1986) in his pre-Act research, and with the following from one of our pre-CPS police areas:

> *BK-A067/A068/A069/J19* – The four defendants were arrested for 'taking a vehicle without consent' (TWOC), reported for summons and summonsed. The police believed in the guilt of all four, although the evidence was 'a bit thin' according to the first prosecutor. The police appeared to agree, the DI endorsing the file 'give all four a run at court'. The case against two was dismissed at committal, and the case against the other two was dropped in the Crown Court. The Crown Court prosecutor was surprised that any of the cases survived committal.

Even this case was eventually dropped only because the victim gave very equivocal evidence at the committal. Had the victim 'come up to proof' the prosecution might have fought the case. In *AH-J59/J60* (another pre-CPS case) the case was fought until the magistrates held that there was no case to answer – an indication of how hopeless this case was. The CPS would now require strong reasons for fighting such cases, albeit that 'strong reasons' include *policy* reasons, often of a dubious kind.

Why this apparent change of heart by prosecutors? First, in many of these cases the weakness was initially identified by the police (see Chapter 7). Second, the simple fact of the power so to do is one factor, but not a crucial one. For the dropping of cases on 'public interest' grounds alone *never* occurred in our research sample, except when the defendants concerned were already sentenced for more serious offences, making the dropped case not worth pursuing. Even the police do not actually claim that the CPS drops many cases on these grounds (Wilkinson and Evans, 1990). The following case is instructive:

> CE-A098 – A098 was involved in a neighbour dispute with V. The police believed A098's claim to have been provoked into assaulting V, but this was no defence. A098 had only one previous conviction several years earlier. There was no medical evidence of injury to V. A098 was prosecuted and elected Crown Court trial. The case was dropped at the Judge's instigation, on 'public interest' grounds, and A098 was bound over. The CPS told us 'As soon as he [the Judge] suggested dropping it [we] agreed.' Yet it did not occur to CPS to initiate this move.

The likelihood of case failure in court is one of only two compelling factors leading to cases being dropped at the instigation of the CPS. Case failure in this context does not mean evidential weakness: rather, it means that a case will be continued even if it is lacking in evidence sufficiency until and unless the defence enters a meaningful challenge. Hence the practice of CPS endorsing files 'Offer bind over if not guilty plea' or even 'Discontinue if the defence go to trial'. The second factor relates to financial concerns contained within two limited 'public interest' factors: where defendants are already charged with, or sentenced for, more serious offences; and where defendants elect for jury trial in minor cases (usually shoplifting). The police complain particularly about the latter (see, for instance, the ACPO evidence to the Home Affairs Committee: House of Commons, 1990).

While, prior to the Act, failure could be regarded as the responsibility of the police, now it is, formally, that of the CPS. This creates for the CPS a meaningful working rule – to drop cases on evidential or financial grounds – that, in each case, is weighed against any police working rule operating in the opposite direction.

Dropping cases on 'public interest' grounds alone, though, furthers no working rules for the CPS or the police, and it therefore does not occur except for financial reasons. The goal of the CPS is not to drop evidentially weak or policy-weak cases. Its goal is to secure a maximally high conviction rate. As we have seen, weak cases do not necessarily fail. So rather than seeking independence from the police, by pursuing the rhetoric of the Code, the CPS compounds its dependency on the police by tying its 'success' rate to the products of the police arrest and charge process. Were the dropping of cases which violate the Code the goal of the CPS, discontinuance rates, rather than conviction rates, would be used as performance indicators. Although both are actually used, discontinuance rates are not published in the Annual Reports for this purpose. The highlighting of conviction rates instead illuminates the working rules of the CPS.

At least evidential standards are discussed in policy-making circles (because of their connection to 'success' rates). 'Public interest' considerations are not mentioned in the most recent Annual Report (CPS, 1989). Whether as a result of the CPS itself minimizing the 'public interest' element or for other reasons, public bodies which scrutinize the CPS also ignore it. It is as though the CPS sets itself a 'conviction rate' agenda and thus sets the standard by which others judge it. Thus neither the National Audit Office (1989) nor the House of Commons Committee on Public Accounts (1990) mention the 'public interest' element. In the Home Affairs Committee Memoranda of Evidence (House of Commons, 1990) 'public interest' is mentioned very briefly by the CPS itself (para 5.4 and Annex 11) and otherwise discussed only by the 'caring agencies' (Probation, NACRO, etc.) if we leave aside the narrow financial aspects of this concept. These agencies concentrate on the VERA study on 'public interest case assessment' (Stone, n.d.) which showed the considerable scope for increased diversion of adults on 'public interest' grounds even within the existing Code and institutional structure. The interest in this of probation bodies is doubtless due to their involvement in the VERA project and in all information schemes of this kind. What is really significant is that the VERA study has not been mentioned in any other official document to which we have had access. Diversion, other than in the traditional police-controlled manner through cautioning, is on the official agenda – that is the agenda of the CPS itself, ACPO, Home Office and so forth – only in the rhetoric of the Code.

Thus in *CC-A102* (shoplifting by an 18-year-old girl) the prosecutor, on being asked why she prosecuted, told us that it was CPS policy to prosecute shoplifters without considering the possibility of a caution and regardless of likely penalty. Indeed, she considered that penalty was a matter for judge and jury to consider not for prosecutors, despite the CPS Code of Practice. Another prosecutor confirmed that CPS did not normally caution adults unless there was something unusual about a case (*CE-A094*). These statements and policies were reinforced time and time again, as by the prosecutor in *AH-A113* who told us that he avoided discontinuances because he was part of a prosecution service. (In cases *CC-A102*, *CE-A094* and *AH-A113* the DPP decided that we could not quote the prosecutors directly.)

The failure to consider the likely penalty in *CC-A102*, despite para 8 of the Code, was commonplace. Not only was that particular defendant given a conditional discharge, but out of 288 sentenced adults (where sentence was known) there were 31 absolute or conditional discharges (10.8 per cent of the total). Some 18 of these 31 were judged by us to be cautionable. Of the 92 sentenced juveniles there were 16 discharges and 28 had no previous convictions (although eight of these had been previously cautioned). There is no reason to believe that these patterns, and the issues that underlie them, are attributable to our research being done in the early days of the CPS or that they are a product of personnel shortages.

Clearly large numbers of prosecuted cases could be discontinued on 'public interest' grounds. The CPS is either unaware of or uninterested in this. This structural problem of the CPS, which the VERA scheme set out to investigate and surmount, has been pursued at length elsewhere regarding prosecutions pre-CPS (Sanders, 1988b). Clearly it persists despite the CPS which, given the structural position of the CPS, is only to be expected.

Plea bargaining

It has been frequently observed that Britain and the USA have guilty plea systems. Adversarial values are replaced by inquisitorial values, and 'Due Process' is on display only in the occasional 'show trial' in the Crown Court (McConville and Baldwin, 1981, p. 7; McBarnet, 1981). This is effected in part through 'deals', which are a structural feature of criminal justice (Hobbs, 1988). Much police behaviour is predicated on deals – including plea bargaining – as is pre-trial prosecutorial work (Baldwin, 1985), right up to the point of trial (Baldwin and McConville, 1977; Moody and Tombs, 1982). In areas like drugs, deals are commonplace. One officer told us that deals were 'always considered' when deciding whether to caution for drug possession if, for instance, the suspects are 'prepared to give evidence about where they bought it from' (*CE-A003*). But it happens in all types of crime, from deception (Sanders and Bridges, 1990) to handling (Sanders, 1985a).

Deals include what an officer in charge described as 'adjusting charges' (*CE-A002*). This means that a lot of plea bargaining is done by the police and presented to the CPS as a *fait accompli*. At other times it involves 'over-charging' and 'top-charging'. Police and CPS are usually happy to drop a level or two, for this is all part of the 'game'. As one officer said, when asked why section 18 wounding with intent was always charged when section 20 unlawful wounding was the usual result, 'Haven't you heard of plea bargaining?' (Sanders, 1988a).

The CPS does not attempt to get behind police accounts or to provide alternatives to them. In so far as prosecutors are aware of the police deals that lie behind specific cases, they do not question them. Plea bargains usually involve CPS acceptance of police construction, rather than the CPS 'seeing through' police accounts. When the CPS gets involved in plea bargaining it is usually not on the basis of their recognition of weakness following independent scrutiny. Rather, it occurs when the defence signals non-acceptance of the case as constructed by the police. As with dropped cases and trial outcomes the eventual product (whether there is a bargain and, if so, of what type) is often a product of what the police do or do not do. It is often the construction failures of the police themselves which create problems for the CPS. Plea bargains cover up these failures:

> *AT-A043* – A043 was charged with possession of drugs with intent to supply (see Chapter 2). He was seen going up to people in the street. The police thought that he was trying to sell drugs, while he said he was trying to buy them; he had on him only fake drugs. The CPS said that 'going equipped to cheat' would have been a better charge: '. . . if the police had got statements from the people who [A043] had approached . . . if they had said that he had approached them and offered to sell them drugs we might have had him on going equipped to cheat.' He eventually pleaded to 'attempted possession'. It was, said the CPS, 'better to get a plea to something'.

This is a common sentiment, echoed by the CPS in *CC-A115*: 'there is a lot of confusion about who did what . . . the merits of the case are served by getting him to plead to what you can prove'. In reality, of course, the many examples in this chapter of bargains made and attempted suggest something rather different: what the CPS seek is not a plea to what they can *prove*, but to what they can bluff or 'arm-twist' defendants into. As Baldwin (1985, pp. 79–81) has also noted, bind overs in exchange for the substantive charge(s) being dropped represent common bargains where the CPS foresees failure at trial and/or considers the case too trivial to be worth fighting. Of the 68 cases dropped in our sample, bind overs were ordered in twenty (29 per cent).

Bargains are often prepared in case of not guilty pleas, but offered only when 'necessary'. Hence in *BW-A083* (theft of light bulb, discussed earlier) the CPS instruction was to accept a bind over 'if not guilty plea', but since A083 pleaded guilty it never arose. Bluff and tactics – rather than Truth, Justice, Guilt or Innocence – are what 'good' prosecution is all about.

The practices and ideologies of defence lawyers

We have argued that the practices of police and CPS fall far short of Due Process ideals and that the way in which cases are constructed undermines the adversarial system. This is because, as McBarnet (1981) persuasively argues, the ambiguities of normal life are rendered one-dimensional by police prosecution practices. The police and courts will not accept the presentation of several competing interpretations, which would allow adversarial processes to flourish. Case construction – in its one-dimensional form – is a Crime Control strategy: the crucial decisions are made at the earliest possible stages, at which around 50 per cent of arrested suspects are ejected from the system without charge, while for the rest conviction is *made* highly probable. Whilst we have argued that police and prosecution control of cases creates these conditions, giving the defence little room for argument, defence lawyers none the less generally contribute to this situation. As this was not a study of defence lawyering, systematic analysis of this dimension is not possible. But brief discussion is essential to provide a rounded picture.

Even where suspects are advised in the station they rarely exercise their right of silence (Sanders *et al.*, 1989). And defendants rarely exercise their right of trial. Why does this section of the poor – the criminally accused – fail to exercise its rights despite having the services of lawyers?

In part, defence lawyers are simply outmanoeuvred, as we have seen, through police and CPS controlling information, charges and procedure. But, as we stated earlier, defence lawyers opt into the Crime Control system. This is because they are *part of*, rather than challengers to, the apparatus of criminal justice. They therefore cannot really subscribe to the Due Process values of silence and the presumption of innocence. They are officers of the court, they often prosecute on an agency basis, they have a common legal training and class culture (Blumberg, 1967; Casper, 1972). As officers of the court they are captured by Crime Control, not Due Process: in a case where access to a lawyer is unlawfully denied, and a confession elicited, even if the confession is inadmissible, the defence lawyer cannot call her client to give evidence rebutting the confession on her own behalf if she told her that the confession was none the less true. In other words, not only do the police and courts benefit from the 'fruit of the poisoned tree', but the defence is bound by it too. Prosecutors and defence lawyers share 'a common code of ethics and have a special allegiance to the court and the demands of justice' (Moody and Tombs, 1982, p. 306).

It is perhaps not surprising that Baldwin and McConville (1977) found that so many defendants perceived themselves to be isolated from their own lawyers, as well as from the other institutions of criminal justice. Material gathered by Baldwin (1985) supports this view, although we shall see that his interpretation is different from ours. He comments that defence lawyers often make concessions to prosecutors even when they need not do so. Defence lawyers often 'agree that it is more important that something be done . . . than that the defendant be encouraged to stand on his rights' (p. 85).

And so we see case after case in this chapter, as well as in Baldwin's (1985) study, of defence lawyers unnecessarily agreeing to bargains. This may seem to them 'fair', but – more importantly – it maintains cordial relationships with other court actors and it helps defence lawyers to gain the trust of the court and of prosecutors. This means that defence lawyers are believed when they make statements of fact and give assurances to the court, which can help clients. Credibility, then, is purchased by the defence lawyers' subscription to Crime Control and the abandonment of all but the shell of adversariness except in the occasional 'show trial'. Thus in their Scottish study Moody and Tombs comment that:

> in the absence of what they call *trust*, trial avoidance arrangements become virtually impossible . . . in return for co-operation the fiscal demands more than the mere communication of information from the defence agent. He expects that the defence will *play fair*. (1982, p. 305, our emphasis)

Pre-trial reviews (PTRs) are important in this context. They can be regarded in three ways: defining the issues, providing a forum for amicable compromise or as a tool of the prosecution to further crime control through pressure and 'deals'. Baldwin (1985) subscribes to the first two views. He observes that criminal solicitors 'are pre-disposed towards a co-operative rather than an antagonistic posture . . . in which settlement of cases on an amicable basis is preferred' (p. 32). He adds that this gives rise to 'deals' and 'arrangements', and that PTRs 'represent a relatively formal acknowledgement and manifestation of (these) unofficial practices' (p. 32). He quotes one defence solicitor as saying 'I'll do some leaning (on D)' (p. 48), and another as saying 'We're going to definitely put pressure on him. Perhaps I shouldn't say that – try to persuade him' (p. 87).

In only two out of Baldwin's 402 cases was the defence solicitor reluctant to disclose 'pertinent details' (and in a further 32 (8 per cent) nothing new was disclosed). Thus in over 90 per cent of PTRs the solicitors co-operated without being legally obliged to do so (p. 44). Baldwin acknowledges in Chapter 1 that defence disclosure is incompatible with the adversarial principles and associated presumption of innocence which supposedly underlie the system. Hence the evidence he presents suggests that PTRs are tools of the prosecution. However, Baldwin resists this conclusion, arguing that the PTR 'represents no affront to basic values enshrined in English criminal procedure' (1985, p. 168). He reaches this conclusion because he 'did not observe a single case in which a bargain could fairly be described as improper' (p. 97). Moreover,

> It did not seem to the present writer that attempts were made to force settlements in cases where there were real doubts or ambiguities in the evidence or where the defence solicitor was clearly not interested in any kind of negotiated settlement. (1985, p. 50)

In such cases, PTRs are simply viewed as short-cuts to inevitable guilty verdicts:

> the prosecutor is concerned to convince the defence solicitor of the accused's factual culpability based on the available evidence and of the futility of contesting the matter. Most defence lawyers, once convinced, are prepared to admit defeat and only exceptionally, it seems, do they [defence lawyers] have difficulty in persuading their clients. (1985, p. 50)

This line of analysis misses two points. The first is that large numbers of defendants *perceive themselves* to have been forced into accepting pleas. The fact that defence lawyers, objectively viewed, may not have to employ great pressure on defendants does not undermine the power of the subjectively experienced pressure highlighted in earlier research (Baldwin and McConville, 1977). Second, the apparent absence of doubt or ambiguity and the willingness of defence lawyers to 'lean on' defendants may have been less a product of overwhelming evidence and more a result of uncritical acceptance of the prosecution case by defence lawyers. Research on other aspects of criminal lawyering does suggest that defence lawyers judge their clients' cases in the light of the police case, which entails some pre-judgment (Sanders, *et al.*, 1989, ch. 7). Both points are illustrated by this case:

> *BW-A088* – A088 was charged with criminal damage. His own solicitor and the duty solicitor tried to persuade him to plead guilty. The clerk said that his solicitors had 'washed their hands of him'. Eventually he entered a guilty plea.
> Bench: 'Is this just to get it over with?'
> A088:   'Yes, I've wasted too much time from work.'
> Bench: 'Well it's unfair on us. You must plead not guilty if you are in doubt.'
> The CP then asked the Bench to accept the guilty plea as the duty solicitor 'had the file and so had advised the defendant with the full facts'.

However, A088 did then plead not guilty and, unrepresented, secured an acquittal.

This case must have seemed, before trial, as having no 'real doubts or ambiguities', but that is only because lawyers on both sides shared the same ideology. This enables PTRs (and prosecutor–defender discussions generally) to function as tools of the prosecution whilst at the same time being generally amicable. In a PTR we saw, the defence lawyer said that there would be a 'probable' plea to handling.

CPS: '... what do you mean "you can't guarantee it"?'
Defence: 'Well normally I can guarantee it mostly, but I don't know this character.'
Clerk: 'I think this is a case of taking this person in a corner and banging his head against the wall.' (*much laughter all round*)
Defence: 'Yes, that's right.'

Baldwin himself says that 'Advice to plead guilty was referred to by solicitors in various ways – from "leaning" on a defendant and "talking sense into him" to "beating him over the head"' (1985, p. 86). In one case cited by Baldwin, the prosecutor said that, although he wanted the defendant bound over, he would drop the case anyway. He told the defence lawyer: 'You can tell [the defendant] that, obviously, but I leave it to you as to the way you do it.' D did accept a bind over despite his lawyer knowing that he need not do so (1985, Case 129, p. 81).

In this case, as in many others observed by both Baldwin and ourselves, the defence lawyer abdicated her responsibilities to her client in the interests of amicable settlement. In the light of such evidence, it is difficult to see why routinized collaboration with the prosecution could not, as Baldwin asserts, 'fairly be described as improper' or as an 'affront to basic values'.

Outcomes are thus often contingent upon considerations other than the weight of evidence (McConville and Baldwin, 1981; Moody and Tombs, 1982, p. 306). The police play a major part in the creation of cases, but their power is not monolithic and constructions are often weak. Those weaknesses rarely emerge in court because neither prosecutors nor defence lawyers subject cases to close scrutiny in either private or public forum.

CONCLUSION

Lost cases, whether dropped or following trial, rarely represent victories of legal skill by defence over prosecution. Nor do dropped cases necessarily represent gracious withdrawals by the CPS. McConville and

Baldwin's observation that 'thin cases are needlessly protracted' (1981, p. 93) is, at one level, as true now as it was in the mid-70s when their research was done. Our interpretation of this now, though, is that by protracting prosecution the CPS secures more guilty pleas or other desired outcomes and generally discourages the fighting of cases by the defence.

It is also important to note that none of the (few) jury verdicts were ever described to us as 'perverse' by police officers or prosecutors. There were, to our knowledge, no ambush defences at all – despite this spectre haunting the current debate on the right of silence. From the adversarial point of view this might be surprising, but the ideology and practice of the legal aid defence lawyer are simply not compatible with 'ambush'.

We are not, of course, claiming that acquittals were always predictable or 'correct'. Many verdicts, even when judge-directed, were impossible to predict. Indeed, most contests, and many non-contested cases, represent intrinsically ambiguous situations or situations in which the 'facts' were simply incomplete in vital ways. These were cases which the police may have been able to clarify but did not, cases in which clarification was not possible or potentially strong cases which – because of their relative or absolute triviality – the police and/or CPS could not be bothered to fight over. All these considerations apply equally to plea bargains as to contests, and indeed to many straightforward guilty pleas: cases which the CPS would have been prepared to concede in whole or part if only they had been pushed by the defence. The idea that the pattern of acquittals and convictions reflects either real situations 'out there' or the product of the obstacle course of Due Process just does not stand up to scrutiny.

The battle, then, which produces acquittals and convictions is rarely fought in court – even in contested cases. Where there is doubt about the evidence, that is usually apparent long before the court case. The issues are largely settled in the police station and through any other investigation which the police might carry out. This is all contrary to the rhetoric of our adversarial Due Process system, where openness and judicial decision making are proclaimed as hallmarks of the Rule of Law.

One important implication of this which is often overlooked is that most people internalize this rhetoric. Even experienced defendants believe that the important forum in which their future will be decided is the court (Baldwin and McConville, 1977; Bottoms and McClean, 1976; Sanders *et al.*, 1989). Only a minority of suspects (even of those charged with criminal offences) seek advice in police stations. Yet most defendants in court have lawyers: both lawyers and suspects believe that this is the more important stage in the process at which to have a lawyer. Sanders *et al.* (1989) found that lawyers were sought largely to get out of custody, rather than to engage in the case *per se*, and the reluctance of lawyers to attend police stations shows that lawyers perpetuate this belief in the greater relevance of court. Very often, lawyers would tell their clients that they 'would see them in court' as if this was all that counted. One suspect, who did ask for a lawyer but never saw one in the station, said that not seeing a lawyer did not matter as 'nothing happened'. What actually did happen was that he had confessed under interrogation and had been charged. The die was cast. But he did not realize that, and neither defence lawyer nor police officer was going to disabuse him.

The rhetoric of Due Process means that suspects and lawyers do not fight as hard as they could when the cases are being initially constructed in the station, when it matters most. The reality of Crime Control (in which, whatever their public postures to the contrary, police and Crown prosecutors join hands) means that courts do little more than endorse constructions according to the quality of workmanship, the combativeness of the defence lawyer and the hand of Fate.

9 Understanding the criminal justice process

The preceding chapters have shown how prosecution cases develop from often vague suspicions to carefully constructed edifices. We have shown how rules and laws assist the police in this task as much as they constrain them or protect the suspect. This is not consistent with the liberal rhetoric by which the criminal justice process is usually characterized. Indeed, the Home Secretary is at this moment considering an erosion of the suspect's right of silence precisely because the criminal justice process is now judged to have shifted 'the balance' in favour of suspects (Home Office, 1989b). The object of this chapter is to assess this alleged disjunction between rhetoric and reality, and to ask what does constrain the police if the law does not do so.

LEGAL RHETORIC AND LEGAL REALITY

Our account of the realities of policing and prosecution should not be surprising for anyone familiar with research on criminal justice. Much of the literature relating to the day to day practices of policing (and, indeed, to the practices of other official actors in the criminal justice process) has been a dialogue with the law. Critics of police behaviour have judged the police either on the basis of their failure to comply with some unstated idealized set of rules or have assumed that police action is in violation of existing legal norms. Interactionist writers, for example, see legal rules as functional only in terms of *justifying* and not as *guiding* police work: rules, in this tradition, are simply presentational devices, actual police work being informed instead by a highly specific police subculture (Manning, 1977; Holdaway, 1979; Punch, 1979).

Now, as Feeley (1976) and McBarnet (1981) have pointed out, these writers have generally assumed that the law incorporates the 'rights' which are said to be violated by the police. McBarnet put the point in this way:

> The assumption has been in effect that the law incorporates rights for the accused, and the problem has been simply to ask why and how the police and courts subvert, negate or abuse them. . . . In conventional sociological studies of criminal justice . . . 'law' stands merely as a supposed standard from which the enforcers of law routinely deviate; legal procedures are simply *assumed* to incorporate civil rights. The 'law in action' is scrutinised but what the 'law in books' actually says is simply taken as read; it remains unproblematic and unexplored. (McBarnet, 1981, pp. 4–5; original emphasis)

If this analysis is accepted, two broad points worthy of discussion emerge: the importance of understanding the law and the unimportance of focusing attention upon the system's low-level officials such as the police. A third issue concerns the nature of legal rhetoric. We shall explore each of these points in turn.

The role of law

It is understandable that researchers, confronted by behaviour of officials which appears to go contrary to the law, should use as the framework of analysis the failure of 'law in action' to come up to the requirements of 'law in the books'. Writers such as Skolnick (1966, 1967), Blumberg (1967) and Cole (1970) described worlds in which the legal order appeared to have been subverted by personal, group or institutional norms of behaviour. As Skolnick wrote, the purpose of his study was 'not to reveal that the police violate rules and regulations – that much is assumed' (1966, p. 22). Similarly, those operating from the interactionist perspective assume that formal legal rules do not condition or determine behaviour but only constrain how official actors account for their behaviour (Feeley, 1973; Carlen, 1976; Manning, 1977; Chatterton, 1979; Fielding, 1984). Properly analysed, McBarnet (1981) argued, it would be found that the action criticized offended only the rhetoric of the law, not the letter of the law itself. To assume 'subversion' by petty administrators, therefore, has the effect of whitewashing the law itself and those who make it. In any discussion of the law in action it follows that deviance cannot be taken for granted, and it is necessary to interrogate the law itself.

When the law is interrogated, it will be found, as McBarnet argued, that a great deal of police practice is perfectly lawful and offends Due Process values alone. The law accords the police extensive discretion and is essentially enabling (Brodeur, 1981). It acts as a powerful resource for the police, covering much of their behaviour (however motivated) with a legal canopy. Individual laws are often open-textured in nature, providing the police with considerable latitude of action; and so many laws are available to cover particular situations that the police can always choose some law which fits their purpose. When subjected to critical scrutiny, police behaviour which offends the sensibilities of civil libertarians or which seems at variance with notions of democratic principles of justice turns out to be perfectly within the law.

Whilst this analysis has much truth in it, it is important that we should not discard the notion of police *illegality*. Although it is true that much police action is legal and that the law provides legitimacy to police behaviour that is either deviant or conducive to deviance (Brodeur, 1981), much of what they do is understood by the police themselves as illegal and some of what they do does contravene legal precepts. This remains true even though most police illegality is insulated from scrutiny and remains unsanctioned.

On the other hand, police behaviour will generally be lawful where they are able to achieve their goals through use of the law, where law assists them in achieving their objectives. The resort to illegal practice by the police should not, therefore, obscure the essentially coercive nature of *legal* powers. Most of what the police wish to achieve is realizable through use of laws relating to stop and search, arrest, detention, restrictions on access to a solicitor and the like. The use of such powers singly and in combination endows the police with an impressive arsenal of weapons to deploy against anyone who attracts their suspicion.

Where, however, the law is considered to be an obstacle to their work, it may be set aside if the goals in question are the dominant or predominant consideration. This will happen, for example, where they are determined to 'get' a particular suspect and, having failed to acquire evidence through use of the law, decide that they should create such evidence through a 'verbal'. The police will 'bend' the law on access to a solicitor; only if this does not work *and* if the police are sufficiently concerned will they then break the law (Sanders and Bridges, 1990). Concentrating on the elasticity of the law should not blind us to the fact that malleability is finite.

Petty officials of the system

McBarnet also argued, in directing commentators back to the law, that less attention should be paid to the petty administrators and their alleged blameworthiness, and more to the judicial and political elites who make the law. In McBarnet's words:

Front-men like the police become the 'fall guys' of the legal system taking the blame for any injustices in the operation of the law, both in theory (on the assumption . . . that they break the rules) and indeed, in the law. The law holds the individual policeman personally responsible for contraventions of legality that are successfully sued, while at the same time refusing to make clear until after the event exactly what the police are supposed to do. (McBarnet, 1981, p. 156)

Whilst it is necessary to interrogate the law, however, it is equally important to evaluate the activities and ideologies of the police.

First, to state that the law is *permissive* of police action supplies the reason to focus attention upon the police rather than giving a reason for diverting attention away from the police. If the law is structured, as it often is, to accord the police freedom to act, police decisions to act outside the rhetoric are a proper subject of enquiry. Indeed, it is precisely because the law is problematic that the explanation for police behaviour must be found outside the analysis of the law itself. While the law tells us what the police *can* do, it does not tell us what the police *do* do. Although this does not exempt the law and its controllers from scrutiny, the police also cannot be exonerated from responsibility.

Second, McBarnet's analysis is based upon the false assumption that the police are consciously utilizing or exploiting the tolerance provided by the law. But much police action is autonomous and not driven by or accountable to the law. And so, in Chapter 6, we saw that the majority of police charge and caution decisions are made *without regard to* the supposedly applicable guidelines. Moreover, even if the police do sometimes use the law as a resource, it is also the case that the police do see important aspects of their activity as involving subversion of the law. This is well established not only in relation to rank and file officers (Reiner, 1978), but has been publicly admitted by senior police officers (Mark, 1978; McNee, 1983). Indeed, in evidence to the Royal Commission on Criminal Procedure, Sir David McNee (then Commissioner of the Metropolitan Police) sought to justify claims for extended police powers on the basis that:

> many police officers have, early in their careers, learned to use methods bordering on trickery or stealth in their investigations because they were deprived of proper powers by the legislature. They have risked civil actions frequently when doing so. . . . One fears that sometimes so-called pious perjury of this nature from junior officers can lead to even more serious perjury on other matters later in their careers. (McNee, 1978, p. 2)

If the police themselves accept that their actions are illegal, why should we not believe them? This does not mean that police action need be routinely illegal or that it be overtly practised: police officers are well-known adherents of the 'cover your back' philosophy and seek to hide their illegal activities from superior officers (unless they can be trusted or are parties to the acts in question) and from researchers (Van Maanen, 1974). Nevertheless, officers routinely admitted to us that, in police euphemism, they 'bent' the rules, 'gilded the lily' or acted unlawfully in a variety of situations. The police cannot be exonerated from critical scrutiny if they knowingly engage in unlawful behaviour.

Third, even if much police action is *lawful*, with the police using the letter of the law to the full, to exempt the police from responsibility misses the point that the law is very much another *police product*. Throughout this century and over the past 20 years in particular, the police have politicized law reform, actively campaigning for laws which will assist in the 'fight against crime' (Reiner, 1980; Kettle, 1980; Taylor, 1980). A persuasive case has been made out which locates the PACE Act itself less in the Report of the Royal Commission on Criminal Procedure (1981) and more in 'the highly assertive evidence presented to the Royal Commission by various police spokesmen and pressure groups' (Bridges and Bunyan, 1983, p. 86).

Apart from political campaigns, 'law reform' is also very much a product of police operational practices. The police are not inhibited by the prospect that their action *might* be unlawful (Gilroy and Sim, 1987); on the contrary, this often stimulates the police first to act and *then* to seek legal validation for what they have done. The police are constantly striving to push out and extend the boundaries of 'legal' behaviour and they do this by their practice. They were not dissuaded from interrogating individuals by occasional judicial rebukes but continued custodial interrogations until these were legitimated by the judges (Judges' Rules, 1912). Police officers prepared their evidence together instead of separately from each other, and continued to testify in courts that their evidence *was* independently prepared until they had a special rule created for them by judicial fiat which legalized their formerly unlawful practices (*Bass*, [1953] 1 Q.B. 680). They did not stop searching people's houses illegally, until they were given judicial sanction (*Ghani v. Jones* [1970] 1 Q.B. 693) and Parliamentary approval (PACE Act, ss.8–22). The same is true of detention purely for the purpose of imposing interrogation conditions likely to secure a confession (*Holgate-Mohammed v. Duke*, 1984; PACE, s.37).

Legal 'reform' is very often nothing more than the legitimation of police practice. Moreover, this has frequently taken place on the basis that, to do otherwise, would result in the continuation of illegal police behaviour: police collaboration in writing up notebooks was created as a special exception to the general rule of evidence that witnesses must act independently because, the judges said, the police would otherwise continue to collaborate and then give perjured testimony denying this; and police were given search powers of a wide nature because the judges acknowledged that the police had assumed these anyway and were likely to continue illegal practices. McBarnet's contention that the focus of interest should be shifted to the 'judicial and political elites' who make the law and away from the police rests then upon a false polarity.

The nature of legal rhetoric

If much police behaviour can be made to fit within legal rules (whatever the precise motivations and understandings of police officers themselves), the question is raised whether the observed social reality of policing offends against the democratic ideology of criminal justice. The answer McBarnet gives is that these practices offend against the rhetoric of the law because the law does not incorporate its own rhetoric:

> A wide range of prosecution evidence can be legally produced and presented, despite the rhetoric of a system geared overwhelmingly to safeguards for the accused, precisely because legal structure, legal procedure, legal rulings, *not* legal rhetoric, govern the legitimate practice of criminal justice, and there is quite simply a distinct gap between the substance and the ideology of the law. (McBarnet, 1981, p. 155; original emphasis)

This analysis sees the rhetoric of the law as unproblematic, but just as it is necessary to problematize the law so it is necessary to interrogate the rhetoric.

For McBarnet, the rhetoric of justice is external to the law and its content is essentially 'Due Process' or civil libertarian. As to the first, Nelken (1987) put the criticism in these terms:

> The view that 'rhetoric' lies *outside* the law rests on an unexamined positivist separation between the rules of law and the broader principles which animate it and ignores the argument . . . that 'rhetoric' serves as the source of principles which can generate or limit legal rule-making even though it does not and cannot function in the same way as rules. (Nelken, 1987, p. 151; original emphasis)

This brings us into the *politics* of criminal justice, the rules and principles which *ought* to infuse the law, fix its purpose and control its interpretations. For McBarnet the underlying rhetoric of the law is clear and identifiable: incriminating evidence is the basis for search and arrest; no individual need supply evidence to incriminate themselves; people should be treated equally; each case should be judged on its own facts; the burden of proof is on the prosecutor; and individuals have the right to trial by their peers (McBarnet, 1981, pp. 154–5).

But why should this be taken for granted? After all, there is a strong, well-established rhetoric which sees the world in a different light: that the police should be able to intervene at the earliest point in order to avert social damage without having to wait for evidence to appear; that early intervention, including arresting citizens, should not be conditional upon the existence of admissible evidence but may be founded wholly on unsubstantiated suspicion; that silence is the first resort of the guilty; that different people should be treated differently on the basis of social danger, their known propensity to commit crimes, their responsiveness to social control mechanisms, etc; that suspects should be required to establish facts over which they have exclusive control; that juries are inefficient institutions which inadequately discriminate between the innocent and the guilty. These illustrations confirm the appropriateness of the observation that within the ideology of legality can be seen 'a process of extracting from the law any elements that can justify a widening of its reach' (Brodeur, 1981). In other words, the rhetoric of the law is also *for* Crime Control.

Whether it is seen as a *source* of law or whether it is seen as a set of principles which is used to interpret the law or inform practice, rhetoric is problematic. Our challenge is to McBarnet's unargued assumption that legal rhetoric does not form part of the law itself. For if legal rhetoric is viewed as the expression of legal principles, Dworkin's insights (1977) teach us that where rules are vague, absent or in conflict, legal principles (i.e. legal rhetoric) can operate instead. And legal principles can conflict. Thus, whilst McBarnet assumes that the fundamental principles of criminal justice constitute, or derive from, Due Process ideology, it is more plausible to see fundamental principles as constituting, or deriving from, *both* Due Process and Crime Control ideologies.

The 'right of silence' is part of Due Process rhetoric, and can be regarded in this analysis as both a legal principle and the source of particular legal rules (s.76 of PACE, for instance, provides that confessions obtained through 'oppression' are inadmissible). But the rights of the police to ask questions (Code of Practice C, Note 1B), and continue detention without charge for up to 24 hours no matter how often a suspect asserts a 'right of silence', are equally valid rules deriving from the Crime Control principle that the police should be allowed to act on their 'reasonable suspicion'.

Principles of Crime Control underlie numerous important common law and statutory provisions. S.24 of PACE is another example. It provides that arrest may be made on the basis of reasonable suspicion *or* the fact of an arrestable offence. This means that arrests not made on the basis of reasonable suspicion can be legitimized by the fact of crime. Similarly, exclusion of evidence is usually discretionary (the mandatory exclusion under s.76 of PACE being applicable in only restricted circumstance), and evidence secured as a result of illegal police behaviour may be admitted in evidence notwithstanding the unlawful way it was obtained (PACE, s.76(4)). These are all classic Crime Control provisions. And it is worth pointing out that the principle so central to liberal legalism – that penal statutes should be strictly construed and any ambiguity resolved in favour of the individual citizen – has *never* been an organizing feature of criminal justice jurisprudence in the courts.

If the rhetoric expresses the law, and the rhetoric contains contradictions, it is hardly surprising that detailed legal rules also contain contradictions and that a wide variety of police practices are permitted by the law. A little-noticed consequence of this was the remarkable terms of reference of the Royal Commission on Criminal Procedure, requiring 'a balance to be struck here between the interest of the whole community and the rights and liberties of the individual citizen' (*Report*, p. 4). The idea that the interests of the community are antithetical to rights and liberties of individual citizens is a Crime Control view, inconsistent with Due Process principles. McBarnet argues that 'due process is *for* crime control' (1981, p. 156) because she can only reconcile Due Process rhetoric with Crime Control rules by arguing that the former camouflages the latter. We would argue that one does not exist for the other; rather both form part of the fabric of law in all its manifestations – principles, rules and practice.

The vision of an unsullied Due Process ideal expressed in legal rhetoric is essentially idealist. Ideology is a product of material conditions. Historically, Due Process has never been the dominant principle of English criminal justice. Thompson (1975) argues that Due Process ideals were created by the bourgeoisie for themselves in their struggle against the divine right ideology of the Stuarts. The law was called in as a shield to protect the ascendant ruling class, and it had to apply to all if it was to succeed in its ideological mission. But the triumph of 'law' over 'state' was never complete, and so Due Process has always co-existed uneasily with Crime Control. If we are now in an era of retreat for Due Process (see e.g. Harman and Griffith, 1979) this may be connected to the massive post-war extension to suspects and defendants of legal advice and representation – to the actual utilization, in other words, of Due Process.

The connection with our previous argument, that much police behaviour is lawful only because much law is a police product, should now be clear: the endorsement of police Crime Control behaviour by law makers is part of the retreat in recent years of Due Process. The letter of the law had no need of change in earlier years when few suspects and defendants sought its protection or challenged police practices.

CONSTRUCTIONS IN CONTEXT

What then of the rhetoric, principles, rules and practices which structure case construction? The policing criteria – that is, the informal rules – which create the official suspect population, govern detention and interrogation, and grade and sift that population are derived from Crime Control principles. Most police practices involved here are lawful because those principles are lawful. There are Due Process rules too – relating to reasonable suspicion, admissions as pre-conditions for cautions and so forth – but they are largely irrelevant not just because they get in the way of Crime Control, but also because they are frequently contradicted by other legal rules. At these points of the process the police are engaged in an inquisitorial task – an attempt to secure 'facts' and identify offenders. Inquisitorial procedures are antithetical to the obstacle course of Due Process, so it is hardly surprising if both law and practice favour the former rather than the latter.

In constructing cases to fit the decisions the police wish to make, the police adopt an adversarial role. Their job is to build the strongest possible case against the defendant. Naturally they do not choose to help defendants, by drawing out their legal defences or emotional problems for instance, but they are not required to by any law or set of guidelines. The guidelines require the 'public interest' to be taken into account only *in so far as it is known*. Again, the absence of a complete fit between these two positions is not surprising once the existence of competing principles is recognized.

This is best exemplified when we consider juvenile bureaux and the CPS. The idea that a Crown *Prosecution* Service could act out a neutral 'Minister of Justice' role in an adversarial system is as incoherent in theory as it is impractical (Sanders, 1987). The 'Minister of Justice' principles are there in the Code, but adversarial principles – which are equally legitimate – are also present. The conflict is inescapable when a defendant against whom there is little or no evidence wishes to plead guilty. The conflict is resolved in a predictable way: the CPS allows the guilty plea to go ahead. The contradictions are even more apparent with juvenile liaison bureaux. Whilst these have traditionally been considered sites for the ideological struggle between 'justice' and 'welfare' principles (Clarke, 1985), the bureaux have developed a corporatist methodology which is replacing both (Pratt, 1986, 1989).

To leave this analysis at the level of competing principles would be as idealist as McBarnet's idealization of legal rhetoric. In reality, different principles rise and fall as a result of power. The preceding chapters have demonstrated the power of the police over all other competing institutions and persons – in itself a manifestation of Crime Control ideology, which is a product of capitalism's requirement of a strong state. This power is at its height in setting the terms of the charge and in creating the information relevant to that charge. How can the CPS act 'fairly' when the only information which forms the basis of its actions comes from the police? The same is true of juvenile bureaux. And defence lawyers are in thrall to the police and CPS in other ways.

When we argue that the case for the prosecution is a construction we are making the following statement. The case is a product of a) low-level officers operating under conditions of low visibility, enforcing b) particular socio-economic and political policies, through c) socially (rather than legally) constructed criteria which incorporate and produce structural bias, within d) a permissive institutional and legal framework riddled with contradictions, in which e) rule breaking is sanctioned in a graded manner, allowing a large amount of rule breaking when the law is insufficiently permissive to the police.

All the components of this framework have been discussed in this chapter with the exception of e). It is to sanctions and constraints that we now turn.

WHAT CONSTRAINS THE POLICE?

We have seen that police behaviour cannot be understood simply in terms of the law, but it operates, as a general rule, within certain bounds of tolerance. These boundaries are defined by the combination of a variety of social constraints (which may be weak or strong) that are accepted as valid by the police. These social constraints are not fixed and immutable but operate to define a general framework for understanding the *regularities* of police practice. The constraints operating upon the police may be identified in terms of (i) legal constraints; (ii) self-preservation; (iii) practicability; and (iv) moral constraints.

Legal constraints

As a general rule, conformity with the detailed substantive and procedural rules is *not* an important consideration for police officers in respect of most of their powers. Thus, powers of stop-and-search do not standardly inform police decision making but rather rationalize behaviour undertaken for other reasons. Detectives and uniformed officers openly admitted, for example, to stopping people in the street and searching them in forces where they had no general power to do so before PACE, relying instead upon bluff, 'consent' or the 'Ways and Means Act'. Even with the powers of PACE available, officers conceded that any 'suspicion' utilized was often generalized rather than individual. The fact that wholesale, random stops are not carried out all the time is thus not a function of the constraints of legality (even if officers know that these constraints are weak and non-specific) but of police motivational rules, such as the need to secure (grudging) acceptance of their presence in certain localities, and the need to dominate the citizen encounter.

Similarly, the legal conditions necessary to ground a lawful arrest do not inhibit officers from employing arrest in circumstances where they know that those conditions are absent, as the following case illustrates:

CC-A048 – X went into a shop and examined the goods on display, at one point approaching A048, a fellow customer, and briefly asking his advice about an item that both were interested in. Later X selected an item and presented a credit card for payment. The shop assistant telephoned the credit card company and discovered that the card in question was stolen. When the shop assistant re-appeared, X ran off. Meanwhile, A048 was still browsing in the shop and took no interest in the departure of X. The police were called and the officer arrested A048. The arresting officer explained to us that 'it was a situation where unfortunately just by his presence there' he had come to be arrested. On interview with the officer in charge of the case, the following exchange took place:

Res: 'So looking at the arrest itself, do you think that the arrest was a proper arrest?'
Officer: 'I don't think he should have been arrested. Personally I wouldn't have arrested him.'
Res: 'Why do you think they did arrest him?'
Officer: 'Because I think it was from the [shop] assistants. They believed they [X and A048] were related, that they were both together, doing the same sort of thing.'
Res: 'So they put two and two together did they?'
Officer: 'And got six.'

Although, therefore, legal rules do not necessarily constrain officers from acting at all, especially in respect of low-visibility behaviour (stop-searches, arrests and interrogation practices), legality may place limits upon the extent to which illegal action *continues* and upon the extent to which it can exercise permanent influence upon the shape of the case. Thus, an arrest may be made purely on the basis that the arrestee is 'known to the police' but without any evidence connecting the arrestee to the offence and without any reasonable suspicion. If the arrestee is guilty and confesses and/or pleads guilty, no-one is likely to mount a plausible challenge to the arrest which may then take on the guise of a lawful arrest. If, however, no confession is forthcoming, and no other evidence implicating the arrestee discovered, the constraints of legality may (subject to what is said below) operate to prevent the case going to court or, where there is a charge, cause the abandonment of the prosecution in court.

Legality is not, however, a strong constraint on police behaviour. Indeed in some cases legality is not a constraint at all, and the reason action is being taken or pursued in a particular form is to cover police *illegality*. Thus, as we have seen, a case may be continued to 'support the Bobby' precisely because abandoning the case might be seen as an acknowledgement that illegal behaviour had occurred, thus exposing the officer to the threat of legal action.

Self-preservation

Although the law may be seen as a resource for the police, it is often forgotten that it also provides a disciplinary framework. An officer may, in all sorts of ways, 'fall foul of the law' or (and this is seen as equivalent by the police) incur the displeasure of senior officers. Self-preservation, therefore, is a central concern of the police (Manning, 1977). It is important to note that this point is *strengthened* not weakened by the observation we have already made that the practice of policing is very often ahead of the law. The very fact that practice is in advance of the law sets up contradictions, uncertainties and doubt in the minds of the police. It acts to undermine their confidence in the legitimacy, moral as well as legal, of their own behaviour. Indeed, it is the very *enabling* structure of the law which can centrally constrain the police. If laws are so organized that police action offensive to the idealised version of liberal legal rhetoric *may* none the less be perfectly legitimate, it also follows that to the officer such action may also be (and retrospectively be held to be) *illegal*. The 'liberating' structure of the law thus operates in some respects as an organizational constraint.

The need for the police to 'cover' themselves thus infuses their everyday world. 'Covering' involves behaviour which is understood to be illegitimate as well as behaviour which is felt to be probably or possibly legitimate. Whilst, therefore, self-preservation includes situations in which the police will interpret the law conservatively, sticking to what they are sure is within the law and avoiding action whose legality is dubious, it is not confined to cautionary and licit behaviour. On the contrary, it includes behaviour (such as 'verballing', the suppression of evidence, altering official records and the use of unnecessary physical force) which is understood by the police as illegal. This is done in order to obscure the true character of their behaviour and to present that behaviour as unambiguously lawful or the evidence as unambiguously strong. The following case illustrates the point:

> CE-A015 – The arresting officer complained to us of the burdensome requirement of creating contemporaneous notes of an interview and said that it was possible to get around this to some extent by talking to the arrestee off-the-record. There were, however, limits:
> 'You've got to be careful because you've got to cover all your [time]. It's no use losing your job for perjury for some toe-rag who's been arrested for some poxy job just to get him convicted. It's just not worth it.'

Although constraints of this kind are related to legal considerations, legality is not the constraining rule. The constraining rule here is self-preservation: behaviour is governed by the extent to which the officer can 'get away with it' and the extent to which it is 'worth' taking the risk. A major element of this is the probability, if a particular rule is broken, of detection and/or significant punishment.

Practicability

Although the success of any attempted case construction may be wholly within the hands of the police officer concerned (in which case, the constraints are few) it very often involves others, whether superior officers, prosecution lawyers, defence lawyers or courts. Especially in the latter event, police behaviour is constrained by the extent to which supporting evidence can be produced and by their success in convincing others to support police action. A failure to gather evidence or elicit support may result in outright failure or displacement of the initial account by a new construction. A clear example is where the police believe that an offence has been committed by the individual, but fail upon investigation to establish any crime:

> BK-A059 – The defendant was seen walking along a country road at 2.30 a.m. carrying a beer glass. He was arrested because, as the officer explained to us, 'you're quite justified in thinking he's walked out of the pub with it; he's stolen it'. On arrest, the defendant said that he had permission to take the glass. At the police station, the licensee was contacted by telephone and he confirmed the defendant's story. In the absence of a complaint, therefore, no further case could be constructed and the defendant was refused charge.

It is necessary to deal here with a *claimed* constraint upon the police. The police claim that in certain inner-city areas, their behaviour is constrained by their estimate of community tolerance for police action. This is usually expressed in relation to (though not confined to) areas with heavy concentrations of ethnic minorities. In some areas we found that officers claimed to have their freedom to act compromised by instructions from their superiors to avoid patrolling certain areas, to avoid 'hostile' acts such as stop-searches and arrests and, generally, to 'cool it', especially when tensions were high. These claims are illustrated in the following case:

CE-A065
Res: 'What about things like stop and search on the street, do you
           ever use those powers?'
Officer: 'Difficult in our area because we've got the ethnic minority area
           and of course tensions are very high. Most of the people you
           want to stop and search are West Indians which has always
           been difficult and I wouldn't say we tend to shy away, but you
           don't do it unless its absolutely necessary.'

Although this claim is projected heavily by the police, it must be recognized as part of the police effort to legitimate themselves. As the Institute of Race Relations point out in *Policing Against Black People* (1987), stories about the police going 'soft' on black areas because of community resistance often appear 'in advance of, or directly following, large-scale police raids against black community institutions and meeting places. In effect, they seek to justify such operations and support police demands for additional powers and resources' (p. 53). Community resistance does not, therefore, prevent heavy policing nor does it prevent police raids. Instead, it only affects police *tactics* – saturation policing, dawn raids, going in 'mob-handed' – all of which are, in turn, justified by singling out the black community for special treatment. In other words, it is not that black criminality justifies the use of such tactics; rather, such tactics are justified by the prior stigmatization of the community as criminogenic. Practicability (the ability to do the job) is, therefore, used in this context not to abandon 'normal' policing but to impose coercive policing upon the black community.

Moral constraints

A final general constraint upon their behaviour is a self-imposed moral constraint. Many police officers have a sense of fairness, justice and equity which pervades their everyday actions. This sense may not accord with the moral sense of others (including that of some other police officers) and may not correspond with legal notions of fairness, but it infuses their routine decision making. This does not, of course, mean that rule bending and rule violation are not condoned by police officers; but it does mean that such 'deviance', subject to limits, is purposive and organized around a moral code of rectitude. Our research, which is littered with examples of this in terms, for example, of administering cautions where charging seemed inevitable, of charging at a level below that which the alleged facts would sustain and of building-in mitigation to the prosecution case, reinforces a long line of studies of police culture (Manning, 1977; Klockars, 1980; Baldwin and Kinsey, 1982; Chatterton 1983; Graeff, 1989).

Although this internal police culture may be largely congruent with sentiments held by people in wider society, internal police moral codes are intimately connected with the police world-view of society and the threats to it. It is not, therefore, a strong constraint in situations where the police confront individuals or groups who rank low in their esteem. Police moral codes act as restraints, therefore, only where police sentiments are not affected by the nature of the suspect or the nature of the crime.

In the police world-view, most if not all of the suspects they deal with are criminals who are likely to hide behind the right to silence, suborn witnesses and meddle with juries, supported by solicitors who assist in the production of false alibis or conjure up off the peg defences. Thus, a senior police officer:

> A very small proportion of both counsel and solicitors are [sic] grossly insulting to police witnesses. Why, goodness knows. A charitable view is that possibly because of their unworldliness, when listening to deceitful men instructing them, they are duped by the lies they hear about you.... With an even smaller proportion of lawyers, the reason is even more sinister – they are as dishonest as the profit-motivated criminals they defend and justify. The motives of this tiny proportion are plain enough – they abuse you because they think it good tactics in the frustrating of justice and the making of money. (Powis, 1977, p. 167)

Rhetoric of this kind, which echoes the views of Sir Robert Mark (1973) that a minority of criminal defence lawyers are 'more harmful to society than the clients they represent', emerged strongly in our research. Such rhetoric legitimates police rules, police traditions, police methods, police rituals and symbols, the network of understandings and relationships that guide police action: it explains and justifies for the police why legal rules can be used or displaced in favour of internal rules. The following points and supportive quotations illustrate aspects of this rhetoric:

   - defence solicitors (or a proportion of them) are not interested in the pursuit of justice or even in the promotion of the interests of their clients. Instead, they are concerned to act for personal financial gain and to obstruct the process of justice. They are on the side of criminals.

CC-J48

Police: 'When an alleged offender has spoken to a solicitor his story is so much more off pat, and not necessarily the truth. This is where the solicitors are obviously trying to get a fee out of it, and they are obviously trying to get a not guilty. And I'm not saying they twist the facts, but of course they put the facts as they want them. . . . It's the solicitor who almost feeds the words into the suspect's mouth.'

   - that the law is organized to enable the escape of the guilty rather than to assist in their conviction.

CE-A032

Police: 'PACE I would describe as a criminals' charter.'

Res: 'You're so cynical. Why?'

Police: 'You see it's all right people making rules and regulations . . . but my view is that we are the good guys, O.K. there are some bad guys amongst the good guys but we are generally good guys. We don't need to be told how to go on by somebody who has never been out on the street, because we know what's right, we know what's wrong, otherwise we wouldn't be doing this job. You know it seems to me that somebody or a load of Law Lords get together and they bring the PACE Act out: I would love to take these people out around —— Road and just say to somebody "Right we're going into a house now" and take them into a house. And when you come out you've got to wipe your feet – there's dog turds everywhere, human turds, everything and the only thing that these people know is that when they are arrested and they come into a police station they get immediate help by so many do-gooders. . . .'

   - that the sanctions imposed by the courts in sentencing convicted individuals are both idiosyncratic and derisory in severity.

BW-A098

Res: 'So what do you think may happen to him in court?'

Police: 'A usual slap on the wrist.'

Now the important point about police rhetoric is that it is not essentially a rhetoric about *the law*. Indeed, it provides for the police the legitimate authority for disregarding the law and its official methods (where necessary) on the basis that these handcuff the police, handicap real police work and provide a charter for criminals. The police follow rules, but these are *police* rules of behaviour not legal rules. They are, as Ericson (1981b) states, rules of *disorder*, rules of deviance.

It is this which explains why PACE, so widely regarded as introducing major changes to the investigative system, has been easily absorbed by the police. Apart from changes to bureaucratic recording practices (custody sheets, stop-search forms, etc.), the basic message from our research is of the *non-impact* of PACE on police practices, as the following quotation illustrates:

CC-J56
Res: 'Do you find that the PACE Act on the whole is working well, working badly or has it not really much affected the way that you go about your job?'
Police: 'I would say that we manipulate it in a way that it doesn't affect it so much. It's about the same. You've got the restraints but you've got the good bits, bad bits; it's about the same I would say. But most police officers adapt it in such a way that it stays the same as it was for us.'

Police rhetoric provides the backbone of resistance to unwelcome law. Police rhetoric is a crime and disorder rhetoric which informs *practice*: it explains how they view certain individuals and certain sections of the community; it defines their attitudes towards defence lawyers, juries and courts; and it provides the moral framework within which they can rationalize their own conduct towards those they process. It locks into police stereotypes of groups and individuals in society and forms a benchmark against which they can judge individuals; it provides a set of values which reinforce their own sense of mission and moral rectitude.

CONCLUSION

The conceptualization of police practices and their relationship to the law has undergone significant transformations in recent years. The old assumption that unacceptable police practices contradict the law can now be discarded, and the law properly understood can now be seen as enabling. Whilst this leads to critical scrutiny of the activities of the political and judicial elites who make the law, we urge as well a return to examining the petty officials of the criminal justice process, their activities and ideologies. The law, which is in important ways shaped by the police, prescribes only what the police can do and not what the police do do. In examining the empirical reality of the police it is an error to assume both that police behaviour offends against the rhetoric of the law and that the law fails to incorporate its own rhetoric. Legal rhetoric is in fact problematic and expresses both Due Process and Crime Control values. The practices of the police are troubling precisely because they are underpinned by a legal rhetoric which legitimates behaviour on the basis that it is expressive of Crime Control values. Police behaviour is not, of course, unbounded and the activities of individual officers are in important ways shaped by the law, by the need for self-protection and by practical and moral considerations. Nevertheless, when set against the demands of police occupational culture, these are weak constraints which, by their very nature, are contingent, of low visibility and not susceptible to any system of public accounting.

10   The problems of law reform

When we began our research we anticipated as one tangible product a set of reform proposals which would address critical points of the criminal justice process causing 'problems' with a view to fixing the system. When we had completed the research we could hardly complain of a lack of things which needed reform: stop and search, arrest, detention, interrogation, the role of custody officers, juvenile bureaux, the Crown Prosecution Service and so on. We do not, however, intend to pursue this kind of analysis because we think it counter-productive. Essentially we believe, as will become apparent in our discussion, that reformist strategies embody the false assumptions of positivism discussed in Chapter 1, and in particular the false promises of liberal legalism: namely, that the law offers significant protection of the person of the individual; that the law assists citizens in making decisions free of restraint, coercion and undue influence; that the behaviour of official actors is normatively ordered according to legal rules and legally recognized principles; that adversarial confrontation is the hallmark of criminal justice; and that all significant decisions are made according to revealed criteria in public settings.

We recognize that this approach will not be welcomed by those of a reformist persuasion and that it holds out little hope for those whose voices are not at present heard, including the victims of assault whose (known) assailant is not prosecuted or otherwise dealt with; the victims whose assailant is given a favourable deal or bargain; and the defendants who are railroaded into co-operating in their own conviction (on the treatment of victims, see Shapland, 1984; Maguire, 1984; Burrows, 1986; Walklate, 1990). But the hope offered for these people by legalistic reform has always proved to be false. Instead, we want to explain why the possibilities of change are so restricted.

THE LEGAL REFORM MODEL

A seductive and understandable response to the findings of our research is to amend the rules in order to increase legal protection of individuals who are susceptible to police interest as 'suspects' or arrestees, and to increase the role of victims in the process. This legal-reform model would seek to identify points of vulnerability for individuals in their dealings with the police and attempt to restrain police power by subjugating it to tighter and more restrictive rules. Police autonomy and discretion would be limited and individual citizens would be dealt with according to rules, procedures and laws known in advance and publicly-announced, instead of principles and norms privately operated by the police. The arbitrary exercise of power would be diminished and the authority of law magnified.

If this approach were adopted, many rules would be candidates for legal redrafting. Thus, for example, powers to stop and search individuals on the street would need to be changed so that stops and searches could be undertaken only where these were *in fact* justified and reasonable. Powers of arrest would be redefined to ensure that individuals were not deprived of their freedom except where this was both justified by reasonably founded suspicion of a criminal offence and necessary in order to prevent continuing criminal behaviour or to secure attendance at court where there was clear danger of flight, and, in the event of an arrest, individuals would be given at the time the true reason for their arrest in particularized language. At the police station, custody officers would be required to make individual determinations as to whether an arrestee should be subjected to any period of police detention, instead of routinely authorizing the detention of all arrestees. Custody officers would also be required to give suspects their rights or even to call out a legal adviser for all detainees, so that everyone in custody would be given legal advice except those who informed the solicitor in person that they did not wish to be represented. Solicitors, for their part, could be required to attend police stations upon request, to advise detainees and to attend any interrogations. Rules could be changed to require all interrogations to be validated by tape-recording, and all non-recorded interrogations could be subject to a strict exclusionary rule. These and other rules would, in short, address critical points of interaction between the citizen and police officer, seek to limit arbitary, selective and discretionary behaviour on the part of the police and envelop the citizen in a protective canopy of law.

To advocate reform of this kind implies that social actors are responsive to changes in legal rules and that the response is that which is contemplated by the advocate of reform. Evidence of responsiveness to changed rules was encountered at every point of our research. Thus, although we found that most custody officers adopted a blanket approach to the detention of arrestees, uncritically reviewed constables' decisions to arrest and charge and took on a collaborative rather than independent relationship toward arresting and investigating officers, we also found that some took a more robust and independent line. Some appeared to be bureaucratic, if not punctilious, in completing custody records, refused charge books and other official documentation. A few custody officers had a reputation for 'doing things by the book', forbidding 'unofficial' interviews with suspects, constantly monitoring how the case was progressing and even harrying investigating officers in order to secure the earliest possible release of detainees. Some investigating officers, for their part, found that the introduction of contemporaneous note-taking during interrogations had the effect of confining questioning to the offence(s) under investigation, curtailing 'fishing expeditions' into any and all the suspect's previous misdeeds and forcing the abandonment of styles of questioning (such as swearing and shouting at suspects, issuing overt threats or utilizing hard and soft or Mutt and Jeff routines) that would not stand up to external scrutiny. The presence of legal advisers practically eliminated bargaining with suspects during interrogation in order to secure criminal intelligence or a confession.

Some hope, therefore, is promised by the legal reform model. Changes in legal rules have had *some* impact upon the behaviour of state officials and further rule revisions might have a wider impact by 'correcting' behaviour thought to be improper or inappropriate; and where behaviour proves unresponsive to rule change, further revision can be made, with the rules constantly subject to recalibration and fine-tuning. Nevertheless, the worth of this model is called into serious doubt by the massive countervailing evidence described in the current research. That evidence includes the fact that the occupational sub-culture of the police – marked by suspicion, conservatism, isolation/solidarity, machismo and racism (Reiner, 1985) – appears resistant to change; that the requirement of reasonable suspicion as a foundation for stop-searches has little relevance to actual police behaviour and is easily displaced by 'consensual' searches; that instead of arrests being founded in reasonable suspicion, arrests may be made in order to acquire evidence sufficient to justify reasonable suspicion; that rights and protections for suspects may be set aside because of the 'needs' of investigation; that officially proclaimed controls on interrogation may be rendered redundant by informal, 'unofficial' interrogation; and that rules of evidence can be used, not as testing and screening devices but as guides to what evidence needs to be created in order to conform to legal demands.

The assumptions underlying the legal reform model

This countervailing evidence injects a sense of realism into uncritical reliance upon law as a protective device. More than this, it questions basic assumptions underlying the worth of the legal reform model. In the first place, the model assumes that the purpose of legal reform is *benign*. In the context of pre-trial criminal justice, this involves a belief that changes to the rules which are expressed to be protective of suspects are intended to have protective effect. Second, it assumes that legal rules have *instrumental* effect. In other words, it involves a belief that there is a direct link between legal precepts and social behaviour, and that the behaviour of potentially deviant officials is constrained by law. Third, it assumes that legal rules may be accurately *targetted*. This assumption entails a belief that rules may be drafted in an unambiguous way so that they are non-manipulable, and a belief that social actors will not adjust their behaviour so as to circumvent or subvert clear legal precepts.

Stating the points in this way helps us to see how shaky the legal reform model is and how dangerous it is as a guide to social change. Whether legal reform is or is not benign cannot be taken as a given. As Abel stated: '[I]t is vitally important to recognize that the attribution of purpose is rationalization, not scientific explanation' (Abel, 1973, p. 207).

The purpose of law reform is therefore an object of enquiry not an unproblematic given, and lends substance to McBarnet's claim that attention must be paid not only to the 'front-men' of the legal system (like the police) but also to 'the judicial and political élites' who make the law (McBarnet, 1981, p. 156). Similarly, it should be abundantly clear, even from a cursory review of the social science research literature, that the relationship between legal rules and social behaviour far from being direct and clear is indirect and contingent. Failure to recognize this, leads inexorably on to the treadmill of permanent law reform in which every 'failing' of the law to deal with certain forms of social behaviour is addressed by a reformulation of the rules. 'Legal reform', as Sarat and Silbey put it, 'ends up being the answer to the problems caused by legal reform' (Sarat and Silbey, 1988, p. 135).

The limits of the legal protection model can be illustrated by tracing through the notion of reasonable suspicion, a concept central to understanding the make-up of the defendant population. We can begin by asking whether changes to the law of stop and search were intended to be protective of the rights of citizens, whether the new law was *benign* in its intent. If the intent was benign, it might be expected to have tried to secure that any suspicion was both *individual* and *reasonable*. This much was claimed by the then Home Secretary in steering PACE through Parliament: 'The safeguards on stop and search powerfully strengthen the rights of the citizen and strengthen the basic safeguard of reasonable suspicion' (*Hansard*, H.C., Vol. 48, col. 103). However, the final proposals rested heavily upon the recommendations of the Royal Commission on Criminal Procedure (1981) whose *Report* casts considerable doubt on the benign-intention thesis.

Although the Royal Commission asserted that the powers were individualized, they explicitly stated that this 'requirement' could be discarded in the everyday world of policing:

> Where the police, from experience, believe that criminal offences are likely to result from a group's activities, because, for example, one or more of them may be carrying offensive weapons, the power of stop and search which we propose should be available. (RCCP, *Report*, 1981, para. 3.23)

Similarly with respect to reasonableness. The Royal Commission was fully aware that broadly drafted provisions maximized police discretion and minimized the opportunity for legal challenge. Indeed, in dismissing concerns of a minority of its members in relation to extending the powers to cover 'offensive weapons', the majority scathingly remarked:

> If there is imprecision in the definition of the offence, the remedy for the difficulty perceived by [the minority] lies in removing that imprecision rather than in refusing the police the power to search. (*Report*, 1981, para. 3.21)

When it came to reasonable suspicion, however, the Commission, whilst acknowledging the risk that 'the criterion could be loosely interpreted', refused tighter regulation as 'impracticable' (para. 3.25).

Nevertheless, it might be argued that the Royal Commission saw the new powers as having *instrumental* effect. On this argument, the Royal Commission could concurrently acknowledge the *potential* ineffectiveness of legal rules controlling police behaviour whilst believing that this would not be an operational reality. In this way, the Commission could reconcile an instrumental view of legal precepts with the theoretical possibility that social behaviour could function independently of legal rules. But why should we accept this when there is evidence to the contrary provided by the Royal Commission itself? Nor is this evidence of the critics (although the interactionist literature provides plenty of that): it is evidence from the best source possible, the police themselves. As the *Report* puts it:

The police favour clarification. They also believe that their powers to stop and search persons and vehicles should be increased in certain respects. They say that they frequently have to lay themselves open to the risk of civil action by stopping and searching in circumstances where they have no power to do so but where equally they will be criticised for failing to act. (RCCP, *Report*, 1981, para. 3.15)

As the Commission knew, therefore, there is no direct link between legal rules and police behaviour, and the ability of legal rules to control potentially deviant police behaviour is at best weak.

Nor can any reasonable claim be made that the Commission's proposals were *targeted* in such a way as to minimize the opportunity for manipulation or subversion. To the contrary: the proposals simply locked into a pre-existing police culture, focused around local powers, which utilized reasonable suspicion to legitimate stop-searches based in police stereotypes relating to who people are, where they (appropriately) should be and when (Cohen, 1979; Brogden and Brogden, 1984; Dixon *et al.*, 1989). There was every prospect, therefore, that police practice would continue unchanged and every indication that it was *expected* to continue unchanged. Moreover, the 'stringent controls' advocated by the Royal Commission, namely 'notification of the reason for the search to the person who has been stopped, the recording of searches by officers, and the monitoring of the records by supervising officers', could hardly have been more badly chosen given the essential feature of police recording systems documented by Bittner in his classic study of the police:

[P]olice departments accommodate a colossally complicated network of secret sharing, combined with systematic information denial . . . the overriding rule [is] that no one tells anybody else more than he absolutely has to. (Bittner, 1970, p. 64)

Police forces, thus, display some of the endemic sicknesses of formal organizations, one of which, as Banton (1964) pointed out, is 'concentration upon reporting procedures to ensure that one is "in the clear" instead of upon the job to be done' (Banton, 1964, p. 108).

The unity of police culture and practice

The foregoing argument indicates that an intending reformer would be unwise to rely simply on changing the legal framework of the criminal justice process. To affect existing police practices in relation to stop-search, for example, would require more than mere rule change, defining and redefining 'reasonable suspicion' with more or less specificity: it would, at a minimum, require an attack upon police occupational culture. It is this culture which gives empirical reality to police interactions with citizens in the street. One of the interesting sociological features of policing is, in fact, a unitary view of the 'world of crime' combined with substantial dissensus among officers on almost any other topic. Whilst an observer is immediately struck by vigorous debates among officers over a wide variety of subjects (the assertion of self being a demonstration of individuality and a form of modest resistance to the demands of 'The Job'), an essentially argumentative streak in police officers (Banton, 1964, p. 144), and the internal divisions and factions within the police organization, the dominance of an institutional consensus on 'law and order' issues is remarkable.

Police culture is heavily defensive and territorial, with society outside being seen as permanently on the brink of chaos and disorder (Holdaway, 1983). The police have a unitary and absolutist view of human behaviour and social organization which disavows the contradictions within liberal capitalist society, that is, the possibilities built into it *for* disorder. Disorder of itself is therefore defined by the police as a problem. Of course only certain types of individual and certain groups are viewed as threatening. As Kettle pointed out:

> [T]he police have been allowed to run their own show, make their own definitions and operate behind a rhetoric of their own choosing. Whatever they decide to do becomes, by definition, in the interests of 'law and order' and therefore of 'society' too. Whoever opposes them is, equally by definition, 'anti-police' and thus hostile to 'law and order' and therefore hostile to 'society'. Some sections of society are already safely consigned to this camp: demonstrators, pickets, squatters, blacks, gays, feminists, immigrants, the Irish. (Kettle, 1980, p. 59)

This world-view of the police is learned as a work skill (Manning, 1977, p. 142). The 'law' is an inadequate guide to appropriate action: everything lacks clarity and certainty and is 'situationally justified' (Manning, 1977, p. 142). Because this learned craft is highly valued within police culture and because it contributes heavily to the cohesiveness, morale and solidarity of the lower ranks, it is especially resistant to change (Manning, 1977, p. 338; Fielding, 1984, pp. 64–6; Dixon *et al.*, 1989, 188–9). The extent of the task facing any reform programme emerges clearly from the detailed analysis of Dixon *et al.* (1989). In order to rescue 'reasonable suspicion' from failure, Dixon *et al.* suggest 'some minimal conditions' for success:

(i) clear expression of the derived standards;
(ii) effective training in order to modify police culture;
(iii) favourable political circumstances;

(iv)   the backing of effective sanctions for non-compliance; and
(v)   public knowledge of rights and the limits of police powers.
       (Dixon *et al.*, 1989, p. 192)

By any standards, this is a formidable agenda.

It should be clear, therefore, that rule changes cannot simply be imposed as if cultural, organizational and historic work-practice constraints did not exist. This is a generalizable point which is not confined to matters such as reasonable suspicion. Thus, for example, the attempt, if genuinely sought, to constitute custody officers as independent scrutineers of other officers' work practices by changing the rules defining their responsibilities was bound to fail, given that it conflicted with an entrenched hierarchical command system which designates as superior all officers of the rank of Inspector and above, a status system which accords superior-knowledge status to detectives to whom others (including custody officers) are expected to defer, a bureaucratically task-oriented system which confers case control upon the investigating officer, a shift system which sets up deep loyalties between arresting officers and their own shift sergeants and an overarching police culture which emphasizes internal cohesiveness and solidarity as fundamental organizational values. Subservience to authority, deference to superior knowledge, submissiveness to others' case control, acquiescence in the decisions of others of the same rank and collaboration with other officers engaged in 'valuable' police work are not aberrational characteristics but part of what it means to be a custody officer.

The unity of criminal justice processes

The legal reform model also fails because it views the criminal justice process as essentially *segmental*, with each component part susceptible to separate analysis and separate reform. On this view, the system is divisible into three linked but independent parts: the investigative, accusative and determinative. The legal reform model assumes that any one of these parts may be isolated and refined without consideration being given to either of the other parts. Indeed, it was precisely this thinking which confined the terms of reference of the Royal Commission on Criminal Procedure to the investigation of offences and their prosecution, with only limited remit to examine the trial process. This form of analysis has also been assumed by researchers who often depict the police in a subordinate position with respect to other institutional actors in the system, as, for example, in the following account by Manning:

The relationship between the police and other components of the criminal justice system is symbiotic – each is dependent upon the other for information and support. One of the reasons why a professionalized police department is so concerned with its public image originates from its inability to control the conviction process. (Manning, 1977, p. 136)

This line of thinking leads to an analysis which sees the symbiotic relationship sustained 'through systematic abrogations of guarantees of Due Process. The denial of Due Process is routinely accomplished through the simple expedient of "bargain justice".' (id.)

Contary to this mode of analysis, it is essential to understand that the criminal justice process is marked by *unity* not disunity, and requires singular not separate analysis. What makes the process unified is the motivations and actions of the police. The police, who do not structurally exercise complete control over juries and magistrates, seek to avoid the decisions of both. They do this by taking decisions themselves which are unreviewable and by constructing the evidence in such a way as to maximize their control over future decisions. The legal reform model assumes that each step in the process can be viewed separately because it sees the process as dispassionate investigation, producing evidence pointing to suspicion and guilt, justifying the bringing of a case. In fact, the police see their role as involving a determination of guilt or innocence *at the outset*. This determination defines for them whether an incident is a crime or not, or whether it needs to be transformed into a crime; and it requires justification either in the form of the creation of an internal record or, if the case is to go to court, the creation of evidence. Thus to redefine 'reasonable suspicion' in order to narrow police discretion misses the point that reasonable suspicion requirements do not limit police decision making but only the way in which the police may legitimately account for their decisions. To introduce tape-recording or video-recording into police interrogations in order to prevent coerced or false confessions is to erroneously see the interrogation as a severable part of the police–citizen encounter whereas, in reality, it is one part of an ongoing relationship the earlier aspects of which can crucially influence what occurs during the interrogation. To advocate a corroboration requirement as an answer to the false confession overlooks the point that the same pressures used to produce a false confession may be used to generate corroborative evidence from a civilian witness or from a forensic expert (McConville, 1989).

In rejecting the utility of the legal reform model, therefore, it is not necessary to engage in extreme rule-scepticism (cf. Reiner, 1985, p. 175; Dixon *et al.*, 1989, p. 192) or to see police culture as fixed and unchangeable. Instead, it is only necessary to recognize that where legal rules cut across well-established cultural norms of actors to whom they are addressed, they are unlikely to have instrumental effect. Historically this has meant, in the case of the police, that rather than the police being socialized into more acceptable and legal modes of behaviour, law 'reform' has had to be increasingly brought into line with police practice, legitimating and 'covering' dubious or illegal behaviour. The legal reform model has done little to address the problems of suspects: 'law reform' has largely been a matter of empowering the police in relation to the suspect.

CHANGING THE ADVERSARIAL SYSTEM

The limits of reform of the rules have aroused interest in reform of a more fundamental nature, and, in particular, has thrown into doubt the basic principles of the adversarial system of justice. The most influential critic of the adversarial system has been Lord Devlin (1979) who has advocated sweeping changes to the existing system. Given the inadequacies of rule-change, it is worthwhile examining these more radical proposals.

According to Lord Devlin, the basic assumptions of the adversarial system are unsound. Under it, the police are required to make enquiries in a quasi-judicial spirit, conducting investigations as much with the object of ascertaining information which will exonerate as of ascertaining evidence which will convict. In Lord Devlin's view, this places unreasonable and unrealistic demands upon the police:

> The role we have assigned to the police is theoretically unsound. There is a great difference between playing fair with an opponent, which the police are rightly required to do, and holding the balance even between him and yourself. The latter activity is discountenanced by the legal maxim that no man can be a judge in his own cause. The police would not be as useful to society as they are if they were not ardent against its enemies and did not make their apprehension and conviction the cause for which they fight. It is unnatural to fight quasi-judicially. . . . When a police officer charges a man it is because he believes him to be guilty, not just because he thinks there is a case for trial. For the policeman the arrest and charge ends the matter; what follows is for him the solemnization which society as a matter of decency requires. (Devlin, 1979, pp. 71–2)

At this stage of the process, i.e. when the police have made up their minds, rather than at the earlier stage when they are still hunting, Lord Devlin proposes the interposition of a judicial mind. The judicial intermediary would be required to investigate both sides, prosecution and defence, using the police as agents.

This institutional reform model has some initial attractions. It would mean, in the first place, the interposition of an independent mind at an early point in the system which would act as some restraint upon the prosecution of cases unsupported by substantial evidence. Second, it could be a counterweight to a leading cause of miscarriages of justice, namely the tendency of the police, once they have decided that the suspect is guilty, to treat as mistaken any evidence that contradicts the evidence upon which they rely (Kennedy, 1961; Devlin, 1979; McConville, 1987). Thirdly, it could lead to earlier and more consistent disclosure of the prosecution's case, with the judicial intermediary being able to direct further investigation of those matters that the police have examined only cursorily or have overlooked altogether. This last point has been highlighted in a number of official reports and was a central factor in the Confait Report of Sir Henry Fisher:

> The evidence which I have heard suggests that the police do not at present see it as their duty to initiate enquiries which might point to the fact they had got the wrong man, or that for some other reason the prosecution should fail. And there is nobody outside the police who regards it as his duty to spur the police on to question the case and to follow lines of enquiry which might be inconsistent with it. (Fisher, 1977, para, 2.30)

A judicial intermediary might, therefore, spot weak cases, correct police bias, and instigate further and more scrupulous investigation.

Although superficially attractive, this institutional reform model is also deeply flawed. In the first place, since the police would retain investigative autonomy and have the initial responsibility of putting together the case dossier, the judicial intermediary's role would be highly circumscribed because she would not see those cases where the police decided not to charge. This would make it impossible to formulate a rational investigative and prosecutorial policy. Second, it assumes that the 'independence' of the judicial intermediaries can be continued and their insulation from the pressures for results which affect the police can be guaranteed, despite evidence to the contrary from inquisitorial systems (Erikson, 1990). Third, it is unlikely to uncover 'weak cases', cases which ought not to be prosecuted because of evidentiary shortcomings. As this study has demonstrated, cases are not 'weak' or 'strong' in terms of some naturally occurring reality: cases are constructions, and cases are constructed in order to conceal some evidentiary shortcoming or in order to create it. Fourth, it will do nothing to overcome the central problem of the present investigative system – the motivations of the police. The last two points can be demonstrated from an analysis of two cases relied upon by Lord Devlin in support of his proposed judicial intermediary – the cases of Timothy Evans and Laslo Virag.

Timothy Evans, under police questioning, made detailed confessions to the murder of his wife and daughter. Subsequent to this confession, the police uncovered evidence from independent witnesses which made Evans' story of hiding the bodies of the victims highly improbable. This did not cause the police to doubt the account of Evans. Instead they simply assumed that, if Evans was telling the truth, the witnesses must have been mistaken (Kennedy, 1961). Similarly in the Virag case, in which an individual, surprised while stealing coinboxes from parking meters, shot and wounded a police officer during the chase. Six witnesses identified Virag as the criminal in question. Sets of fingerprints were found on four of the coin boxes and, although these were not those of Virag, the police belief in his guilt was not shaken. Far from supporting the creation of a judicial intermediary, these cases provide powerful evidence against the proposal.

In each case, once the police had decided upon the guilt of the suspect, they constructed the case to ensure a conviction. Thus, in the case of Timothy Evans, the two independent witnesses were re-interviewed by the police and persuaded to make new statements altering their earlier accounts in such a way that they were now consistent with Evans' confession. Since the police then suppressed the original statements and withheld them from the defence and the court, it is obvious that they would not have made their existence known to a judicial intermediary. Exactly the same thing happened in the case of Virag. There the evidence of the fingerprints (which later proved to be those of the real culprit) was suppressed by the police and Virag wrongly convicted. The short point is that motivations which are strong enough to cause the police or forensic scientists to mislead courts of law would be just as effectively deployed through case construction against any judicial intermediary.

THE CONSENSUS MODEL OF JUSTICE

The reform strategies discussed above are marked by legalism and a faith in incremental change effected by internal reform of the criminal justice process. At their core, the strategies assume or promote a *consensus* model of justice. In this view, events are marked by a single truth and it is the purpose of the criminal justice process to identify that truth in such a way that *all* parties agree upon it. It is this feature of the system which links the philosophies and motivations of prosecutorial officials and defence lawyers, the methods of investigators and courtroom actors and the nature of institutional forms of liberal capitalist society, and which conspires against more radical change. It is necessary at this point to expand upon this analysis.

The criminal justice process does not recognize as valid the disorder and disagreement which is endemic to liberal capitalist society. Conflict is accepted only as existing *outside* the legal system: indeed, its existence in the external world is advanced as the *justification* for the criminal justice process. Since conflict is seen as dysfunctional, the criminal justice process can be depicted as a voice of reason in an otherwise disorderly world: rational and restrained, it mediates and solves external disputes. It is a force *for* order.

This consensus view is first apparent during police investigations. The police and prosecutors are not required to, and do not, present cases *about* incidents, but cases *against* individuals. Doubts and uncertainties, and competing versions of reality, are not accorded legitimate status. Indeed, they are, as we have seen, discomforting for state officials who seek their removal at every opportunity. This is entirely understandable given the police mandate, well expressed by Manning in the following passage:

> [T]he police role conveys a sense of *sacredness* or awesome power that lies at the root of political order, and authority, the claims a state makes upon its people for deference to rules, laws, and norms. The ideology or belief system in our society makes this secular sacredness and authority a direct function of the state itself. This belief, or ideology, contains three interrelated axioms: it posits the existence of an *absolutistic morality, links it with the state and makes them equivalent,* and *it attaches to policing the obligation to defend these two entities.* (Manning, 1977, p. 5, citation omitted; original emphasis)

This dominant value system built into policing also infuses the role definition of prosecutors so that 'cases' project a single, unitary view of reality. This unitary view of reality would be of little importance if it were not for the fact that the system is organized to ensure that this view acquires *primacy*.

The state's view acquires primacy because it is buttressed by enabling institutional structures, incentives and legal forms. Thus, juvenile liaison bureaux (themselves creations of the police) are designed to sanction and legitimate police decisions and police determinations in an atmosphere of co-operative harmony which defers to the authoritative position of the police. Similarly, Pre-Trial Review systems attempt to isolate and remove conflict, encouraging, through disclosure and informal discourse, defence lawyers to become privileged 'insiders', further empowering them to pressurize their clients into accepting the validity of the state's case. At every step of the process, defendants are confronted with incentives to conform – the non-prosecution of a partner, a reduced charge, a reduced sentence, the abandonment of the charge(s). These incentives can be held out by police, prosecutors, solicitors, barristers and judges, because the legal forms ensure *privacy*: in the case of the police, the privacy secured by according a right to hold the suspect in custody; in the case of lawyers, the privacy accorded by the lawyer–client privilege and by the corridors of the court; in the case of judges, the privacy accorded in plea bargaining by the *Turner* Rules which permit judges (lawfully) to use barristers as their messengers.

The process, in common with other areas of social organization (Johnson, 1972), also secures consensus because of its attitude toward public disclosure of its own mechanics. Nothing attracts such violent disapprobation as when one of the 'inner circle' actually reveals the private reality. What attracts particular censure is the police officer who admits to bail bargaining (*Zaveckas* [1970] W.L.R. 516) or engaging in deliberate deception of a lawyer (*Mason* [1987] 3 All E.R. 481), the barrister who concedes that structured coercion of defendants in order to extract a guilty plea is common practice, not simply an isolated occurrence (*Llewellyn* (1978) 67 Cr. App. R. 49), and the judge who describes what he does as 'plea bargaining' (*Grice* (1977) 66 Cr. App. R. 167; *Plimmer* (1975) 61 Cr. App. R. 264; *Atkinson* [1978] 2 All E.R. 460). Revelation invokes a sense of betrayal and is visited with wrath.

Trials are similarly disapproved: they threaten the ideology of consensual truth which is the hallmark of the system (cf. Banton, 1964, p. 144). Trials not only display unwholesome dissent; their outcomes are also uncertain. Consensual truth can be *ensured* only by private determinations legitimated by public displays of unity. The most effective of these displays is the plea of guilty because this ensures that the accused is a party, an agreed not an aggrieved party, to her own downfall, and because it is the only way of ensuring that result. Whilst, therefore, co-operativeness is in part accounted for by exchange-relationships among official actors of the system (Cole, 1970), it is a central *demand* of the adversarial system's claim to truth-determination.

At each point, therefore, the system is able to present itself in terms of consensus because consensus is an *ideological production* of the system. In this presentation, people are stopped and searched with their consent; those who are released without charge accept the propriety of police action and show no resentment; cautions are administered only to those who accept their guilt; confessions flow freely out of a suspect and are usually attended by abject apologies, themselves the product of volition; and pleas of guilty are entered by those who acknowledge responsibility for their misdeeds. This is a world in which conflict is dysfunctional, even unseemly. Everything is made to be predictable: victims hand over their complaints so that the police can determine the best course of action or inaction and they routinely sign statements that they will accept the decision of the police, *whatever* it is; defendants are guilty and convict themselves; prosecution witnesses are co-operative and tell a story consistent with the police case, and, if they do not, they *fail* to come up to proof, or are officially designated as *hostile*; the propriety of the prosecution is a fact, and challenges to this will be seen as 'mud-slinging'; and any defences must be fully disclosed before hearing the case for the prosecution, otherwise they will be regarded as involving an 'ambush' and thus likely to be discredited. In this world consensus triumphs through its own power. The very utilization of the criminal justice process transforms conflict and removes it, as if by magic without threats or blandishments, trade-offs or deals, coercion or bargains. And nothing could be clearer demonstration of the correctness of the system's values and the efficacy of its procedures than the disposition of cases in an agreed manner, without trial: in this way, the investigation, adjudication and sanctioning decisions appear as both appropriate and inevitable.

As this study has sought to show, however, consensus describes only the external public image of the system, not its inner workings. External consensus is achieved despite internal conflict, and it might be the first aim of any legalistic reform to expose and maximise this conflict rather than to suppress and minimize it. This, as Nils Christie pointed out, is not likely to happen in respect of lawyers:

> Lawyers are particularly good at stealing conflicts. They are trained for it. They are trained to prevent and solve conflicts. They are socialised into a sub-culture with a surprisingly high agreement concerning interpretation of norms, and regarding what sort of information can be accepted as relevant in each case. (Christie, 1976, p. 6)

What is true of lawyers is even more true of the police. And what would be the function of Devlin's judicial intermediary? Why, precisely to discover and proclaim 'the truth', thus even more effectively concealing conflict.

CONCLUSION

Internal, legalistic reforms would leave untouched the class, gender and race biases of the system. Attention should be focused away from extending ineffective 'protections' to a captive and largely unchanging suspect population, and towards altering the composition of this suspect group by removing the bias of state legality against the weak and powerless.

Within the legal system, a start in this can be made by overturning police culture, by redefining the policing mandate and by instituting new forms of accountability. Police culture is important because it significantly affects who gets drawn into the criminal justice process:

> [T]he occupational culture favours a law-enforcement approach to policing over a broader problem-solving approach. This in turn leads to stereotyping and the labelling of people in terms of the way they impinge upon the job of law enforcement or detract from its pursuit. (Southgate, 1986, p. 56)

Changing police culture is not possible on its own, for it derives from the policing mandate. At present, the police mandate is heavily geared towards public order, social hygiene and the protection of physical property backed up by a criminal law which is comprehensive, discretionary and enabling (Brogden, 1982). Most concern centres on publicly disreputable behaviour which is easiest to observe. But the result of this is to further magnify the bias against the weak and powerless, whose social relations are conducted in public and who often have no private space to themselves (Stinchcombe, 1963). In this way, the constant supply of relatively low-level arrests satisfies the demands both of the organization and the occupational culture for a regular volume of relatively easy and trouble-free transactions to process, in the interests of 'efficiency' (Brogden *et al.*, 1988). The outcome is an emphasis upon the crimes of the poor and weak and not those of the powerful (Box, 1983) even though the crimes of the powerful entail more loss and greater injury to society (Reiman, 1979). Indeed, the rich and the powerful are generally not under scrutiny from the police but instead have their own 'control' agencies which generally espouse non-prosecution policies (Sanders, 1985b; Clarke, 1990). To police the suites rather than the streets properly would require new strategies, new technologies and new methods of criminal investigation. None of these are needed for street policing which continues to operate with nineteenth-century methodologies. That the police are able to concentrate on their ancient mandate, with the rich and powerful immune from scrutiny, is a testimony to the pervasiveness of the myth which associates crime with poverty (Brogden, 1982) and to the success with which liberal capitalist ideologies of equal treatment and full enforcement of the law have been produced so as to capture the public mind and to form and constitute the social relations and practices of all those connected to or processed by the criminal justice system. The issue, therefore, is not just the methods and methodologies of policing, but its *objectives*. As Rumbaut and Bittner put it:

> The problems of policing are not simply problems of finding 'efficient' and 'effective' means; they are problems of ends, of competing social values, interests, and priorities, the resolution of which raise fundamental moral and political issues to be decided by an informed citizenry, not only scientific or technical issues to be decided by experts and technocrats. Hence, the most hopeful prospect for substantive police reform is the influence an informed public can exert on the direction of change in the police agencies. (Rumbaut and Bittner, 1979, p. 284)

Just as the redefinition of the police mandate cannot be left to the police themselves, new forms of police accountability will be required. Though there is no shortage of proposals for new forms of accountability (e.g. Hewitt, 1982; Jefferson and Grimshaw, 1984; Lea and Young, 1984; Reiner, 1985; Lustgarten, 1986; Shapland and Vagg, 1987) two recent developments indicate a decline in police accountability. First, *accountability* is being displaced in favour of *consultation*. Police/ community consultative committees, set up under section 106 of the Police and Criminal Evidence Act, 1984, do not involve greater accountability of constabularies and provide little more than 'talking shops' (Morgan, 1987). Second, control of the police is becoming less *local* and more *central*. As Reiner (1989) has pointed out, the emphasis on the independence of chief constables from control by local police authorities, which has tended to dominate accountability debates, has diverted attention away from the growing control of policing by central government. The much criticized activities of the National Reporting Centre which co-ordinated police operations during the miners' strike (Coulter *et al.*, 1984; Reiner, 1984; Fine and Millar, 1986) and the readiness of the Home Secretary to authorize, against the wishes of the local police authority and without any proven need, a chief constable to acquire CS gas, plastic bullets, etc. (*R v. Secretary of State for the Home Department ex parte Northumbria Police Authority*, 1987, 2 All. E.R. 282) do not give confidence in central control providing policing accountable to the interests of the policed.

But accountability in the rhetoric of the law has little meaning in terms of our data. Liberal modes of accountability, termed 'explanatory' by Marshall (1984), which enjoin and direct the police to offer after-the-fact explanations for their conduct and decision making, can have little value given that the police are able to *construct the fact*. Accountability, if it is to have any relevance to police-work practices, must be both prospective and able to penetrate the control networks which the police utilize to perpetuate police values and ideologies and screen out external inspection mechanisms.

It is, of course, hardly necessary to emphasize that there is no real possibility of major changes to police culture or forms of police accountability. Law reform does not have a dynamic separate from and independent of state interest. The criminal justice process not only imposes order but reproduces a particular form of social order which involves class, race and gender biases and which differentially distributes opportunity, wealth and power between different groups in society. As Manning put it, in relation to the police:

> The ineluctable fact is that *the police deal in and dispense violence in protection of the interests of the state*. They are not autonomous entities. They are inextricably linked to the political status quo and are, in effect, duty bound to sustain and uphold it. (Manning, 1977, p. 361; original emphasis)

Understood in this way, it is obvious that there is no constituency of any note for reform which involves real protections for vulnerable citizens or substantive changes to existing modes of policing. For the state, existing modes of law enforcement *work*. And this is so even when they sometimes fail or encounter resistance: indeed, occasional failure and the possibility of resistance is a *requirement* for an effective *legal* system (Foucault, 1978; Sarat and Silbey, 1988).

The result is the continuance of a 'model' criminal justice process, focused on the deprived and the powerless, affirming the dominant values of the wider society through modes of adjudication which favour private decision making over public accountability, and celebrating the localization and removal of conflict in the relentless imposition of consensus. The official memoranda, accounts, records and files have no room for other readings, perspectives and discourses. The voices of defendants, victims, witnesses and even official actors are disembodied or stilled. These, and other alternative realities, have no place in the case for the prosecution.

Appendix

Our analysis of case construction arises out of a long-term empirical study of police and prosecutorial decision making in three English police forces which began in 1986 and was funded under ESRC's 'Crime and the Criminal Justice System' initiative (Grant no. EO 6250019). We selected two police sub-divisions from each force as the sites from which the case samples would be taken. The forces were chosen in order to represent different policing and prosecutorial systems, and to represent different crime problems in inner-city, suburban and rural areas. Force A is a large urban force; area AH is an ethnically mixed inner-city area with very little owner-occupation, while area AK is largely white working class with more owner-occupation (in old terraced housing) than AH but (like AH) with the majority of inhabitants in council accommodation. This force had had a prosecuting solicitors' department prior to the Prosecution of Offences Act, 1985, but since it handled only a small proportion of the force's cases, the introduction of the Crown Prosecution Service (CPS) in 1986 had a major impact on the force's prosecution procedures.

Force B is a largely rural force; both areas (BK and BW) were based on medium-sized towns and included some outlying rural districts. They therefore included all socio-economic groups, but the populations of both areas were largely white. The force acquired a prosecuting solicitors' department only shortly before the introduction of the CPS, which therefore had an even greater impact on procedures than it did in force A.

Force C had had a prosecuting department which handled all that force's cases, and the police were accustomed to accepting prosecutors' advice about cases. The impact of the CPS was therefore expected to be small, and by comparing decision making in the three forces the impact of the legal changes (particularly s.23 of the Prosecution of Offences Act: the power of the CPS to drop cases) could be isolated. For logistical reasons we had to take two sub-divisions (CC and CE) from one division (both in the same city). One was a city centre and the other included extensive working-class suburbs, both with ethnically mixed populations. Both areas were under the same police decision-making unit and CPS branch. In force A the areas were in different police divisions and under different CPS branches. In force B the two sub-divisions were in different divisions, but under the same CPS branch.

We collected our samples in the same way in each site in order to ensure comparability between areas. In each area we collected all new non-Road Traffic Act arrests and reports for summons from a set date (our entry on to the site) until our pre-set totals were reached. These were, for each of the six sites, 120 adult and 60 juvenile cases. Data collection began simultaneously in our first two sites (AH and BK), in March 1986. These samples were collected before the introduction of the CPS, although later decision making in some of these cases occurred after the Prosecution of Offences Act (POOA) came into operation. Our entry into the other four sites began after the introduction of the CPS. The Police and Criminal Evidence Act, 1984 (PACE), came into operation before any of the research began.

In each area, we extracted all information relevant to the case contained in the police station custody record. We contacted all police officers in the case and sought tape-recorded interviews with each independently. Where cases took a long time to be disposed of or where decisions in the case were delayed or changed, repeat interviews were sought. Each interviewee was given a guarantee of confidentiality and anonymity. Table 16 sets out the number of cases in which we obtained a substantive interview with police officers.

Although Table 16 discloses a very high success rate in terms of interviews obtained, it understates the number of interviews actually conducted for a number of reasons. In some cases more than one reporting/arresting officer was involved and interviewed, and some officers were interviewed several times in respect of the same case where the case evolved over time. The table counts only those cases in which there was a *substantive* interview and excludes those where the officer agreed to be interviewed but was unable to recall the case in detail. This point is particularly relevant in respect of custody officers many of whom in busy stations were unable to remember a case after a few days.

Cases which survived the police station were then tracked as they progressed through the court system, where we interviewed prosecutors. Although there were fewer cases here than in the total sample, the logistical difficulties were greater because of the dispersal of cases to a variety of courts and because advocates were often in no position to

Table 16 The number of cases in which police officers were interviewed according to the status of the officer and the police force studied

a) *Adult cases*	Force A		Force B		Force C	
	n	*%*	*n*	*%*	*n*	*%*
Arresting or reporting officer	214	89.2	226	94.2	233	97.1
Custody officer	112	46.7	126	52.5	151	62.9
Other officer	61	25.4	39	16.3	75	31.3

b) *Juvenile cases*	Force A		Force B		Force C	
	n	*%*	*n*	*%*	*n*	*%*
Arresting or reporting officer	95	79.2	107	89.2	112	93.3
Custody officer	43	35.8	52	43.3	39	32.5
Other officer	51	42.5	10	8.3	42	35.0

Table 17 Persons prosecuted for indictable and either-way offences: national and research sample figures

Offence category	National statistics*		Research sample	
	n	*%*	*n*	*%*
Violence against the person	71,341	16.7	52	12.3
Sexual offences	8,298	1.9	6	1.4
Burglary	68,778	16.1	72	17.0
Robbery	6,362	1.5	3	0.7
Theft/handling	213,795	49.9	210	49.7
Fraud/forgery	26,371	6.1	12	2.8
Criminal damage	14,497	3.4	40	9.5
Drug offences	18,757	4.4	28	6.6
Total	428,199	100.0	423	100.0

* *Source:* Home Office Statistical Department (unpublished)

comment upon a case before final disposition. Nevertheless, we obtained interviews with reviewers and advocates in over one-third of relevant adult cases (37.2 per cent in force A, 35.2 per cent in force B and 36.4 per cent in force C) and in over one half of relevant juvenile cases (51.4 per cent in force A, 68.2 per cent in force B and 38.3 per cent in force C).

We conducted the empirical research in these ways to ensure that our sample of cases was reasonably representative of different types of case and different types of police decision making so that generalization was possible. The indictable and either-way offence mix of our sample is indicated in Table 17, and compared with the national statistics for 1987 (when the bulk of our data was collected).

There is a remarkably high degree of correspondence between these two sets of figures albeit that violence and fraud are rather under-represented in our sample, and criminal damage over-represented. Our sample is at variance with national figures in one important way: summary non-motoring offences form around 22 per cent of the prosecutions in our sample, but 50 per cent of national prosecutions. We expect that this is in part because of the over-representation of juveniles in our sample, in part because so many of our summary non-motoring offences were cautioned (see Table 9) and in part a product of the particular areas in which the research took place.

NEW HOME OFFICE GUIDELINES ON CAUTIONING

The Home Office Guidelines on cautioning, which were current during the research on which this book is based, have now been replaced by new guidelines, published in 1990 (Home Office, 1990). The guidelines are stated to be drawn up in the light of findings of research commissioned by the Home Office and conducted by the Department of Social Work and Social Policy of the University of Birmingham (Wilkinson and Evans, 1990; Evans and Wilkinson, 1990).

The two factors which apparently prompted the publication of the new guidelines were first, the wide variations in cautioning rates between forces, and second, the sharp fall in cautioning rates for offenders over 17. Both factors had been anticipated by the 1985 guidelines which were designed 'to promote more effective and consistent cautioning on a national basis' and had stated that for adults 'criminal offences should not automatically be the subject of prosecution' unless 'the public interest requires it'. Thus, the new guidelines do not promote a change of policy, but rather reassert policies embodied in the 1985 guidelines.

Under the 1990 guidelines the pre-conditions for cautioning are evidence of guilt sufficient to give a realistic prospect of conviction and an admission of guilt and consent to the caution by the offender (or parent in relation to a juvenile). It is stressed that where the criteria for caution are met but the offender refuses to consent to be cautioned, prosecution should not be the only option considered. As under the previous guidelines, the criteria for cautioning are: the nature of the offence; the likely penalty; the offender's age and health; the offender's criminal record and her or his attitude towards the offence. It is emphasized that the presumption in favour of not prosecuting juveniles and the elderly 'should now extend to other groups – young adults and adults alike – where the criteria for caution are met'.

The influence of the 1985 guidelines on decision making by police and prosecutors is discussed in chapters 6 and 7. There is no reason to think that the publication of new guidelines, embodying similar policies will, of itself, change current practice.

Bibliography

Abel, R. (1973) 'Law books and books about law', *Stanford Law Review* 26: 175.
Balbus, I. (1973) *The Dialectics of Legal Repression*, New York: Russell Sage.
Baldwin, J. (1985) *Pre-Trial Criminal Justice*, Oxford: Basil Blackwell.
Baldwin, J. and McConville, M. (1977) *Negotiated Justice*, Oxford: Martin Robertson.
—— (1978a) 'The new Home Office figures on pleas and acquittals: what sense do they make?', *Criminal Law Review* 1978: 196.
—— (1978b) 'The influence of the sentencing discount in inducing guilty pleas', in J. Baldwin and A. Bottomley (eds) *Criminal Justice: Selected Readings*, London: Martin Robertson.
—— (1979a) *Jury Trials*, Oxford: Oxford University Press.
—— (1979b) 'Police interrogation and the right to see a solicitor', *Criminal Law Review* 1979: 145.
—— (1981) *Courts, Prosecution and Conviction*, Oxford: Clarendon Press.
—— (1982) 'The role of interrogation in crime discovery and conviction', *British Journal of Criminology* 22: 165.
Baldwin, R. and Kinsey, R. (1982) *Police Powers and Politics*, London: Quartet Books.
Banton, M. (1964) *The Policeman in the Community*, London: Tavistock.
Barnes, J. and Webster, N. (1981) *Police Interrogation: Tape Recording*, Royal Commission on Criminal Procedure Research Study No. 8, London: HMSO.
Baxter, J. and Koffman, L. (1983) 'The Confait inheritance – forgotten lessons?', *Cambrian Law Review* 1983: 14.
Becker, H. (1963) *Outsiders*, London: Macmillan.
Bevan, V. and Lidstone, K. (1985) *The Police and Criminal Evidence Act, 1984*, London: Butterworth.
Bittner, E. (1967) 'The police on skid-row: a study of peace keeping', *American Sociological Review* 32: 699.
—— (1970) *The Function of the Police in Modern Societies*, Rockville, MD: National Institute for Mental Health, Center for Studies of Crime and Delinquency.
Black, D. (1970) 'Production of crime rates', *American Sociological Review* 35: 733.
Blumberg, A. (1967) 'The practice of law as confidence game: organizational co-optation of a profession', *Law and Society Review* 1: 15.
Bottomley, A. and Coleman, C. (1976) 'Criminal statistics: the police role in the

discovery and detection of crime', *International Journal of Criminology and Penology* 4: 33.

—— (1981) *Understanding Crime Rates*, Farnborough: Gower.

Bottoms, A. and McClean, J. (1976) *Defendants in the Criminal Process*, London: Routledge.

Bowden, J. and Stevens, M. (1986) 'Justice for juveniles – a corporate strategy for Northampton', *Justice of the Peace* 150: 326 and 345.

Box, S. (1981) *Deviance, Reality and Society*, New York: Holt, Rinehart & Winston.

—— (1983) *Power, Crime and Mystification*, London: Tavistock.

Box, S. and Russell, K. (1975) 'The politics of discreditability', *Sociological Review* 23: 2.

Bridges, L. and Bunyan, T. (1983) 'Britain's new urban policing strategy – the Police and Criminal Evidence Bill in context', *Journal of Law and Society* 10: 85.

Brodeur, J-P. (1981) 'Legitimizing police deviance', in C. Shearing (ed.) *Organizational Police Deviance*, Toronto: Butterworth.

Brogden, A. (1981) 'Sus is dead: what about "SaS?"', *New Community* 9: 44.

Brogden, M. (1982) *The Police: Autonomy and Consent*, London: Academic Press.

—— (1985) 'Stopping the people – crime control versus social control', in J. Baxter and L. Koffman (eds) *Police: The Constitution and the Community*, Abingdon: Professional Books.

Brogden, M. and Brogden, A. (1984) 'From Henry III to Liverpool 8: the unity of police powers', *International Journal of the Sociology of Law* 12: 37.

Brogden, M., Jefferson, T. and Walklate, S. (1988) *Introducing Policework*, London: Unwin Hyman.

Brown, D. (1989) *Detention at the Police Station Under the PACE Act, 1984*, London: HMSO.

Burrows, J. (1986) 'Burglary investigations: victims' views of police activity', *Policing* 2: 172.

Burton, F. and Carlen, P. (1979) *Official Discourse*, London: Routledge & Kegan Paul.

Cahill, D. and Mingay, D. (1986) 'Leading questions and the police interview', *Policing* 2: 212.

Cain, M. (1973) *Society and the Policeman's Role*, London: Routledge & Kegan Paul.

Cameron, M. (1964) *The Booster and the Snitch*, New York: Free Press.

Carlen, P. (1976) *Magistrates' Justice*, London: Martin Robertson.

Casper, J. (1972) *American Criminal Justice: The Defendant's Perspective*, Englewood Cliffs, NJ: Prentice-Hall.

Chambers, G. and Millar, A. (1983) *Investigating Sexual Assault*, Edinburgh: Scottish Office.

—— (1986) *Investigating Rape*, Edinburgh: Scottish Office.

Chatterton, M. (1976) 'Police in social control', in J. King (ed.) *Control Without Custody*, Cambridge: Institute of Criminology.

—— (1979) 'The supervision of patrol work under the fixed points system', in S. Holdaway (ed.) *British Police*, London: Edward Arnold.

—— (1983) 'Police work and assault charges', in M. Punch (ed.) *Control in Police Organization*, Cambridge, Mass.: MIT Press.

Christie, N. (1976) *Conflicts as Property*, University of Sheffield: Centre for Criminological Studies.

Cicourel, A. (1968) *The Social Organization of Justice*, London: Wiley.

Clarke, M. (1990) *Business Crime: Its Nature and Control*, Cambridge: Polity Press.

Clarke, J. (1985) 'Whose justice? The politics of juvenile control', *International Journal of the Sociology of Law* 13: 405.

Cohen, P. (1979) 'Policing the working class city', in B. Fine, R. Kinsey, J. Lea, S. Picciotto and J. Young (eds) *Capitalism and the Rule of Law*, London: Hutchinson.

Cohen, S. (1985) *Visions of Social Control*, Cambridge: Polity Press.

Cole, G. (1970) 'The decision to prosecute', *Law and Society Review* 4: 331.

Coulter, J., Miller, S. and Walker, M. (1984) *State of Siege*, London: Canary Press.

CPS (1989) *Annual Report of the Crown Prosecution Service*, London: HMSO.

Cross, R. (1985) *Evidence*, London: Butterworth.

Davies, G., Boucherat, J. and Watson, D. (1989) 'Pre-court decision making in juvenile justice', *British Journal of Criminology* 29: 219.

Davis, K.C. (1969) *Discretionary Justice*, Baton Rouge: Louisiana State University Press.

de Gama, K. (1988) 'Police process and public prosecutions', *International Journal of the Sociology of Law* 16: 339.

Dell, S. (1971) *Silent in Court*, London: Bell.

Devlin, Lord, (1960) *The Criminal Prosecution in England*, Oxford: Oxford University Press.

—— (1979) *The Judge*, Oxford: Oxford University Press.

Ditchfield, J. (1976) *Police Cautioning*, London: HMSO.

Dixon, D., Bottomley, A., Coleman, C., Gill, M. and Wall, D. (1989) 'Reality and rules in the construction and regulation of police suspicion', *International Journal of the Sociology of Law*, 17: 185.

Dworkin, R. (1977) *Taking Rights Seriously*, London: Duckworth.

Edwards, S. (1989) *Policing 'Domestic' Violence*, London: Sage.

Elliman, S. (1990) 'Independent information for the CPS', *New Law Journal* 140: 812.

Ericson, R. (1981a) *Making Crime*, London and Toronto: Butterworth.

—— (1981b) 'Rules *for* police deviance', in C. Shearing (ed.) *Organizational Police Deviance*, Toronto: Butterworth.

Erikson, K. (1964) *Wayward Puritans*, New York: Wiley.

Erikson, T. (1990) 'Confessions in evidence: a look at the inquisitorial system', *New Law Journal* 140: 884.

Evans, R. and Wilkinson, C. (1990) 'Variations in police cautioning policy and practice in England and Wales', *Howard Journal of Criminal Justice* 29: 155.

Feeley, M. (1973) 'Two models of the criminal justice system: an organizational perspective', *Law and Society Review* 7: 407.

—— (1976) 'The concept of laws in social science: a critique and notes on an expanded view', *Law and Society Review* 10: 497.

Fielding, N. (1984) 'Police socialisation and police competence', *British Journal of Sociology* 35: 568.

Fine, B. and Millar, R. (eds) (1986) *Policing the Miners' Strike*, London: Lawrence & Wishart.

Firth, A. (1975) 'Interrogation', *Police Review*, November: 1507.

Fisher, Sir Henry (1977) *Report of an Inquiry by the Honourable Sir Henry Fisher into the circumstances leading to the trial of three persons on charges arising out of the death of Maxwell Confait and the fire at 27 Doggett Road, London SE6*, London: HMSO.

Foucault, M. (1978) *The History of Sexuality: vol. 1*, Harmondsworth: Penguin.

Freedman, D. and Stenning, P. (1977) *Private Security, Police and the Law in Canada*, Toronto: Center of Criminology, University of Toronto.

Gelsthorpe, L. and Giller, H. (1990) 'More justice for juveniles: does more mean better?', *Criminal Law Review* 1990: 153–64.

Gemmill, R. and Morgan-Giles, R. (1980) *Arrest Charge and Summons: Current Practice and Resource Implications*, Royal Commission on Criminal Procedure Research Study No. 9, London: HMSO.

Genn, H. (1987) *Hard Bargaining*, Oxford: Clarendon Press.

Gill, P. (1987) 'Clearing up crime: the big "con"', *Journal of Law and Society*, 14: 254.

Gilroy, P. and Sim, J. (1987) 'Law, order and the state of the left', in P. Scraton (ed.) *Law, Order and the Authoritarian State*, Milton Keynes: Open University Press.

Gobert, J. (1989) 'The peremptory challenge: an obituary', *Criminal Law Review* 1989: 528.

Goffman, E. (1961) *Asylums*, Chicago: Aldine.

Goldstein, J. (1960) 'Police discretion not to invoke the criminal process: low visibility decisions in the administration of justice', *Yale Law Journal* 69: 543.

Graeff, R. (1989) *Talking Blues*, London: Collins Harvill.

Greenwood, P., Chaiken, J. and Petersilia, J. (1977) *The Criminal Investigation Process*, Lexington: Heath.

Gudjonsson, G. and Clark, N. (1986) 'Suggestibility in police interrogation: a social psychological model', *Social Behaviour* 1: 83.

Gudjonsson, G. and MacKeith, J. (1982) 'False confessions: psychological effects of interrogation. A discussion paper', in A. Trankell (ed.), *Reconstructing the Past: The Role of Psychologists in Criminal Trials*, Deventer, The Netherlands: Kluwer.

—— (1988) 'Retracted confessions: legal, psychological and psychiatric aspects', *Medicine, Science and the Law* 28: 187.

Hall, S., Critcher, C., Jefferson, T., Clarke, J. and Roberts, B. (1978) *Policing the Crisis*, London: Macmillan.

Hamer, J., Radford, I. and Stanko, E. (1989) *Women, Policing and Male Violence*, London: Routledge.

Harman, H. and Griffith, J. (1979) *Justice Deserted*, London: National Council for Civil Liberties.

Hay, D. and Snyder, F. (1989) *Policing and Prosecution in Britain 1750–1850*, Oxford: Oxford University Press.

Henry, S. (1983) *Private Justice*, London: Routledge.

Hewitt, P. (1982) *The Abuse of Power*, Oxford: Martin Robertson.

Hobbs, D. (1988) *Doing the Business*, Oxford: Clarendon Press.

Holdaway, S. (ed.) (1979) *British Police*, London: Edward Arnold.

—— (1983) *Inside the British Police*, Oxford: Basil Blackwell.

Home Office (1985) *The Cautioning of Offenders*, Home Office Circular 14/1985.

—— (1989a) *Criminal Statistics for England and Wales, 1988*, London: HMSO.

—— (1989b) *Report of the Working Group on the Right to Silence*, London: Home Office.

—— (1990) *The Cautioning of Offenders*, London: Home Office.

House of Commons (1990) *Report of the Home Affairs Committee on the Crown Prosecution Service*, London: HMSO.

Inbau, F. and Reid, J. (1967) *Criminal Interrogations and Confessions*, Baltimore: Williams & Wilkins.

Institute of Race Relations (1987) *Policing Against Black People*, London: Institute of Race Relations.

Irving, B. (1980) *Police Interrogation: A Study of Current Practice*, Royal Commission on Criminal Procedure Research Paper No. 2, London: HMSO.

—— (1985) 'Research into policy won't go', in E. Alves and J. Shapland (eds) *Legislation for Policing Today: The Police and Criminal Evidence Act*, Leicester: British Psychological Society.

Irving, B. and Hilgendorf, L. (1980) *Police Interrogation: The Psychological Approach*, Royal Commission on Criminal Procedure Research Paper No. 1, London: HMSO.

Irving, B. and McKenzie, I. (1989) *Police Interrogation: The Effects of the Police and Criminal Evidence Act 1984*, London: The Police Foundation.

Jefferson, T. and Grimshaw, R. (1984) *Controlling the Constable: Police Accountability in England and Wales*, London: Muller.

—— (1987) *Interpreting Policework*, London: Unwin Hyman.

Johnson, T. (1972) *Professions and Power*, London: Macmillan.

Jones, T., MacLean, B. and Young, J. (1986) *The Islington Crime Survey*, Aldershot: Gower.

JUSTICE (1979) *Pre-Trial Criminal Procedure: Police Powers and the Prosecution Process*, Evidence submitted to the Royal Commission on Criminal Procedure, Mimeo.

Kennedy, L. (1961) *Ten Rillington Place*, London: Gollancz.

Kettle, M. (1980) 'The politics of policing and the policing of politics', in P. Hain (ed.) *Policing the Police: vol. 2*, London: John Calder.

Kitsuse, J. and Cicourel, A. (1963) 'A note on the use of official statistics', in *Social Problems* 11: 131.

Klockars, C. (1980) 'The Dirty Harry Problem', *The Annals* 1980: 452.

—— (ed.) (1983) *Thinking about Police*, New York: McGraw-Hill.

Lambert, J. (1970) *Crime, Police and Race Relations: A Study in Birmingham*, London: Oxford University Press.

Landau, S. (1981) 'Juveniles and the police', *British Journal of Criminology* 21: 27.

Laycock, G. and Tarling, R. (1985) 'Police force cautioning: policy and practice', in D. Moxon (ed.) *Managing Criminal Justice*, London: HMSO.

LCD (1988) *Judicial Statistics*, London: Lord Chancellor's Department.

Lea, J. and Young, J. (1984) *What Is to Be Done About Law and Order?*, Harmondsworth: Penguin.

Lemert, E. (1967) *Human Deviance, Social Problems and Social Control*, Englewood Cliffs, NJ: Prentice-Hall.

Lipton, J. (1977) 'On the psychology of eyewitness testimony', *Journal of Applied Psychology* 62: 90.

Lustgarten, L. (1986) *The Governance of the Police*, London: Sweet & Maxwell.

McBarnet, D. (1981) *Conviction*, London: Macmillan.
McCabe, S., and Purves, R. (1972) *By-passing the Jury*, Oxford: Oxford University Penal Research Unit/Blackwell.
McCabe, S. and Sutcliffe, F. (1978) *Defining Crime*, Oxford: Blackwell.
McCabe, S., Wallington, P., Alderson, J., Gostin, L. and Mason, C. (1988) *Police, Public Order and Civil Liberties*, London: Routledge.
McConville, M. (1983) 'Search of persons and premises: new data from London', *Criminal Law Review* 1983: 605.
—— (1987) 'Bent by the burden of proof', *The Times Higher Education Supplement* 885: 13.
—— (1989) 'Justice in the frame', *The Times Higher Education Supplement* 887: 13.
McConville, M. and Baldwin, J. (1981) *Courts, Prosecution and Conviction*, Oxford: Clarendon Press.
McConville, M. and Morrell, P. (1983) 'Recording the interrogation: have the police got it taped?', *Criminal Law Review* 1983: 158.
McKenzie, I. and Irving, B. (1988) 'The right to silence', *Policing* 4: 88.
McKenzie, I., Morgan, R. and Reiner, R. (1990) 'Helping the police with their inquiries: the necessity principle and voluntary attendance at the police station', *Criminal Law Review* 1990: 22.
MacKenzie, J. (1990) 'Silence in Hampshire', *New Law Journal* 140: 696.
McNee, D. (1978) *Evidence of the Commissioner of the Metropolis to the Royal Commission on Criminal Procedure*, Mimeo.
—— (1983) *McNee's Law*, London: Collins.
Maguire, M. (1984) 'Meeting the needs of burglary victims: questions for the police and the criminal justice system', in R. Clarke and T. Hope (eds) *Coping with Burglary: Research Perspectives on Policy*, Boston: Kluwer & Nijhoff.
—— (1988) 'Effects of the "PACE" provisions on detention and questioning', *British Journal of Criminology* 28: 19.
Manning, P. (1977) *Police Work*, Cambridge Mass.: MIT Press.
Mansfield, G. and Peay, J. (1987) *The Director of Public Prosecutions*, London: Tavistock.
Mark, R. (1973) *Minority Verdict*, London: BBC Publications.
—— (1978) *In the Office of Constable*, London: Collins.
Marquis, K., Marshall, J. and Oskamp, S. (1972) 'Testimony validity as a function of question form, atmosphere, and item difficulty', *Journal of Applied Psychology* 2: 167.
Marshall, G. (1984) *Constitutional Conventions*, Oxford: Oxford University Press.
Mason, J. (1986) 'Expert evidence in the adversarial system of criminal justice', *Medicine, Science and the Law* 26: 8.
Matza, D. (1969) *Becoming Deviant*, Englewood Cliffs, NJ: Prentice-Hall.
Mawby, R. (1979) *Policing the City*, Farnborough: Saxon House.
Mirfield, P. (1985) *Confessions*, London: Sweet & Maxwell.
Mitchell, B. (1983) 'Confessions and police interrogation of suspects', *Criminal Law Review* 1983: 596.
Moody, S. and Tombs, J. (1982) *Prosecution in the Public Interest*, Edinburgh: Scottish Academic Press.
Morgan, R. (1987) 'The local determinants of policing policy', in P. Willmott (ed.) *Policing and the Community*, London: Policy Studies Institute.

Morris, A. and Giller, H. (1987) *Understanding Juvenile Justice*, London: Croom Helm.

Morton, J. (1975) 'To combat verbals', *New Law Journal* 125: 830.

Mott, J. (1983) 'Police decisions for dealing with juvenile offenders', *British Journal of Criminology* 23: 249.

Murphy, D. (1986) *Customers and Thieves*, Farnborough: Gower.

National Audit Office (1989) *Review of the Crown Prosecution Service*, London: HMSO.

Nelken, D. (1987) 'Criminal law and criminal justice: some notes on their irrelation', in I. Dennis (ed.) *Criminal Law and Justice*, London: Sweet & Maxwell.

O'Hara, C. (1970) *Fundamentals of Criminal Investigation*, Springfield, Ill.: Charles C. Thomas.

Packer, H. (1968) *The Limits of the Criminal Sanction*, Stanford, Ca.: Stanford University Press and Oxford University Press.

Pepinsky, H. (1984) 'Better living through police discretion', *Law and Contemporary Problems* 47: 249.

Piliavin, I. and Briar, S. (1964) 'Police encounters with juveniles', *American Journal of Sociology* 70: 206.

Policy Studies Institute (1983) *Police and People in London*, Aldershot: Gower.

Powers, P., Andriks, J. and Loftus, E. (1979) 'Eyewitness accounts of females and males', *Journal of Applied Psychology* 64: 339.

Powis, D. (1977) *The Signs of Crime: A Field Manual for the Police*, London: McGraw-Hill.

Pratt, J. (1986) 'Diversion from the juvenile court', *British Journal of Criminology* 26(3): 212.

—— (1989) 'Corporatism: the third model of juvenile justice', *British Journal of Criminology* 29(3): 236.

Prosecuting Solicitors' Society (1979) *Written Evidence to the Royal Commission on Criminal Procedure: Part II Police*, Mimeo.

Punch, M. (1979) *Policing the Inner City*, London: Macmillan.

Quinney, R. (1977) *Class, State and Crime*, New York: David McKay Co.

Ramsay, M. (1987) *The Effectiveness of the Forensic Science Service*, Home Office Research Study No. 91, London: HMSO.

Reiman, J. (1979) *The Rich Get Richer and the Poor Get Prison*, New York: Wiley.

Reiner, R, (1978) *The Blue-Coated Worker*, Cambridge: Cambridge University Press.

—— (1980) 'Fuzzy thoughts: the police and law and order politics', *Sociological Review* 28(2): 377.

—— (1984) 'Is Britain turning into a police state?', *New Society*, 2 August 1984.

—— (1985) *The Politics of the Police*, Brighton: Wheatsheaf.

—— (1989) 'Thinking at the top', *Policing* 5: 181.

Reiss, A. (1971) *The Police and the Public*, New Haven, Conn.: Yale University Press.

Richardson, S., Dohrenwend, B. and Klein, D. (1965) *Interviewing: Its Forms and Functions*, London: Basic Books.

Riley, D. (1986) 'Sex differences in teenage crime: the role of lifestyle', *Home Office Research and Planning Research Bulletin, no. 20*, London: Home Office Research and Planning Unit.

Royal, F. and Schutt, S. (1976) *The Gentle Art of Interviewing and Interrogation: A Professional Manual and Guide*, Englewood Cliffs, NJ: Prentice-Hall.

Royal Commission on Criminal Procedure (1981) *Report*, London: HMSO.

Rubenstein, J. (1973) *City Police*, New York: Farrar, Strauss & Giroux.

Rumbaut, R. and Bittner, E. (1979) 'Changing conceptions of the police role: a sociological review', in N. Morris and M. Tonry (eds) *Crime and Justice: An Annual Review of Research: vol. 1*, Chicago: University of Chicago Press.

Samuels, A. (1989) 'Forensic evidence for the defence', *Medicine, Science and the Law* 29: 293.

Sanders, A. (1979) 'Guilt, innocence and jury acquittals', *Howard Journal* 18: 7.

—— (1985a) 'Prosecution decisions and the Attorney-General's guidelines', *Criminal Law Review* 4: 19.

—— (1985b) 'Class bias in prosecutions', *Howard Journal* 24: 76.

—— (1986) 'An independent Crown Prosecution Service?', *Criminal Law Review* 1986: 27.

—— (1987) 'Constructing the case for the prosecution', *Journal of Law and Society* 14: 229.

—— (1988a) 'Personal violence and public order', *International Journal of the Sociology of Law* 16: 359.

—— (1988b) 'The limits to diversion from prosecution', *British Journal of Criminology* 28: 513.

Sanders, A. and Bridges, L. (1990) 'Access to legal advice and police malpractice', *Criminal Law Review* 1990: 494.

Sanders, A., Bridges, L., Mulvaney, A. and Crozier, G. (1989) *Advice and Assistance at Police Stations and the 24 Hour Duty Solicitor Scheme*, London: Lord Chancellor's Department.

Sanders, W. (1977) *Detective Work*, New York: Free Press.

Sarat, S. and Silbey, S. (1988) 'The pull of the policy audience', *Law and Policy* 10: 97.

Shapland, J. (1984) 'Victims, the criminal justice system and compensation', *British Journal of Criminology* 24: 131.

Shapland, J. and Hobbs, R. (1987) *Policing on the Ground in Highland*, Working Paper, Oxford: Centre for Criminological Research.

—— (1989) 'Policing priorities on the ground', in R. Morgan and D. Smith (eds) *Coming to Terms with Policing*, London: Routledge.

Shapland, J. and Vagg, J. (1987) 'Using the police', in R. Reiner and J. Shapland (eds) *Why Police?*, Special Issue on Policing in Britain, *British Journal of Criminology* 27: 54.

—— (1988) *Policing by the Public*, London: Routledge.

Shearing, C. (1981) 'Deviance and conformity in the reproduction of order', in C. Shearing (ed.) *Organizational Police Deviance*, Toronto: Butterworth.

Shepherd, E. (1984) 'Values into practice: the implementation and implications of human awareness training', *Police Journal* 57: 286.

—— (1986a) 'Interviewing development: facing up to reality', *Police Journal* 59: 35.

—— (1986b) 'The conversational core of policing', *Policing* 2: 294.

Shepherd, E. and Kite, F. (1989a) 'Training to interview', *Policing* 4: 264.

—— (1989b) 'Teach 'em to talk', *Policing* 5: 33.

Silberman, C. (1978) *Criminal Violence, Criminal Justice*, New York: Random House.

Silver, A. (1967) 'The demand for order in civil society: a review of some themes in the history of urban crime, police and riot', in D.J. Bordua (ed.) *The Police: Six Sociological Essays*, New York: Wiley.

Skolnick, J. (1966) *Justice Without Trial*, New York: Wiley.

—— (1967) 'Social control in the adversary system', *Journal of Conflict Resolution* 11: 52.

Smith, D. and Gray, J. (1983), see Policy Studies Institute.

Softley, P. (1980) *Police Interrogation: An Observational Study in Four Police Stations*, Royal Commission on Criminal Procedure Research Study No. 4, London: HMSO.

Southgate, P. (1986) *Police–Public Encounters*, Home Office Research Study No. 90, London: HMSO.

Southgate, P. and Ekblom, P. (1984) *Contacts Between Police and Public*, London: Home Office Research Unit.

Steer, D. (1980) *Uncovering Crime: The Police Role*, Royal Commission on Criminal Procedure Research Study No. 7, London: HMSO.

Stern, W. (1938) *General Psychology: From the Personalistic Standpoint*, New York: Macmillan.

Stinchcombe, A. (1963) 'Institutions of privacy in the determination of police administrative practice', *American Journal of Sociology* 69: 2.

Stone, C. (n.d.) Public Interest Case Assessment, New York: VERA Institution of Justice.

Taylor, I. (1980) 'The law and order issue in the British General Election and Canadian Federal Election of 1979', *Canadian Journal of Sociology* 5: 3.

Taylor, I., Walton, P. and Young, J. (1973) *The New Criminology*, London: Routledge and Kegan Paul.

Thompson, E. (1975) *Whigs and Hunters*, London: Penguin.

Tuck, M. and Southgate, P. (1981) *Ethnic Minorities, Crime and Policing*, Home Office Research Study No. 70, London: HMSO.

Tully, B. and Cahill, D. (1984) *Police Interviewing of the Mentally Handicapped: An Experimental Study*, London: Police Foundation.

Tutt, N. and Giller, H. (1983) 'Police cautioning of juveniles: the practice of diversity', *Criminal Law Review* 1983: 587.

Unger, R. (1976) *Law and Modern Society*, London: Macmillan.

Van Maanen, J. (1974) 'Working the street', in H. Jacob (ed.) *The Potential for Reform of Criminal Justice*, Beverly Hills: Sage.

Vennard, J. (1985) 'The outcome of contested trials', in D. Moxon (ed.) *Managing Criminal Justice*, London: HMSO.

Vennard, J. and Riley, D. (1988) 'The use of peremptory challenge and standby of jurors and their relationship to trial outcome', *Criminal Law Review* 1988: 731.

Vincent-Jones, P. (1986) 'The hippy convoy and criminal trespass', *Journal of Law and Society* 13: 343.

Vogler, R. (1982) 'Magistrates and civil disorder', *LAG Bulletin* November: 12.

Walklate, S. (1990) *Victimology: The Victim and The Criminal Justice Process*, London: Unwin Hyman.

Walkley, J. (1987) *Police Interrogation*, London: Police Review Publishing Co.

West, R. (1986) 'Police superintendents and the prosecution of offences', in J. Benyon and C. Bourn (eds) *The Police: Powers, Procedures and Proprieties*, Oxford: Pergamon.

Westley, W. (1953) *Violence and the Police*, Cambridge, Mass.: MIT Press.

White, R. (1986) 'A public prosecution service for England and Wales', in J. Benyon and C. Bourn (eds) *The Police: Powers, Procedures and Proprieties*, Oxford: Pergamon.

Wilcox, A. (1972) *The Decision to Prosecute*, London: Butterworth.

Wilkinson, C. and Evans, R. (1990) 'Police cautioning of juveniles', *Criminal Law Review* 1990: 165.

Williams, G. (1979) 'The authentication of statements to the police', *Criminal Law Review* 1979: 6.

Willis, C. (1983) *The Use, Effectiveness and Impact of Police Stop and Search Powers*, Research and Planning Unit Paper 15, London: Home Office.

Wilson, J. (1968) *Varieties of Police Behavior*, Cambridge, Mass.: Harvard University Press.

Zander, M. (1972) 'Access to a solicitor in the police station', *Criminal Law Review* 1972: 342.

—— (1974) 'Are too many professional criminals avoiding conviction?', *Modern Law Review* 37: 28.

—— (1979) 'The investigation of crime: a study of cases tried in the Old Bailey', *Criminal Law Review* 1979: 203.

Index

For Product Safety Concerns and Information please contact our EU representative GPSR@taylorandfrancis.com
Taylor & Francis Verlag GmbH, Kaufingerstraße 24, 80331 München, Germany

www.ingramcontent.com/pod-product-compliance
Lightning Source LLC
Chambersburg PA
CBHW070405270326
41926CB00014B/2712

* 9 7 8 0 8 1 5 3 7 2 4 6 2 *